Trans World Airlines
A Book of Memories

Edited By

Jon Proctor

and

Jeff Kriendler

International Standard Book Number 13: 978-1-60452-122-1
International Standard Book Number 10: 1-60452-122-8
Library of Congress Control Number: 2016944569

BluewaterPress LLC
52 Tuscan Way Ste 202-309
Saint Augustine FL 32092
http://bluewaterpress.com

This book may be purchased online at - http://www.bluewaterpress.com/twa

Please note that address information is subject to change. At the time of printing, the address was correct, but may have changed since. Please check our website for the latest address information for BluewaterPress LLC.

Unless otherwise credited, TWA historic images are from the collection of Jon Proctor.

Contents

Introduction

Trans World Airlines - A Book of Memories represents another form of merger in the extended airline industry as it is a collaboration between two veteran airline employees, Jon Proctor of TWA and Jeff Kriendler of Pan Am. Jon enjoyed a career of 27 years with Trans World Airlines and has continued his love for the airline by writing about TWA and posting images of the famed carrier on his web site (www.jonproctor.net). In this endeavor, Jon has joined with a colleague from Pan Am, Jeff Kriendler, a 50-year industry veteran who was the Vice President - Corporate Communications and chief spokesman for the airline during the last 10 years of the company's existence.

Last fall, Jeff reached out to Jon, suggesting they share their mutual passion for history and creative writing to edit an anthology about TWA. Jeff's suggestion follows on the heels of two similar works he had completed over the past few years on Pan Am and Eastern Air Lines. To him, TWA was a natural choice for a third creation of stories written by employees of a defunct airline whose appeal continues unabated despite its disappearance from the skies.

Although TWA and Pan Am were cutthroat competitors, they were without question pioneers in the U.S. commercial aviation industry and they had similar footprints. They were both representative of high quality of service on the ground and in the air. The two airlines were symbols of the United States and thus were victims of the scourge of international terrorism that struck the airline industry. In the 1970s and persists today. Although neither of the carriers operates today, both of the brands continue with high consumer value.

The book is presented in a different manner and a most unique format – through the eyewitness experiences of its employees and friends of the fabled carrier. In creating the book, the editors first developed a list of stories they wanted to be covered and then sought the employees who were first hand participants in these events. TWA friends were also solicited to share their tales. The result is a compilation of more than 60 stories.

Reading these pages will surely stimulate your own fond recollections of a by-gone era, which will never be replicated. These are stories from the heart by employees who often dedicated their entire professional careers to TWA and were personally involved in some of the incredible achievements that brought Trans World Airlines to greatness.

We hope the readers will enjoy each of these TWA memories.

The Editors

JON PROCTOR

JEFF KRIENDLER

Jon Proctor is a seasoned airline industry veteran and served in a variety of positions with Trans World Airlines over a 27-year span. His father was a pioneering airmail and airline pilot for American Airlines and his brother flew for TWA. Jon has written two books and co-authored a third. His numerous magazine articles on commercial aviation have appeared worldwide over the years. The former Senior Editor of *Airways Magazine* and Editor-in-Chief of *Airliners Magazine*, his original airline images appear throughout this book. He maintains two websites: www.jonproctor.com, plus www.twdcs.org for the TWA DCS Alumni Association. Jon resides in Sandpoint, Idaho.

Jeff Kriendler has spent most of his 50-year professional life in and around the aviation industry, holding many posts at Pan American World Airways during a 24-year career that included 10 years as the airline's Vice President—Corporate Communications. A native New Yorker, Jeff now resides in Miami Beach where he is contributing editor for *Airways Magazine*. He also serves on the Board of the Pan Am Historical Foundation. This TWA anthology is his third such airline-employee book, following similar projects featuring Pan Am and Eastern Air Lines.

Dedication

To my late brother, Bill Proctor, TWA career pilot, who constantly encouraged me to follow my aviation dreams. After my eyesight prevented a commercial pilot avenue, he kept me focused on the airline industry, and paid the $7 "jet surcharge" for my first turbine-powered ride, on a Boeing 707. When I got into aviation journalism, Bill was my biggest fan. He was a great brother. – *Jon Proctor*

To my late parents, Florence and Bob Kriendler, who had the foresight and the graciousness to teach me a love for travel and aviation at an early age. Following in their footsteps, I have attempted to instill a love for world travel and the benefits accrued by meeting different peoples in this diverse world in my daughter Catherine, to whom I likewise dedicate this work. My hope for her is that she may one day experience the elegant service provided aloft by the iconic carriers of yesteryear, Pan Am and TWA, which set the standards for elegance aloft. – *Jeff Kriendler*

Foreword

By Mark E. Abels

On December 1, 2001, I flew as a passenger on TWA Flight 220. It was not the most momentous or memorable flight in my three decades of flying TWA as both a customer and an employee (that flight was three years earlier, when I was privileged to travel on Pope John Paul II's TWA *Shepherd One* flight from St. Louis to Rome). But Flight 220 on 12/1/01 was probably my most historic TWA flight. After 76 years of "firsts" for TWA, Flight 220 was the last – the last flight ever under the TW flight code. When Captain Bill Compton (who also was TWA's CEO) parked the MD-80 at the gate in St. Louis, our historic airline officially became history.

The story that drew to a close that day in December would make a pretty good Hollywood block- buster. It had at least a few of each of the ingredients – and often a generous helping of some of the tastier items – that make a box-office hit.

The narrative was epic. It started with the birth of one of the most exciting, most dynamic and most important American industries – the airline industry. It spanned three-quarters of a century, as long as the lifespan of air transport itself. When critical events occurred, when vital innovations were needed, this great airline invariably was at center stage.

Its characters were larger than life. There was the young airmail pilot whose daring and courage literally had stunned the world. There was the swashbuckling tycoon who built it into an international powerhouse of a company and earned a fortune on top of his fortune, but was finally forced out of the business he loved. There were the airmen and women who performed unrecognized acts of accomplishment, some of them heroic, in the service of what they regarded as a true vocation, not just a job. There were movie stars, celebrities, politicians, presidents and Popes. There were skillful and daring leaders with a vision of the future and the courage to build it, and there were financial manipulators who almost destroyed it.

It was the first at so many things. It was the first to span the continent, coast-to-coast. It claimed many technological firsts, often initiated in cooperation with the great aircraft manufacturers. Its contribution to launching, with

Douglas Aircraft, the legendary series of modern twin-engine "DC" airliners made the modern airline industry possible. It worked with Boeing to develop a lesser-known but perhaps no less significant aircraft, the Stratoliner – the world's first pressurized airliner. Its owner's perfectionist insistence with Lockheed was the driving force behind the creation of the incomparable Constellation. It was the first airline to turn its back on propellers and boast of an all-jet fleet.

This was TWA, the Lindbergh Line, the transcontinental airline, the trans world airline, the airman's airline, the airline of the stars, the airline of the Popes, the airline of legend. Howard Hughes, the legendary former owner of TWA, also produced silver-screen epics – but even Hughes's best screenwriters could not have dreamed up a more exciting saga than the true story of his own airline. This worldwide corporation achieved such cosmopolitan fame that the name TWA became a household word, synonymous with "airline."

TWA's globe-girdling days ended fifteen years ago, but even today the TWA name remains one of the best-known in commercial aviation throughout the world, from North America to Europe and through the Middle East to Asia.

But the story of an airline – especially this airline – is much more than one of routes and planes. It is very much about people, just as the airline business is very much a people business. TWA was populated by walking repositories of airline history, employees who gave 20, 30, 40 or even more years to the company. Their dedication, their courage, their professionalism and, above all, their loyalty – not to mention many of their best stories – are captured here.

Here are the stories of great events, some triumphant, some tragic, told from the unique vantage point of those who lived them. Here are the personal tales of day-to-day airline life, replete with memories of special friends and special challenges. Here are the reflections that can help you understand how airline folks come to have "kerosene in their veins" and a love of commercial aviation that can make work in any other business seem just not worth the time.

Treasure these stories and savor them as you would a fine wine. Like that vintage wine, they took decades to create, and the stuff and times that created them now are gone forever. But the memories live on, and as long as they do, so will TWA.

Mark E. Abels
Vice-President - Corporate Communications,
1996-2001

A Tribute to TWA

By Chris Sloan

Never an employee of Trans World Airlines, I was not even even much of a TWA frequent flyer, with maybe 10 flights under my belt. I was simply a fan. When asked by Jon Proctor and Jeff Kriendler to write a passage for this book, it had never occurred to me to delve into my inner AvGeek for some introspection as to why this is the case. In considering my love for this long since departed carrier, I discovered a number of themes, inspirations, and milestones that dovetailed with and explain my passion for the airline industry.

I grew up in Tulsa, Oklahoma. What many may not realize is that Tulsa is a first-rate aviation hub anchored by being the locale of the American Airlines' maintenance and engineering base, one of the world's largest. And as the city's largest private employer, American reigned supreme and loomed large in my life. Many of my friend's parents worked for American in "AA City". Perhaps desiring to not follow the herd and be a bit iconoclastic, my first airline dalliance began not with AA, but with TWA.

Stuck in my mind is the instant this love affair was kindled. Tulsa was served in the late 1970s by primarily domestic carriers of the time, flying short-haul, rather pedestrian DC-9s, 727s, and 737s, along with a motley collection of propliners. But in our town, one airline stood out for being a little different then the rest, perhaps a bit more exotic and worldly.

TWA occasionally flew Boeing 707s to Oklahoma City and St Louis from Tulsa. Yes, by the late 1970s, they were elderly aircraft about to embark on their retirement, but to this young 7-year-old boy they represented a connection to the dawn of the Jet Age; Intercontinental and transcontinental long-haul travel. When I saw a mighty four-engine 707 blocking into the humble TUL terminal I was hooked, dreaming of far flung European and Asian destinations that this aircraft had been a portal to. Quite simply, it opened my world. Audaciously, TWA displayed a large-scale 6-foot long-Boeing 747 jumbo jet cutaway model at its gate. Oh, how so very badly I wanted to shrink myself and climb inside that glorious vessel of wood and plastic. The chances of that happening were about on par with flying the real thing.

What was it about TWA that stood out as special and iconic? As a youngster, the airline to me represented a paradox long before I knew what that word meant. On one hand, TWA plied the milk run point-to-point routes of Amarillo, Oklahoma City, St. Louis, Kansas City, and Chicago. On the other, Trans World Airlines could whisk us to such far-flung exotic locations to Paris, Cairo, Athens, and Rome. Unlike the imperial chosen instrument, Pan Am, TWA was really the first U.S. carrier with a domestic and international route network, its headquarters and soul seemingly contradicting image. It was a tale of two cities and mindsets between the urbane East Coast and down-to-earth Midwest: New York City and Kansas City/St. Louis. And somehow culturally it worked, much of the time

As much as I admired and respected the high and mighty Pan Am, TWA felt a little more accessible, humble, like an underdog that never quite received the respect it deserved. After all, it served my progressive and beautiful hometown of Tulsa – an under-estimated city in spite of all of its virtues.

TWA was often the first, a real pioneer but as time went on the credit was assigned to others. Here's a smattering, though by no means a comprehensive list of firsts:

• Beginning in 1930, TWA offered the first all-plane (no train) scheduled service from coast to coast, taking 36 hours.

• International carriers like Lufthansa, Ethiopian, and Saudi Arabian have, in part, TWA to thank for their beginnings, as do many airlines whose flight crews trained there (see *Growing Up With Ethiopian Airlines*).

• In October 1953, TWA was the first airline to operate nonstop transcontinental service, though AA was first to operate in both directions (see *Howard Hughes and TWA's Constellation Transcon Nonstops*).

• To this day, TWA holds the record for the longest-scheduled time-aloft flights with Lockheed1649A Starliner (referred to a "Jetstream") between Europe and California, in excess of 22 hours duration (see *The Longest Day*).

• The first airline to show modern in-flight movies, way back in 1961. "By Love Possessed" starring Efrem Zimbalist, Jr. and Lana Turner was the first feature screened, initially to first-class passengers only.

• TWA had the vision to create the first real iconic terminal of the Jet Age: The Eero Saarinen-designed Trans World Flight Center (see *Saarinen's Soaring Structure*). First opening in 1962, it survives to this day as an icon of early Jet Age travel and will be preserved as part of a hotel instead of raised like many of its early peers.

• In 1985, TWA became the first airline to regularly operate twinjets (using Boeing 767-200ER's) equipped with ETOPS capability over the Atlantic (see *Aviate, Navigate, Communicate*). This changed intercontinental travel as we know it and shifted the market from tri and quad-jets to twins.

And as far as seconds are concerned, TWA was often just slightly behind by weeks or days so as not to get true credit for their pioneering work including:

• Second airline, after Pan Am to operate the Boeing 747, beginning in March 1970.

• Second airline, after American Airlines to fly regular domestic transcontinental jet service, beginning in March 1959, between New York-Idlewild and San Francisco.

• Second U.S. airline, after Pan Am, to operate an around-the-world network, via India, Bangkok, Hong Kong, Taiwan, Okinawa, Guam, and Hawaii.

• And though this is subjective, TWA was symbolized by the most iconic and symbolic airline insignia of all time – Raymond Lowey's "Double Globe" logo. The Pan Am meatball does seem to garner most of the attention today, probably due to TWA prematurely retiring its own in 1974.

• TWA was the first U.S. airline to offer a non-smoking section on all of its aircraft, in July 1970.

Beyond the litany of lists, TWA was known for drama. The lead players in this story include colorful and controversial characters, both good and not so good. Jack Frye who took TWA to heights unimagined during his tenure, the mysterious aviator and Hollywood producer Howard Hughes, who vacillated between hero, heel, and hinderer, Charles Tillinghast, Jr., who inherited the thankless job of trying to repair the wrongs of the past

At the end of the day, and right up to the end of TWA the word that sticks me with the most is one of resiliency. Even following decades of mismanagement, heart-breaking tragedies like Flight 800, three bankruptcies in 10 years, a dramatic downsizing at the end, and at times just bad luck, the TWA family stuck together. They never lost hope. They never abandoned their quest to be the best even until the bitter end of the post-9/11 era when it would be impossible for an independent TWA to survive. This ignominious time was when American acquired the remaining assets and dismantled most of what was left of this historic, legacy airline. Now, 15 years after TWA's last flight on Dec 1, 2001 symbolically between St. Louis and Kansas City, the TWA Museum in Kansas City and Employee Groups continue to thrive. Few other defunct, let alone current airlines continue to be celebrated like this, not only by their former employees but former customers and current fans alike.

In my own way, I too celebrate Trans World Airlines and its place not only in history and but in my personal passion. Remember that Boeing 747 cutaway? I purchased an exact copy and spent four years restoring it to exact late 1970s configuration and aesthetic. It is being relocated for display at Miami International Airport. It is my hope that it inspires others to fly "Up, Up, and Away," the way it inspired me.

As founder and editor-in-chief of the aviation news site, AirwaysNews.com, Chris Sloan is a lifelong "Av-Geek" whose aviation journalism has taken him around the globe in pursuit of the industry's biggest stories. He is president and founder of 2C Creative + Content, a television production and promotion company that produces TV shows and promos for national cable and broadcast networks.

A Salute to Ed Betts

By Jon Proctor

TARPA Topics

Born on August 31, 1920, in Santa Monica, California, Edward G. Betts studied mechanical engineering and was in his senior year at the University of California at Berkeley when Pearl Harbor was attacked, launching the United States into World War II.

Ed had enlisted in the Army Air Corps a few days earlier and trained as a bomber pilot. He flew 74 B-25 combat missions, earning two Distinguished Flying Crosses and a Purple Heart after a forced landing at sea during a mission in the African theater. He was honorably discharged in August 1945 with the rank of major.

Hired by TWA as a DC-3 co-pilot the same month, Ed was assigned to the San Francisco base. A year later he flew with a new hostess, Donna Breckenridge and the two were married. Living in the Bay Area, they raised three children and Ed stayed busy as a member of the American Legion and Masonic Lodge. As his two boys grew up, he also became active in the Boy Scouts of America.

TWA's history, particularly the early years, became a passion for Ed. He spent New York layovers searching through the company archives and repeated the same process in Washington, D.C. at the Smithsonian Institution. His stories became regular reading in the TWA Skyliner company newspaper. These and other efforts led to an Award of Excellence in 1976 and later the President's Award. Ed worked his way through the ranks and retired as a 747 captain, based at Los Angeles. His last trip was the polar flight to London, in August 1980. He continued researching TWA's history and wrote multiple stories that appeared in TARPA Topics, the retired pilots organization journal. Several also appeared in journals of The American Aviation Historical Society.

This author corresponded with Ed over the years and met with him on occasion. He was always approachable and happy to help with my own efforts, which paled in comparison to a man who became a literary role model for me.

Ed Betts passed away March 30, 2001 in Pacific Palisades, California, but he will be long remembered by many, especially his TWA family friends.

Captain Ed Betts Retires

Capt. Ed Betts (LAX-I), examines flight plans of his last pre-retirement trip, a Polar roundtrip Los Angeles-London. With him is his wife, former TWA flight attendant Donna Breckenridge. Capt. Betts retired August 31 after 35 years with TWA. He has been a frequent contributor to *Skyliner*, and in 1976 received an Award of Excellence and the President's Award (now the Tillinghast Award) for his work in researching and chronicling TWA's history.

TWA Co-Founder – Paul E. Richter 1896 - 1949

By Ruth Richter Holden, daughter of Paul E. Richter, first Executive Vice President and co-founder of TWA

"Not thrill seekers, but visionaries reaching for the stars. These men tested their machines and their mettle, their engines and their endurance. As warriors of wind and weather, these men-in-machines searched and researched the sky. Aviation pioneers, they shared the love of flight, a vision of the future of aviation and a life-long bond of brotherhood. Together, they were known as the Three Musketeers of Aviation and founded TWA, the airline run by fliers, a global airline and an aviation legacy."

"Give me enough power and I can fly a barn door."

A true pioneer during the Golden Age of flying, Paul E. Richter played a decisive role in creating and building all aspects of commercial aviation and military air transport. From flight instructor to stunt pilot with Hollywood's famous 13 black Cats to Trans World Airlines co-founder and Chief of Staff for the Navy Air Transportation Service during World War II, Richter soared high in his 53 short years.

Author's Collection
Ruth Richter Holden

Paul Richter, center, with TWA President Jack Frye at Kansas City, in front of the Lockheed 12A "Electra Junior," which was used as a high-altitude and weather research aircraft. In the background is a Lockheed 18 Lodestar.

A Colorado rancher turned visionary California pilot in the 1920s, Richter saw the endless opportunities for commercial aviation and made a career of staying ahead of the curve. He founded some of America's first airlines, flying schools and maintenance facilities. He promoted the skills of female flying students, created high school flying clubs and became one of the world's first Air Sheriffs. Richter co-founded Aero Corporation of California and Standard Airlines in the 1920s. He co-founded Trans World Airlines through mergers and restructuring in the 1930s and led the growth of commercial aviation from regional to transcontinental to international operations in the 1940s.

With a reputation and passion for the advancement of ground and air safety through research, aircraft design, and technology, Richter spoke frequently on the subject and shared his company's knowledge with the aviation industry at large. Under his stewardship, TWA made advancements in de-icing, studied electrical phenomena and the benefits of high-altitude flying, and implemented the "Homing" radio direction finder, the anti-range static radio finder, the written flight plan and navigation logs, air brakes or landing flaps, and automatic pilots.

Hundreds of newspaper and magazine articles covered his innovations and accomplishments —noting his two world altitude records, his numerous air race results, his expertise in running airlines, and his influential role as a decorated Navy Officer. The respect of his peers was reflected by his early induction into the exclusive Quiet Birdmen, and also in well-documented personal correspondence.

Richter was a loyal man of principle, integrity and creativity. He adored flying and its enormous potential and did everything in his power to further its development and innovation. In 1949 at the age of 53, Paul Richter died. His contribution to aviation will always be remembered.

TWA/Courtesy of Gary Smedile

*Paul Richter appears in his U.S. Navy uniform at Las Vegas during
acceptance of the first Constellation to wear TWA Colors. Others include
(left to right) Jack Frye, John Collings, Joe Bartles and Lou Goss.*

Author's Collection

The beautifully restored Electra Junior poses for the camera.

Captain Harold F. Blackburn

By William F. Cass

Fifteen years after commanding the Constellation's first revenue flight, Blackie posed in the left seat of a Boeing 707.

Born on Christmas day 1901, Harold F. Blackburn grew up on the western Nebraska prairie, dreaming of becoming a pilot. After his first flight in a Curtiss Jenny in 1919, he was forced to shelve his dreams of flying because he had to support his mother and brother when his father abandoned the family. After success as a regional orchestra leader, he graduated from the Air Corps cadet program in early 1932 and joined the prestigious Eleventh Bombardment Squadron in San Diego. With that squadron, he became a co-winner of the prestigious Mackay Trophy for flying mercy missions to stranded Native Americans in Arizona and New Mexico during the blizzards of early 1932. Unable to secure a permanent Army commission during the Great Depression, he finally signed on as a TWA co-pilot in 1935 after several years as a successful small businessman Los Angeles. Among his more interesting flights were those as co-pilot for Captain John Zimmerman when TWA was the secret charter line for J. Edgar Hoover and his FBI agents.

Hal Blackburn and Co-Pilot Joe Carr are seen at Paris on arrival of the Constellation inaugural flight.

After flying out of Glendale, Kansas City, and New York, "Blackie" became a check pilot in 1940 and was soon in charge of TWA's B-24 Liberator school, the "Eagle Nest Flight Center" in Albuquerque which trained the first Army heavy bomber pilots in 1941-42. His first Atlantic crossing occurred in the summer of 1942 when he flew Harry Hopkins, General George Arnold, and Admiral Ernest King to Britain in a Boeing 307 Stratoliner for meetings with Winston Churchill. Although most of his wartime flying was for TWA's Intercontinental Division (ICD) over the South and North Atlantic Ferry Routes, it was later revealed that Blackie had flown clandestine missions over Occupied Europe in 1944 in the photo version of the Lockheed Lightning fighter. He also was a co-winner of the Collier Trophy in 1942, which was given to those airlines supporting the Army Air Force's Air Transport Command and its vital work of carrying personnel and high priority cargo to Europe, Africa, and Asia.

Although his wartime flying to Scotland, Africa, and Asia was primarily in C-87 Liberators and DC-4s, his postwar reputation was made on what is probably the most elegant piston-engine airliner of all time, the Lockheed Constellation. Shortly after checking out in the Connie, he first flew to Paris in a C-54 while still managing TWA's Intercontinental Division. That was followed by a brief assignment to TWA's foreign route planning department culminating in the two flights for which he is best remembered: the proving flight to Paris in December 1945 and the first revenue flight to Paris on February 5, 1946 – both in Constellations.

In the immediate years following the war, Blackie was very much at a career crossroads. He was held in very high esteem by Jack Frye, TWA's

CEO, and by Otis Bryan, the former chief pilot, in whose footsteps he had followed at Eagle Nest, ICD, and TWA's postwar International Division. Blackie turned down two vice-presidency offers during the late 1940s simply because he wanted to spend his time in the cockpit instead of an executive office swivel chair. Looking for a change, Blackie accepted an interim and challenging assignment before coming back to flying the line: launching and managing the state airline in Ethiopia. Ethiopian awarded him its pilot wings as did other countries whose airlines he helped to rehabilitate after the war, including Ireland, France, Italy, Saudi Arabia, and eventually, Germany. Blackie enjoyed his time with Ethiopian because it reminded him so much of his early TWA days, flying DC-3s into what were new airports for him.

Returning to the United States, Blackie settled down by flying all models of the Connie from New York to European airports. First it was the usual route via Gander and Shannon to Paris and Rome. As TWA's routes were approved, Blackie started flying into London, Athens, Cairo, Lisbon, Frankfurt, and Zurich.

In the early to mid-1950s, the very articulate Blackie, whose appearance matched every casting director's image of an airline captain, contributed significantly to TWA's already positive image. In 1952, TWA selected him to star in *Overseas Run*, a film by RKO in which he portrays Captain Bill Barrett, who takes a Connie to Paris and in the process helps deflate passenger' fears about international flying and its cost. Just three years later TWA selected Blackie to appear on the popular Walt Disney series, *The Mickey Mouse Club*. That program had several segments entitled "What I Want To Be," designed to show middle school age children a range of career choices. Disney planned to extend the career exploration to other professions but arguments between the producer and writers killed the project, fortunately after all of the Blackburn airline pilot segments had aired in late 1955.

With Captain Blackburn having appeared on both the little screen and the big screen, *The New*

Yorker Magazine came calling. That was just after Blackie appeared in TWA metro-area newspaper advertising campaign promoting low fares from the East Coast to the West Coast. *The New Yorker* article, written by John Bainbridge, was one of the magazine's regular personality feature profiles, but the long arm of Gordon Gilmore, TWA's public relations ace, was clearly involved too. The article, although written in late 1955 appeared in 1956, designed as a market development tool designed to encourage more people to consider flying to Europe.

Blackie had always had a streak of wanderlust, and the mid-1950s brought two opportunities his way. He had grown up in Mitchell, a small town in Nebraska's panhandle, and was always interested in the great out-of-doors. Many of Blackie's closest friends were sons of farmers,

Blackie's retirement photo.

and indeed, two of his closest TWA friends were farmers too: Otis Bryan and Frank Busch, the late 1950s operations vice president, who had beef farms back in Kansas. Looking to his FAA-required retirement at age sixty coming up in 1961, Blackie started searching for a small farm to which he would eventually retire. Although initially searching from Maine to Virginia, he settled on something much closer to New York. His choice was a derelict, run-down dairy farm near Kutztown in the Pennsylvania Dutch farming country. Martha Blackburn and daughters Bonnie and Be were just simply crushed when they first visited the place.

Blackie envisioned it as it would be in several years and promptly set about turning "Hidden Brook Farm" into a showcase operation where he would become a Black Angus breeder. As an airline pilot, he had ample time between flights to work on the place. Although his domicile was technically New York, he was actually about to be based elsewhere. The new location was Germany, and the logos on the hangars were not red and white, but rather the gold and blue of Lufthansa.

In late 1956, Blackie joined the contingent of TWA pilots assigned to breathe new life back into Lufthansa, which was being re-constituted as an international airline. In 1955, Lufthansa was establishing domestic service in Germany and was looking to restore its North and South American routes. It began by recruiting surviving Luftwaffe pilots with whom senior TWA pilots flew as instructor/check pilots. Most of the aviators Blackie worked with were former bomber, transport and night fighter pilots. The new Luftwaffe, which was re-formed as a part of NATO in 1955, absorbed only surviving day and jet fighter pilots. Blackie had a high opinion of his new charges' flying ability and initially flew with them between Frankfurt and New York. As Lufthansa's routes expanded, so did the new entries in Blackie's logbook, including capitals on both coasts of South America.

The tour with Lufthansa satisfied some of the Blackburn wanderlust, provided him with a reasonable amount of time to work on the farm, and kept his mind off TWA boardroom intrigue. By that point, Blackie had tired of the progression of TWA CEOs and their fights with TWA's principal owner, Howard Hughes.

Blackie's tour with Lufthansa ended in 1959 as TWA's contract was winding down. With less than two years to go before hitting the wall at age 60, Blackie was asked by Marv Horstman to consider flying the new 707s. At that point, Blackie was resigned to finishing his career on the model 1649A *Jetstream* Constellation. Horstman took Blackie into the TWA hangar at what was then Idlewild Airport, and let him explore a Boeing 707-331 Intercontinental. Blackie was transformed by the encounter, saying that he had experienced the same sensation only once before: the first time he sat in the Curtiss Jenny that had taken him on his first airplane flight in 1919. Several months later, Blackie graduated as top man in his Boeing 707 class at the Kansas City training facility.

Blackie fell in love with the power, speed, range and ceiling of the 707; he also praised the reliability and simplicity of its jet engines. Gone were the days of stopping at Gander and Shannon – Blackie could then take Flight 800 nonstop to Paris. But it all came to an end on Christmas Day 1961 when he turned 60 years of age.

But go out in style he did. First, there was another profile in *New Yorker* – this time there was more emphasis on the advantage of jet flying, but there was some nostalgia in the article too. Blackie looked back to his early days flying Curtiss Condor bombers in the 1930s and the war years with flights to Scotland in abysmal weather worsened by the possibility of interception by long-range Luftwaffe aircraft.

Word of the upcoming *New Yorker* article had leaked out in New York City's media circles, and Blackie soon found himself as the focal point of *Blackie*, a film by the award-winning documentary producer Robert Drew. The film is essentially the movie version of the second *New Yorker* article as made more dramatic with motion and sound. But then the inevitable happened. Blackie left the cockpit, but not TWA. He became a "captain emeritus" and served as a goodwill ambassador, giving speeches across the country as TWA's Manager of Travel Development. He also kept on flying. Granted the planes were light, general aviation aircraft such as Cessna 182s and Piper Cherokees, but he was still flying and continued to do so until he was in his mid-seventies.

He did briefly come out of retirement with a former TWA navigator, Earl Korf, for a little cloak and dagger business on behalf of the CIA, which had come into temporary possession of the new, Russian AN24-B transport aircraft. In 1965, the CIA needed some low-key ferrying of the airplane, which it had completely disassembled and re-assembled, looking for new technology.

By that point, Blackie was busy with Hidden Brook Farm and managing a small herd of Black Angus. He had also become something of a folk hero in Berks County – an international jet captain and at the same time a progressive farmer whose wife's tomatoes always won the blue ribbon at the Kutztown fair. And so it went for several years until the love of Blackie's life, Martha, passed away in 1975. Blackie soon remarried – to the former Helen Jones who had been his high school sweetheart back in Nebraska. The Blackburns became regular attendees at TARPA and TWA Seniors gatherings, and eventually moved to the Phoenix area. With Helen's passing, Blackie moved to California to be with son Bob and his family. Looking out from the deck of Bob's home above Oakland, the old flyer could see below him TWA's giant 747s taking off from SFO, but also in his mind's eye were the DC-2s and 3s from another era along with the Boeing Stratoliner and the ever-graceful Constellation. Blackie flew west on August 4, 1989.

This story is abridged from the new book, *"Blackie," A Pioneering, Twentieth Century Pilot in Peace and War* by William F. Cass. It is available at amazon.com or as an E-book at kindle.com, also from the publisher, Branden Books, www.brandenbooks.com

William F. Cass is a graduate of Washington College (B.A. Economics) and Syracuse University (M.B.A.). He is a former commercial pilot and is now retired from an advertising and public relations career. Two of his previous aviation titles are The Last Flight of Liberator 41-1133 and Alaska's Father Goose, the biography of Alaskan bush pilot, Bud Bodding.

Ida Staggers – Her Gifts of Service to TWA
By Helen E. McLaughlin

Ida was modest about her achievements. "People aren't interested in me personally. People who are first just get attention. Being number two doesn't count," says Ida Staggers, TWA's airline hostess of 1936. Ida retired on July 24, 1972 at age sixty. She had logged 10 million miles aloft. During her time inflight she had chalked up three and a third years of constant flying as a hostess, accumulating 29,000 flying hours.

Her last flight was a Military Airlift Command flight from Honolulu to Travis Air Force Base, California. The aircraft carried 165 Vietnam servicemen and their families and continued as a ferry flight to San Francisco after military passengers deplaned.

A large group of well wishers greeted Ida's flight at San Francisco with flower leis and placards reading: "Good Luck Ida!" and "Ida, Sweet As Apple Cidah!" It was her 60th birthday and people were showing their respect and love. To sum up her career as a TWA hostess, she said, "I've had the good time of our profession."

Ida seen in a 1937 TWA summer hostess uniform.

Ida grew up on a Hill City, Kansas farm. In 1936, she was a registered nurse employed at Saint Luke's Hospital in Kansas City, working in the operating room and also doing some private duty for two years. During this time she lived in the same apartment building with the secretary to TWA Vice President Paul Richter. The secretary, knowing Ida was an registered nurse (RN), a prime requirement for the airline hostesses TWA was starting to hire, suggested Ida apply for the job. She followed the secretary's suggestion and interviewed for the position. Her acceptance as a hostess trainee began a 36-year career that she loved.

Ida's training in Kansas City was brief. It included a 12-hour familiarization flight to Los Angeles. She started her long hostess career in July 1936. On September 15, 1937, Ida flew on the first DC-2 flight into San Francisco. She liked the Bay area and transferred there a year later. During this time TWA had noted the likeable, dependable Ida and chose her to train several classes of new hostesses. "I remember one two-week class consisting of three hostess students. The salary was $100 a month for more than 100 hours of flight time," related Ida.

In 1940, Ida was designated chief hostess and sent to TWA's La Guardia base in New York. In one year she was became the system chief hostess, back at Kansas City. "It was during this time that I found myself more in the office than in contact with hostesses," said Ida. "In 1946, I requested the La Guardia base once again. TWA began overseas service that year, and I trained hostesses for the international flights."

After six weeks at La Guardia, Ida was given a leave of absence to train Scandinavian Airline hostesses in Sweden. "I like to think I helped them get their flight service started," Ida proudly related. "I went back to La Guardia but wanted to return to my first love, flying the line, instead of training hostesses." She got her wish but was periodically pursued to train, supervise and to line-check the hostesses and pursers in Paris and Cairo. When Ida left her job as chief hostess TWA had 187 line hostesses.

Her favorite flight was an international route from New York to Paris, on an 18-passenger sleeper Constellation with one hostess and two pursers. "We provided a personal touch what was so important for early hostesses. Today there are too many passengers for such a thing. Too bad!" reflected Ida.

Training a new-hire class in the 1930s,
Ida became TWA's Chief Hostess.

Ida's Memories

Ida had many celebrities and well-known passengers on board her many flights. "To me they were just regular folks," she said. "Some were nice and some were blown up with their own importance. I treated everyone the same."

One charter flight was especially interesting. In 1937 Ida was chosen to work a DC-2 two-week charter for the Honorable A.E. Guinness of England, who brought a party to the United States.

"We flew them across the U.S. and Canada, and then left them in Chicago to board his yacht. In 1939 he returned for a similar trip, and we left them this time in Seattle. Those were the happy days. It is all vivid, and my memories are all good"

Regarding the many uniforms that Ida wore in the decades from 1936 to 1972, she didn't like the mini-skirt of the '60s, and thought the 1968 paper uniforms were a disgrace. They were worn on transcontinental flights and were made of high-fiber material. One size fit all, and the length was altered with scissors. There were four uniforms: a French gold lame cocktail dress, a British pub wench dress, a Roman toga, and New York penthouse black lounging pajamas. The uniforms were to give the international flavor of each country, and to compliment the culinary specialties of the country. However, it wasn't long before menus didn't match the uniform of the particular country because of uniform shortages. The replacement fabric was easily torn. Disgusted, Ida refused to wear the uniforms.

Ida said, "I was sorry to see the hat go. I think the uniform hat finished off a put-together look. It's the RN attitude, I guess."

Ida's memories of the people she served were important to her. She was totally dedicated to excellence and to all the work "hostess" implies: gracious personal consideration, as if the passengers on her flight were in her own home. She was always aware of her actions, wanting to represent TWA in the best manner. In a way, Ida had a love affair with TWA. It has been said, "She married TWA."

On the ramp at Kansas City, Ida models an updated, 1941 uniform.

Her long career of 36 years as a TWA hostess ended in a unique way. On June 21, 1972, TWA's board of directors honored their number one flight attendant, with a retirement party in San Francisco. The guest list included TWA people past and present who would honor Ida. They included: Chairman of the Board Charles Tillinghast, Jr.; retired Captain, Lee Flanagen of Los Angeles, who helped Ida check in for her first flight; Mrs. Vivian McCanna, the 1972 president of TWA's Clipped Wings International; TWA hostess Barbara Maloney who traced her birth to "Aunt Ida," who as a registered nurse had attended to her mother when Barbara was born; Colonel Dan Jacobs, Inspector General of the 22nd Air Force Military Airlift Command.

Colonel Jacobs commented on Ida's reputation of excellence in her care of military personnel and their families on TWA MAC flights to Travis Air Force Base.

A letter was read from then-California Governor Ronald Reagan, in recognition of Ida's 36-year career.

TWA Public Relations manager Jerry Cosley prepared a tribute in the form of a trial. The charges brought to Ida were:

(A) "That at the sacrifice of many personal considerations you have devoted 36 years to the feeding and care of passengers."

(B) "While in the employ of TWA, you have sought to subvert Murphy's Law to achieve a standard of excellence in morale and performance as a TWA hostess with good humor. Physical evidence consists of mounds of newspaper clippings from around the world."

Ida was then asked how she pleaded. More than 240 people rose with a standing ovation to show their respect and love for Ida Staggers.

Ida was tearful and speechless as the jury announced the verdict: "Ida Staggers is guilty of endless love for people."

Ida trembled and whispered, "Thank you, one and all."

Officials and guests said, "Goodnight Ida. Thank you from the bottom of our hearts."

Upon returning home, Ida opened a letter from the White House written on behalf of President Nixon and signed by Director of Communications Herbert G. Klein, honoring her impressive achievements from the days of the DC-2s to the 747s, and her million miles in the air:

```
          THE WHITE HOUSE
             Washington
           July 28, 1972

Dear Miss Staggers:
     On behalf of the President, I want to
offer you belated congratulations on the
event of your retirement as a stewardess
for Trans World Airlines.
     You have, during your career, compiled
some impressive statistics - 36 years
of flying, service to 100,000 servicemen
on the flight to and from Vietnam, not
to mention some 10 million miles in the
air! I am sure that you must have some
fascinating tales to tell from the DC-
2's to 747's. I join the President in
saluting these impressive achievements,
and wishing you the very best in the
years ahead.

Sincerely,
Herbert G. Klein
Director of Communications
for the Executive Branch
```

Ida returned to New York in 1980 after working for TWA's Canteen Corporation, at the North Rim of the Grand Canyon following her retirement. She was always a good ambassador for TWA, the airline she had dedicated most of her life to offering "Ambassador Service" all the way.

Ida Staggers died January 11, 1993 in New York City at the age of 81. Affection for Ida and her contributions to TWA will always be remembered and written in aviation's logbook.

The noted aviation author, Robert Serling wrote of Ida, "She wore her wings in two places: on her uniform and in her heart."

Helen Elizabeth McLaughlin was one of the earliest hostesses for Continental Airlines flying with them from 1943 to 1945 when she joined United Airlines for a two-year stint. She has written several books on the venerable position of service aloft and authored this tribute to TWA's renowned Ida Staggers, which has been reprinted with permission from her book, Footsteps in the Sky - An Informal Review of U.S. airlines' In-flight Service from the 1920s to the Present.

TWA Skyliner

*Ida speaks with soldiers
returning from Vietnam.*

The First Transcontinental Football Charter

By Captain Phares McFerren

Originally published in TARPA Topics, April 1982, and reproduced with permission.

In these days when athletic teams of all sorts and sizes are using air transport for getting to the game sites, sometimes halfway around the world, and every day across the continent, we give little thought to what it was like more than 60 years ago, when a team had to spend days in a stuffy train getting to and from the game location. Those long trips were tiring and expensive, and too much classroom time was lost.

TWA predecessor Transcontinental Air Transport (TAT) may well have flown the first-ever college football charter, way back in 1929, utilizing a Ford Tri-Motor to carry the University of New Mexico team to Los Angeles for a match against Occidental College.

Against this background, it was not too surprising when in the fall of 1939, Pittsburgh's district traffic manager, Robert Montgomery, talked the people at the University of Pittsburgh into signing for an Air Charter, with TWA to take their football team to Seattle to play the University of Washington. It was the first transcontinental college football charter in history.

A pair of TWA DC-3s operated the charter.

"Pitt" had a hotshot quarterback, one "Special Delivery" Jones, who had caught the public's attention. The combination of Jones and flying to the West Coast was too attractive for them to resist. So it was all set up. On the September 26, two DC-3s picked up the team in Pittsburgh, with coaches, trainers and others, and took off for Chicago. I was the regional chief pilot in Chicago at the time, and

An earlier charter trip, albeit not across the country, occurred in October 1929, when the University of New Mexico football team traveled on a TWA Ford Tri-Motor from Albuquerque to Los Angeles to play Occidental College.

had been designated by Operations Vice President Larry Fritz to be in charge of the charter.

Captain Ardell Wilkins and First Officer Bob Gandy flew the second DC-3. I took over at Chicago along with Deane Officer as co-pilot. I had prepared myself with route information, maps, charts, and was instructed by Mr. Fritz not to fly instruments or on top. None of the crew members had ever flown over routes, so we would be over strange terrain until reaching San Francisco on the return flight.

Bob Montgomery was the official representative of the company and responsible for the comfort of the passengers. The planes landed at Midway airport about lunchtime. I was waiting for them and I remember wondering about the gross takeoff weight as the huge young men come off the plane. I made a mental note to check the weights very closely, and I was alerted.

We were scheduled to overnight at Minneapolis, and arrived there early in the evening. I have no recollection of anything out of the ordinary happening that night, and my logbook has no notation.

The second day we had planned to land for fuel at Bismarck, and did so without incident. We also planned to refuel at Billings, which we did, then overnight at Spokane. Proceeding west from Billings, high clouds were encountered, which lowered as we went on. About the time we passed over Helena, Montana, the clouds were getting quite heavy. Since our forecast was good, I became concerned. It obviously was a front; a radio contact with the tower at Helena confirmed this. My maps showed a "Mullins Pass" up ahead, and as I went on beyond Helena, it became certain that I would have to proceed on instruments, into an unknown mountainous area.

I called Wilkins and told him I did not like what I was looking at and would return to Helena and check the weather. He replied, "I'll be waiting there for you". After looking at the weather sequences, we decided to spend the night in Helena. The team members received this news with glee; none of them had ever been out West, so this was great! They managed a full practice during the stop and, from the new hats and boots in evidence the next morning, I am sure they all had a good time.

I took some pictures of the team and crewmembers and we were off again, but not before cleaning about three inches of snow off the airplanes before. With the weather all cleared out, it was an easy flight to Spokane, our last fuel stop before Seattle.

Approaching the Seattle area we could see a pall of smoke in the western evening sky, but with the sun just a few degrees above the horizon we did not identify the cause of it. To further complicate matters, we eventually tuned in the Seattle tower and were then told the radio range was off the air, and the visibility was down to about half a mile, in smoke.

A Western Air Lines flight landed about ten minutes ahead of us, and the pilot immediately advised the tower that if we did not know the area, we were in trouble. As luck would have it, the setting sun reflected the outline of the bay in such a manner we could identify the position of the airport, and we were able to circle down from directly over the airport for a landing. I will always appreciate what the Western pilot did, as the tower was alerted to assist us.

With a day to use up before the game and some contacts made us, we enjoyed ourselves. I went fishing on the bay with the other three crewmembers, and while we caught no fish, the food and drink served us on the boat was delightful. We attended a party that night at the hotel, put on by someone I did not know, but no matter, it was a good day.

Saturday, game day, featured excellent weather, and we all attended as the guests of the University of Pittsburgh. The Pitt quarterback, "Special Delivery" Jones, lived up to his reputation and his team won the game before a capacity homecoming crowd.

We had planned on leaving early Sunday morning, but Seattle Airport was weathered in, so we spent day "on the town." About 6 a.m. Monday, the crewmembers gathered in the hotel lobby of. The weather was just clearing out, so we got things going and finally departed about 10 o'clock. Since there it was overcast and we had to land for fuel at Portland, I called Larry Fritz for permission to fly on top and make a descent through the cloud deck at Portland. This was given and the landing at Portland was routine.

We continued without incident to San Francisco, and were again in contact with TWA personnel. That was a good feeling. Again, none of us were familiar with the route to Burbank, so we took our maps with us to review the route, checked the forecast, got our clearance, and were on our way, with food provided on the plane.

About mid-way to the next stop we encountered some clouds, so I pulled out the map, only then to discover that somehow we had picked up the wrong chart at San Francisco! We had only the Burbank approach charts. With the mountains ahead of us this was not good. I was in contact with Wilkins, who was ahead of me, and asked him to check the headings into Burbank for me, and call out the minimum en route altitude. After passing Mt. Pinos we finally broke out in the clear, about 50 miles northwest of Burbank. I did not enjoy that situation!

According to my logbook we had flown 6 hours and 34 minutes from Seattle, and had been on duty for about 15 hours. At Burbank, we were told that Kansas City expected us to take the flights on to Kansas City, with a fuel stop at Albuquerque. I checked with the others and then advised Kansas City that we would take the charters on to Albuquerque, but would require either crew rest or a relief crew at that point. They did not really like that, but we were fully aware that fatigue had already eroded our efficiency to a very low level; another three and a half hours of flying would be stretching it far enough. I do remember a few words with the good Kansas City folks before we got them to agree on a relief crew.

Meanwhile the weather was good and the hot food at Burbank revived us. With our map supply replenished, we took off. Wilkins was off about 5 minutes ahead of me and even though I talked repeatedly with him by radio en route, not once did I establish visual contact.

We landed without incident at Albuquerque around 2 a.m. local time, happily turned the charter over to a relief crew and headed for the hotel. We had flown 10 hours and 23 minutes from Seattle with an on-duty time approaching 20 hours. Dehydration and low oxygen make a bad combination for good health and it took me three days to fully recover from the fatigue built up.

Fortunately we were all young and full of energy. I did wonder about the effects on the team members their next game. Bob Montgomery continued with the flight and they completed to Pittsburgh. I stopped off at Kansas City en route home to Chicago and gave a verbal report to Larry Fritz. He was very understanding and quite happy to learn the entire charter had been completed without incident.

We were all sold on the idea of air charters for athletic teams. But who would have ever imagined the extent of air charters for athletic teams such as are commonplace now.

Members of the Pittsburgh University football squad—33 strong—are shown here at Pittsburgh just before boarding two TWA Sky Sleeper planes for their 2,336-mile journey to Seattle, Washington, where they defeated Washington, 27 to 6, as the climax of the first transcontinental air trip ever made by a university football team.

TWA Skyliner

The Pittsburgh University football squad is shown at Pittsburgh before embarking on their 2,300-mile journey to Seattle.

Howard Hughes and TWA's Constellation Transcon Nonstops

By Jon Proctor

The only Constellation to wear TWA "Transcontinental Line"
titles never flew for the airline in revenue service.

Numerous publications have credited Howard Hughes for designing the graceful Lockheed Constellation; he did not. Nevertheless, Hughes was the driving force behind this elegant-looking, triple-tailed airliner, having proposed specifications for the aircraft.

The original Model 49 Constellation was on the drawing board in July 1939 as a 44-passenger, 6-crew transcontinental airliner. Hughes wanted to replace five Boeing 307 Stratoliners that entered TWA service in 1940 The first airliner with a pressurized cabin, seating 33 passengers and featuring Pullman-size sleeping berths, it lacked transcontinental, nonstop range.

Hughes wanted transcontinental capability within 8 hours, which meant an average speed of 312 mph for the California-to-New York, 2,500-mile segment. Assured the Constellation could do the job, he ordered nine aircraft, insisting the contract be kept secret until the first prototype flew.

By mid-1940, the number had been increased an $81-million, 40-aircraft contract, including

Frank Lennon Collection

This first-flight cover, carried on the record-breaking flight, was signed by Frye and Hughes.

exclusive rights to the first delivery positions off the assembly line, giving TWA a 2-to-3-year monopoly over its competitors. Hughes financed the entire deal himself.

The Constellation's distinctive appearance was also functional, with a fuselage resembling an airfoil. Its cross-section was a perfect circle, designed for the strength needed for cabin

TWA/Courtesy of Gary Smedile

Wearing parachutes, Jack Frye, left, and Paul Richter, right, are seen during a Connie test flight in April 1944.

pressurization. The tripletail design allowed use of existing hangar space and better engine-out control. Except for fabric rudders the airplane was an all-metal design.

When American entered World War II, TWA's Stratoliners were conscripted to the military and all new airliner production was halted by government order, but Lockheed continued building the prototype Connie, having proposed it as a troop carrier designated the C-69. It first flew January 9, 1943 while a second prototype took to the air a month later.

Sensing a publicity coup, Howard Hughes was to buy the first airplane destined for the military, for use on shakedown flights, then immediately sell it to the government at cost. Early on April 17, 1944, he and TWA president Jack Frye flew it from Burbank nonstop to Washington, DC, in the record time of 6 hours, 57 minutes, 51 seconds.

The airline's public relations department set up an elaborate arrival ceremony at Washington National Airport, hastily constructing two wooden boarding steps. Among the bevy of political and military leaders was General Henry "Hap" Arnold, there to accept the Connie on behalf of the Army Air Force.

Hughes took full advantage of the publicity opportunity by having TWA's markings applied to the Connie by Lockheed at Burbank. Among the bevy of political and military leaders there to accept the Connie on behalf of the Army Air Force was General Henry "Hap" Arnold. As the gleaming airliner taxied up in front of the Washington terminal building, the General was furious to see red airline colors instead of military markings but it was too late, and he graciously posed for the ceremonial handover.

The Constellation remained at Washington for a few days, where military markings applied, then ferried to Dayton, Ohio's Wright Field (now Wright-Patterson Air Force Base) for official handover to the government. On April 26 the first person to complete a heavier-than-air flight, Orville Wright, was given a ride and chance to briefly handle controls from the co-pilot seat.

Regular TWA 049 (the internal Model 49 designation) Constellation service began on February 5, 1946, first to Europe and shortly thereafter on transcontinental flights. Across the Atlantic double crews were assigned in observance of regulations limiting pilots to 8 consecutive flying hours, but the added cost on domestic flights was considered too expensive and an intermediate stop was made at Chicago.

Model 749 and 749A Constellations brought increased range, particularly on overseas segments, while the original 049s were relegated to domestic-only flights and converted to coach configuration in 1951. A year later stretched Model 1049 Super Constellations came on-line and with its added speed, began the first transcontinental nonstops, initially eastbound only, in October 1953.

Faster 1049G "Super-G" Connies entered TWA service in 1955, and became first in the United States to offer dual first-class and coach service with transcontinental nonstop low-fare flights. A handful of Model 1049H, convertible Super Constellations were acquired, initially for military passenger and cargo charter work and sold off in less than four years.

Lockheed 1649A Starliners began flying coast-to-coast in May 1957. Called Jetstream by the airline, these ultra-long-haul airplanes were designed for overseas routes but also provided the most luxurious accommodations of the day on transcon nonstops. But the competitive advantage was short lived. Within two years, Boeing 707s cut travel time in half and piston-powered airliners were quickly made obsolete.

Trans-Atlantic service was all jet by October 1961 with the remaining Connies relegated to domestic flying. The Super Connies and Model 049s were retired by year's end, when weather radar became mandatory; none had been so converted. The last passenger fleet was completed April 6, on a multi-stop New York-to-St Louis trip. A few 1649A freighters soldiered on until May 11, closing 21 years of Lockheed Constellation flying.

Howard Hughes had a lot of be proud of.

*General Hap Arnold and Howard Hughes disembark following a brief
tour of the Connie interior. Arnold managed a smile despite his anger after
seeing the airplane arrive in TWA colors instead of military markings.*

TWA/Courtesy of Gary Smedile

Several groups of dignitaries enjoyed scenic flights following the Connie's arrival
in Washington DC. Among them was then-Senator Harry Truman, seventh from left
and standing next to Howard Hughes. Elected Vice-President of the United States
that fall, Truman became President barely a year after this picture was taken.

Some of TWA's iconic Super-G Constellations were equipped with
removable wingtip tanks, each carried 600 gallons of fuel.

Airline Infantry – TWA's Mechanics

By Robert J. Serling

An abridged version of this story appeared in the July/August 2001 issue of *Airliners Magazine*.

They are the unseen warriors of every air carrier, unglamorous men and women who labor behind the scenes to assure safe flight.

TWA's mechanics, as a group, were no different than dedicated brethren on other carriers.

TWA Skyliner

Roy Davis sits at the desk in his O'Hare Airport office. He was seldom spotted without a cigar.

Yet through the years, they developed a tradition of their own, for they were not immune from the vicissitudes that marked TWA's turbulent history. What the mechanic's corps contributed was forging a reputation of maintenance excellence that actually helped keep the airline afloat during its most stormy periods. Maintenance certainly is vital in the crucial element of safety; like all carriers, TWA suffered its share of fatal accidents, but the overwhelming majority was caused by circumstances beyond the control of the airline or its personnel. And not one was directly attributed to poor maintenance, including the Boeing 747 that was the ill-fated Flight 800.

Even as TWA lost its corporate identity, its under-utilized maintenance facilities and people were among the major assets that attracted American Airlines to the debt-ridden airline.

It is a reputation that has spread beyond the United States, for through the years TWA provided technical support and training to such airlines as Saudi Arabian, Philippine, Ethiopian, TACA and Germany's Lufthansa. The latter was the first foreign airline from a former enemy to seek American help in its postwar, civil aviation operations.

During World War II, TWA contributed not just pilots, but scores of mechanics to the newly created Air Transport Command (ATC), the first full-scale military airlift in history. In 1940, President Jack Frye had anticipated just such a wartime role by establishing an Intercontinental Division (ICD), with headquarters in Washington, DC. He also promised that, in the event of war, TWA would turn over its five Boeing Stratoliners to the Army, at the time the only long-range, four-engine transports available. After Pearl Harbor, mechanics assigned to ICD began fashioning a new collection of legendary achievements. For example, a Stratoliner landed at an overseas station and couldn't take off again because of an inoperative starter. There wasn't a replacement on hand, but salvaging a starter from a captured German bomber being stored on the premises solved the dilemma. The part was retooled to fit the Stratoliner ignition system. It worked perfectly.

Roy Davis joined TWA in 1942 as an apprentice mechanic at La Guardia Airport, putting on DC-3 deicer boots and changing wheels. For the next 20 years, he lived the peripatetic life of virtually all airline employees, transferring from one base to another until he acquired enough seniority to have a little say in where he worked. No matter where Roy was stationed, however, he earned the reputation of a man who never goofed off, was never late and never complained about any task. You had to know him to realize that behind his no-nonsense was a heart as soft as wet oatmeal.

Just after war broke out, Roy was assigned to the ICD maintenance base at Washington, D.C. Early on, he was asked if he'd be willing to work at an overseas base, "just for a couple of weeks," he was assured. Those couple of weeks lasted through the entire war.

Returning again to Paris after the hostilities, Davis became known for his trouble-shooting abilities and later worked at New York-Idlewild and Pittsburgh before spending his last 23 years as TWA's General Foreman at Chicago's O'Hare International. It was there he caught the attention of author Arthur Hailey, who spent time at the airport while researching a book. Thus did Hailey create the fictional character, Joe Petroni, for Airport, which was later made into a motion picture. Actor George Kennedy played the part and became a close friend of Roy's.

When schedule cuts hit Chicago, Davis retired a year earlier than planned in order to save the job of one of his supervisors. It was pure Roy Davis, and an example of the airline's unsung heroes who kept 'em flying.

Author

During more than a half-century of aviation writing, Robert J. Serling won numerous awards for his objective reporting and contributions to public understanding of commercial aviation's problems and accomplishments. Among his 24 published books is Howard Hughes' Airline – An Informal History of TWA. He passed away at 92, in May 2010.

Remembering the Forgotten Mechanic

Through the history of world aviation
many names have come to the fore …
Great deeds of the past in our memory will last,
as they're joined by more and more.

When man first started his labor in his quest to
conquer the sky,
he was designer, mechanic and pilot
and he built a machine that would fly.
But somehow the order got twisted,
and then in the public's eye,
the only man that could be seen
was the man who knew how to fly.

The pilot was everyone's hero,
he was brave, he was bold, he was grand,
as he stood by his mattered old biplane
with his goggles and helmet in hand.
To be sure, these pilots all earned it.
To fly you have to have guts,
and they blazed their names in the hall of fame
on wings with bailing wire struts.

But for each of these flying heroes
there were thousands of little renown,
and these were men who worked on the planes
but kept their feet on the ground.
We all know the name of Lindbergh,
and we've read of his flights to fame.
But think, if you can, of his maintenance man.
Can you remember his name?

Now pilots are highly trained people,
and wings are not easily won.
So when you see mighty aircraft
as they mark their way through the air.
The grease-stained man with the wrench in his hand
is the one who put them up there.

—Anonymous

Jean Salvadore – TWA's Roman Queen of Glitterati

By Andrea Salvadore
Photos: courtesy of Andrea Salvadore

I was truly a TWA baby as both my parents worked for TWA in Rome, Italy. They were in their 20s, fluent in English and that was enough in those early days of trans-Atlantic travel. My mother handled public relations for TWA while my father was in marketing. What a great team.

To be the public face for the company in the late 1940s through the mid-60s meant meeting every celebrity coming to Rome or passing through and the list of dignitaries was immense from Ingrid Bergman to Ava Gardner, Elizabeth Taylor, Joan Fontaine, Lana Turner, Montgomery Clift, Richard Burton, Gary Cooper, Humphrey Bogart just to name a few. For my mom, being the public face of such a well-known company, which flew to the United States, was like being an ambassador of the two worlds.

In 2011, just a year before her death, she completed her memoirs and devoted a large part of the book to her 20-year career at TWA. She wrote, "Even though I spent 20 years working in public relations for TWA and thus for Howard Hughes, I have to confess that I never actually met

Jean greets Irish Premier Eamon de Valera at Rome's Ciampino Airport in 1948.

William Holden deplaning as his TWA flight arrived from the United States at Ciampino Airport.

him. I like to refer to Howard Hughes as my boss because he owned 78% of the shares of TWA and I reported directly to him via his office and spoke frequently with Noah Dietrich, his right-hand man. I received requests to handle all the film stars and Hollywood gossip columnists travelling to Rome via TWA. One thing was made crystal clear to me when I worked for him: Howard Hughes didn't want to be mentioned in the papers and I was told that nothing would please him more than never to see his name in print."

Mom loved her job and had a 20-year romance with TWA. She would nurse me between one VIP arrival and another, racing around Rome on her motorbike. She organized many mega parties including one, which celebrated the inaugural flight of TWA from Rome to New York. In 1962 she attended the inauguration of the TWA flight center at Kennedy Airport in New York.

There are many images of my mother greeting very famous people, but one was particularly meaningful to me. When she met Shirley MacLaine disembarking in Rome they were both wearing matching Chanel dresses; the only

difference was that my mother's was a perfect copy created by her beloved seamstress. In her book, *My Dolce Vita*, she wrote that her 20 years with TWA were the most exciting of her life where she made life-long friends. She left TWA after 20 years because my father had taken a job with the noted Italian publisher Rizzoli in Milan.

In those days, Rome was the city where many celebrities lived "la dolce vita" and it was the birthplace of the paparazzi of which she wrote, "I believe the birth of the paparazzi took place on March 20, 1949, when the one and only Ingrid Bergman stepped off the TWA plane in Rome and was immediately surrounded by dozens of photographers who went absolutely crazy as they chanted 'Ingrid, Ingrid!' I tried to shield her from the assault, but she towered over me and I was afraid that we would be trampled to death."

In her book she noted that Jacqueline Kennedy flew on TWA en route to Greece and made a 45-minute stopover in Rome but did not want the U.S. Embassy to get involved, as it was a private trip. Mrs. Kennedy had recently lost her

Jean Peters leaving Rome to return to Hollywood in 1953 after completion of the filming of Three Coins in the Fountain. *It was her last movie before marrying Howard Hughes.*

Jean met Richard Burton in 1962 when he took a day's leave from shooting Cleopatra *and flew to Paris for a cameo in* The Longest Day.

baby son Patrick Bouvier Kennedy who died a few days after birth.

"When the flight arrived, I met Mrs. Kennedy on the ramp. She was left to disembark and I asked the most obvious thing that came to mind: How was the flight? Without looking at me, and staring into space, Mrs. Kennedy whispered, 'delicious.'"

During my mother's 20 years with TWA what she enjoyed most was meeting journalists and authors who flew to the Eternal City on TWA. These included Walter Lippmann, Art Buchwald, Robert Ruark, Joseph Heller, John LeCarré and so many more.

My mother had a deep passion for TWA and the work ethic I saw in my mother was typical of pioneers. Working for an airline company in those years was probably like working in Silicon Valley today, but much more fun.

Mom was appointed as full-time public relations rep for TWA in 1948 when she was just 20 years old. She witnessed the rise of the celebrity-driven media industry first hand.

When any of these writers were going to pass through Rome and needed to be met, Mom would read about them and read their books and columns in an effort to carry on intelligent conversations when in their presence. She wrote, "To me, that was what public relations was all about. I always looked forward to meeting members of the press because that is what I wanted to become myself."

Karen Nelson wrote, "Jean was my treasured friend from the moment we met in 1960 during the Olympics until her death in 2012. Even though she migrated north to Milan, she and her airline were never far from each other. I was fortunate enough to work as a summer intern while in college, at Fiumicino airport in 1961, and was welcomed into her home and family and cherished her friendship

Jean was always on hand to meet celebrities, including the greatest gossip columnist of them all, Hedda Hopper.

for the rest of her life. Naturally, Giovanna had a twinkle in her eye and her favorite color was the cardinal red of TWA."

Giovanna was perfectly trained for her next position in life when she moved to the Milan area as she was director of public relations for the world famous Italian hotel resort Villa d'Este on the banks of Lake Como. Ironically, she left Hollywood's outpost in Rome to work in a similar job function with much the same clientele as Villa d'Este was known as "Hollywood on Lake Como." Like TWA, it was no stranger to notoriety and Mom took care of the world's elite, including royalty, bold face

Heartthrob Errol Flynn arrives at Ciampino Airport in 1949.

names and entertainers at the fabulous hotel, which continues to draw the crowds that are often the subject of gossip page columns.

Throughout her years at Villa d'Este she never forgot her roots at TWA and the unique lifestyle, which that great American company afforded her and the family.

Montgomery Clift is shown arriving at Rome in 1953.

Celebrities Aloft - A Pictorial

*Bob Hope receives a royal welcome at the JFK
Airport International Arrivals Building.*

Andrea Salvadore

*Lauren Bacall and Humphrey
Bogart depart from Rome.*

*Among the celebrities departing on a
special Burbank–New York Connie flight on
February 15, 1946, was Cary Grant, center.*

Jon Proctor

*Desi Arnez posed for a young photographer
at LAX in December 1960.*

Jon Proctor

*Gary Moore is seen on the ramp at LAX during
a television show filming in April 1966.*

Retired and living in Independence, Missouri, President Harry Truman flew on TWA often after leaving office.

The lovely Grace Kelly was a frequent TWA passenger during her silver screen career.

Vice-President Hubert Humphrey chartered a TWA 727 for his 1968 Presidential campaign.

Jane Russell boards a TWA DC-3 at Burbank. The actress was signed to a seven-year contract by Howard Hughes in 1940 and made her motion-picture debut in The Outlaw, *a Hughes production.*

Pat and Richard Nixon pose for the camera, shortly before the future President was elected to the United States Senate, from California.

Future baseball Hall of Fame inductee Willie Mays and his wife board a TWA 1649A Jetstream at New York.

President Dwight Eisenhower greets TWA press charter flight hostesses.

*Joe DiMaggio and his bride Marilyn Monroe are seen
departing on their honeymoon in January 1954.*

*TWA Director of Customer Service Jim Spaeth attempts a future booking from Lassie
aboard an L-1011, as the canine star's owner and trainer, Rudd Weatherwax, looks on.*

Ozark Air Lines

By David H. Stringer

Jon Proctor

Ozark's early DC-9s featured integral staircases both forward and aft. N973Z is seen at Peoria, Illinois, on October 6, 1967.

Ozark Air Lines was born on a spring day in 1943, when Homer Dale "Laddie" Hamilton met with his friend, Floyd Jones, and two attorneys, Barak T. Mattingly and Arthur Heyne, in the Title Guarantee Building on Chestnut Street in Downtown St. Louis. They were there to discuss forming an intra-state airline that would operate within Missouri.

A charter was granted and Ozark Airlines was officially in business (note that "Airlines" was one word in the original incarnation of Ozark). The founders intended for the company to eventually become one of the new "feeder" carriers that the Civil Aeronautics Board (CAB) was contemplating. They felt that the CAB would look favorably upon a company that had intra-state operating experience when it came time to issue the federal Certificate of Public Convenience and Necessity.

Scheduled service began January 10, 1945, when three Beech Model F-17D Staggerwings

David H. Stringer Collection
Initially designed for corporate use, three Beech Staggerwings introduced the first Ozark scheduled service in January 1945.

opened two routes from Springfield, Missouri: one to Kansas City via Clinton, the other to St. Louis via Rolla. From those terminals the aircraft would proceed to Columbia, and then repeat the pattern back to Springfield. Warrensburg was substituted for Clinton in April.

That summer, Ozark replaced its Staggerwings with two twin-engine Cessna

T-50s. Columbia was eliminated and Fort Leonard Wood was added. By November 1945, the company had yet to turn a profit and the little airline was shut down. The intra-state version of Ozark had lasted just shy of 10 months.

David H. Stringer Collection

Meanwhile, the company's executives applied to the CAB for a feeder airline certificate to operate a network reaching 28 cities in six states.

In the Board's Mississippi Valley Case, Ozark's application was not approved. Instead, the CAB selected Parks Air Transport as the carrier to be certificated for feeder routes reaching from St. Louis to Memphis, from St. Louis to Tulsa, and from Tulsa to Kansas City. Each route embraced several small intermediate cities, which was the purpose of the new feeder carriers. Oliver L. Parks owned Parks Air Transport.

Parks was well known in aviation circles. He had formed his pilot training school in 1927 and, by the mid-1930s, was operating a full-fledged aviation academy, Parks Air College, located at the Parks Metropolitan Airport in East St. Louis.

When the U.S. military required thousands of pilots during World War Two, Parks trained flyers in several different locations. After the war he merged his assets into Parks Aircraft Sales and Service, which offered fixed-base operations at various airports.

Thus, it was no surprise when Parks Air Transport won five of the feeder routes awarded in the CAB's North Central Case, three routes in the Great Lakes Area Case, and others in the above-mentioned Mississippi Valley Case.

Ozark Air Lines/Proctor Collection

The Prairie Aviation Museum purchased DC-3 N763A in February 1984 and applied this circa 1950 Ozark livery.

Parks was selected over Ozark Air Lines (now separating "Air Lines" into two words) by the CAB because of Park's "long and varied experience in aviation." The Board found Parks "fit, willing and able," and stated that the selection of Parks to serve such a large area, "will demonstrate the effectiveness of increased size of local operations in meeting the problems of operating costs, equipment, equipment utilization and financing." The Board would come to regret its decision.

While other feeder carriers began operations, the Parks system remained dormant. This was particularly disturbing because it had been awarded such a large network and the cities that had lobbied for this new air service were expecting it. When Parks Air Transport, now calling itself Parks Air Lines, had not inaugurated service over any of its routes by March 1949, the CAB decreed that the company would have a 102-day period in which to get its act together; service over the certificated routes should be inaugurated by July 1, 1949.

Oliver Parks and his executive team had faced problems raising capital. Specifically, they had been unwilling to risk much of their own money on the feeder operation. When Parks applied to the Reconstruction Finance Corporation (RFC) for a loan to help get his airline off the ground, he was refused because of a lack of sufficient equity capital.

Parks and his associates approached the board of Mid-Continent Airlines, a financially healthy trunk carrier, with a plan for Mid-Continent to acquire Parks through an exchange of stock. This would, of course, put money into the pockets of Mr. Parks and his cohorts. Mid-Continent was to operate Parks Air Lines as a wholly owned subsidiary. The plan required approval of the CAB and a public hearing was set for September 28, 1949 in Washington, D.C.

CAB members were livid, and the Parks Investigation Case was initiated. The Parks team contended that circumstances beyond their control prevented them from obtaining the necessary financing. They requested that acquisition by Mid-Continent be approved and, if not, that Parks be allowed to retain its certificate and conduct operations with small, single-engine aircraft.

The CAB stated that approval of the acquisition by Mid-Continent would not only condone the unreasonable delay in inaugurating service but would also permit Oliver Parks and his associates to profit from their inaction.

Then, on May 17, 1950, Mr. Parks announced that he had found "new capital" and could activate the routes with twin-engine aircraft. The change of fortune had come from the "merger" of a struggling non-scheduled carrier, Twentieth Century Airlines, into the Parks organization. With Twentieth Century came DC-3s and two founders of that airline: Rev. Chris A. Bachman, an ordained minister and president of Twentieth Century, and Glenn O. Shaver, the company's general manager and a pilot. But the CAB told Oliver Parks that it was too late. "There must come a time when administrative proceedings of this nature are brought to a close". The Board was ready to give all of the Parks routes to some other applicant.

Oliver Parks would not go down without a fight. On June 21, 1950, Parks Air Lines inaugurated service over the St. Louis to Chicago route with intermediate stops in Springfield, Decatur and Champaign/Urbana, Illinois. Parks stated that he now had the organization and the financing to activate his entire system by November 6, 1950. But the CAB would have none of it. On July 28, 1950, Parks Air Lines' certificate was revoked.

Arthur G. Heyne, the attorney who had been one of Ozark's founding executives, received a phone call in late July from his friend, Clyde Brayton of Brayton Flying Service. Brayton was also an instructor at Parks Air College. Heyne recalled the conversation:

"Congratulations!"

"For what?" Heyne replied.

"I see you just got a certificate from the CAB!"

"Aw, you're pullin' my leg. It's been seven years. Are you sure it's us?" Heyne asked.

Indeed it was. The CAB had awarded Ozark most of the Parks route system.

Then, according to Heyne, because of the recently instigated Korean War, "All those World War II surplus DC-3s and C-47s vanished." Something had to be done to get a very big feeder airline up and operating quickly. Ozark wanted what Parks could now offer: DC-3s, pilots and other personnel. A deal was struck and Heyne added, "Ozark, in essence, merged Parks Air Lines into its organization – the only solution since each badly needed one another."

Ozark's certificate became effective on September 26, 1950. On the evening of September 25, the Ozark group gathered at the Statler Hotel in Downtown St. Louis and waited for the stroke of midnight. At 12:01, they signed paperwork officially accepting the certificate and the airline was in business. At 6:58 that morning, Ozark's first flight took off from Lambert Field bound for Springfield, Champaign/Urbana and Chicago with one passenger aboard.

By August 8, 1951, Ozark had inaugurated service to 29 airports covering all of the routes awarded as a result of the Parks Investigation Case. This could not have been accomplished without the manpower, expertise and equipment provided by the Parks team. Many former Parks Air Lines employees went on to enjoy long careers with Ozark.

The airline grew steadily, adding new stations and deleting unproductive points as allowed by the CAB. On May 19, 1955, U.S. President Eisenhower signed the bill that gave permanent certification to Ozark and the nation's 12 other Local Service Airlines, as the Feeders were now called. This acknowledgement of a permanent place in the U.S. airline system made investors much more confident about betting their money on Ozark stock. Ozark ended 1955 with 535 employees and 16 DC-3s.

In order to keep its aging fleet as competitive as possible, the company undertook a modification

Convair 240 N2404Z is seen during a 1963 open house at Lambert Field, St. Louis.

Fairchild-Hiller FH-227Bs entered service in December 1966.

program for its DC-3s, producing higher performance standards by installing wheel well doors, flush-type antennas, and other improvements. Ozark's DC-3 fleet became the most efficient in the industry. The program was completed by September 1957 when all aircraft had been standardized with the new equipment and each was configured with 27 passenger seats.

In December 1958, Ozark placed an order for three new jet-prop Fairchild F-27s, which carried 40 passengers and, because the wing was above the fuselage, gave every passenger an unobstructed view of the world below.

Laddie Hamilton resigned from his positions as president and chairman of the board in 1959, due to failing health. Floyd W. Jones was selected to take over as board chair and, on October 16, 1959, Joseph H. FitzGerald became president of the company.

The F-27s debuted on January 4, 1960. With introduction of the Fairchilds, Ozark adopted a new logo, described as "Three sets of two overlapping elliptical curves arranged to suggest the graceful swept-back wings and deeply forked tail of the swallow." The 3 Swallows symbol became so associated with Ozark Air Lines that its use continued until the end of the company's existence.

Ozark purchased four 40-passenger Convair 240s to accommodate an expanded schedule at Peoria and Springfield, Illinois, and at Joplin and Springfield, Missouri, when American Airlines abandoned service at those four cities in 1962 and '63. Now the sole carrier at all four points, the "little" airline with the green airplanes was soon carrying more total traffic out of each of these cities than had ever been generated before.

By 1964, twelve Ozark stations were each boarding more than 20,000 passengers per year with Chicago at the top of the list enplaning almost a quarter of a million. The company introduced the slogan, "Go-Getters Go Ozark!"

Joseph H. FitzGerald resigned as Ozark's president at the end of July 1963 and Thomas L.

Grace was recruited from Northeast Airlines to fill the vacancy. He dove headlong into the issues facing Ozark and worked out an agreement with Mohawk Airlines to take that company's fourteen Martin 404s in exchange for cash plus Ozark's Convair 240s. The first Martins went into service on Ozark's system on December 1, 1964.

Big news came in January 1965 at the dedication of Ozark's new general office building and maintenance facility at Lambert Field. Thomas L. Grace announced that Ozark would be entering the ranks of pure-jet operators in 1966 with the arrival of three Douglas DC-9-15s.

Grace's plans did not stop there. He ordered 21 Fairchild-Hiller FH-227Bs, an enlarged and modernized version of the F-27, to replace both the Martins and the F-27s. The new airplane had stronger Rolls Royce turbine engines, carried its own Auxiliary Power Unit (APU), and could accommodate 48 passengers. Grace's goal was to turn Ozark into an all-turbine powered carrier by the end of 1967.

The first scheduled DC-9 service took to the skies on July 15, 1966, from St. Louis to Chicago via Peoria. On board that inaugural jet flight was Arthur B. Skinner of Kirkwood, Missouri, who had been Ozark's very first passenger back in September 1950.

The FH-227B entered service on December 15, 1966. Ozark spent the next several months operating five different aircraft types: DC-3s, Martin 404s, F-27s, FH-227Bs and DC-9s.

The airline embarked on three memorable advertising campaigns in succession in the late Sixties. In 1967, the award-winning "Hostess Campaign" featured St. Louis model Pat Christman wearing an Ozark flight attendant uniform. Photos of her in different poses were presented along with two-line copy, such as: "I can't bear to think of you driving all the way to Kansas City. No one to spoil you." The Hostess Campaign was followed in 1968 by the introduction of "Go-Getter Bird," a cartoon bird dressed in an Ozark pilot uniform, and finally, in 1969, a campaign entitled "Letting George Do It", which featured young comedian, George Carlin.

"Have a sudden meeting in another city? We'll rise to the occasion."

Serving Mid-America from Minnesota to Oklahoma . . . from Indiana to Colorado.

go-getters go **OZARK** AIR LINES

David Stringer Collection

*An advertisement from the airline's 1966 annual
report featured Pat Christman, a St. Louis model.*

Ozark retired its last Martin 404 on August 14, 1967, and the final F-27 service took place in October of that year.

After the company's last scheduled DC-3 flight operated on October 26, 1968, Ozark finally met Tom Grace's goal of becoming an all-turbine powered airline.

On April 27, 1969, service was introduced to Washington, D.C. (Dulles) and New York (LaGuardia) from Peoria and from Champaign/ Urbana, Illinois. The award also allowed flights from Waterloo, Iowa and Springfield, Illinois, to the East Coast. The 956-mile Waterloo–New York authority was the longest segment awarded to a local service carrier at the time.

In 1971, with a modern fleet of DC-9s and FH-227Bs the airline introduced its new slogan, "Up there with the biggest!"

Thomas L. Grace passed away in July 1971, and Edward J. Crane, executive vice-president and treasurer, took Grace's place as Ozark's president.

Innovations such as the internationally themed Flair meal service and wine tasting flights brought attention to Ozark's cabin service, and the company boarded its 30 millionth passenger on May 19, 1975.

Unbridled competition among the nation's airlines became inevitable after President Jimmy Carter appointed pro-deregulation economist, Alfred Kahn from Cornell University, to head the CAB. The U.S. Deregulation bill was signed into law on October 24, 1978, and the entire industry began to change.

Ozark's expansion after passage started out in an orderly fashion. Unlike Braniff and other carriers, Ozark met the challenges of the new environment by expanding judiciously. Sadly, many smaller cities that had been the reason for Ozark's existence in the first place were abandoned by the company.

Now Ozark was heading in a new direction, forced, some would say, by circumstances beyond its control. The company's last FH-227B flight operated on October 25, 1980, leaving a fleet of 30 DC-9-30s, two DC-9-30LRs and seven DC-9-10s. In order to generate cash during a flight attendant strike, two factory-fresh Boeing 727-200s were sold without ever entering service.

No longer in business to feed passengers to other carriers, Ozark's new goal was to feed passengers to itself through the St. Louis hub. Ozark had the disadvantage of competing with another strong player at its hometown airport: TWA. To have two airlines centering domestic operations in a market the size of St. Louis was a recipe for trouble.

On July 28, 1983, Ozark placed an order with McDonnell Douglas for four new McDonnell Douglas MD-80s (previously referred to as DC-9 Super 80s), each equipped with 152 passenger seats. Sanford N. McDonnell, CEO of McDonnell Douglas, noted at the time that Ozark was the largest exclusive operator of DC-9s in the world.

When the new D Concourse at Lambert Field opened for business it gave Ozark a state-of-the-art locale for its hub operation. Dubbed AIRPLEX, the company now had 22 gates available for exchanging passengers among its flights. Ozark entered into an agreement with Air Midwest to provide feed from smaller stations to its St. Louis hub, effective October 1, 1985. Named Ozark Midwest, the operation provided the same type of feed that Ozark formerly provided for other airlines. All service into Springfield, Illinois, once an Ozark stronghold, was now turned over to the commuter carrier.

In 1985, two things happened that would change everything for Ozark: Southwest Airlines, the low-cost carrier that did not follow the pack, entered St. Louis, going right into the St. Louis–Chicago market among others. Then, through a hostile takeover, Carl Icahn gained control of TWA. Icahn went to work reducing labor costs at TWA and reducing passenger fares, making it a more formidable competitor. Ozark was forced to meet new challenges. Ozark

made money during the first half of 1985, but then went into the red. Cash flow was critical. In December, Crane approached Ozark's unions proposing profit sharing and stock ownership in exchange for wage concessions. It was all happening a little too late in the game.

Edward J. Crane, the accountant, had abandoned Ozark's smaller stations and built the airline into a national player with routes radiating solely from St. Louis, which wound up being the corner that he painted himself and his company into. The Crane management team had produced a few profitable years for Ozark since Deregulation but the clock was running out for the airline of the 3 Swallows. It had not grown big enough to withstand major players and it was too late to totally change its game plan and become a low-fare point-to-point carrier like Southwest. When Carl Icahn made an offer to buy Ozark for $19 per share, he had the upper hand. The offer was accepted and announced to the public in February 1986. Ozark employees certainly wondered why their company, which had been profitable for the past few years, should now be up for sale. Ozark management felt that TWA and the low cost carriers would crush Ozark if the company tried to remain independent so they took advantage of an offer that might not have been made a second time.

Icahn merged Ozark into TWA and got rid of the 3 Swallows and the green paint, along with the company name that had been associated with Midwestern states for so many years. The official merger date was October 27, 1986.

Ozark's successful rise from a four DC-3 operation to a national airline with a fleet of 50 jets was the result of the dedication and hard work of its loyal employees, proud to work for the great "little" airline that was "up there with the biggest".

Douglas Historical Archives

Two long-range McDonnell Douglas DC-9-34s, including N928L, were acquired in 1980, allowing the startup of nonstop St. Louis–San Diego service and lengthier charter flights.

David H. Stringer is the History Editor of Airways Magazine *and a member of the Editorial Board of* The Aviation Historian (TAH), *a British publication. His airline career spanned 32 years with Southern Airways, Republic Airlines, and Northwest. David's research and writing are focused on preserving the stories of the companies, the aircraft and the people who are now part of commercial aviation's past.*

TWA Ambassador Service – Traveling in Style

By Jon Proctor

Mel Lawrence photo/George Hamlin Collection

The Golden Age of air travel. Polar Flight 870 awaits customers at Los Angeles.

Purser Russ Robbins prepares a champagne service for his guests aboard an all-sleeper luxury Ambassador Service Constellation flight to Europe.

A similar service was initiated with TWA's new New York-London route, and sleeper flights were increased to twice-weekly frequencies.

The Ambassador name was carried over to domestic with TWA's introduction of 1049 "Super" Constellations, referred to as "Ambassador Service in the U.S." Although restricted to domestic flights, the 64-seat, all-first-class Super Connie cabins were equipped with eight convertible berths for use on night flights. A fold-down table in the "cozy" seven-seat lounge provided space for an elaborate snack buffet presentation.

Ambassador Service was greatly enhanced with the introduction of 1049G "Super G" Constellations in April 1955, the first dual-class aircraft in the United States. Passengers seated in the noisier forward cabin received "Golden Banner Deluxe Coach Service" that featured hot meals for purchase, along with

In 1948, just a year before TWA began offering "Sky Coach" flights within the United States, the airline took its trans-Atlantic service to a higher level by introducing weekly, all-sleeper "Paris Sky Chief" flights between New York and Paris with a scheduled stop at Gander; westbound, it became the "New York Sky Chief." Limited to 18 passengers, the cabin layout included a cocktail lounge in the forward section of the main cabin. Advertisements spoke of champagne dinners and a pre-arrival hot breakfast "served in bed, if you prefer!" With the delivery of longer-range 749A Connies, TWA moved these trips from La Guardia to Idlewild Airport with its longer runways, beginning nonstop flights in November 1951, although weather conditions still dictated occasional en route landings for fuel.

The upgraded flights became known as Paris and New York "International Ambassador" service, while the Sky Chief name was reassigned to domestic first-class segments.

The Super G Constellation lounge where well-dressed passengers enjoyed the lap of luxury.

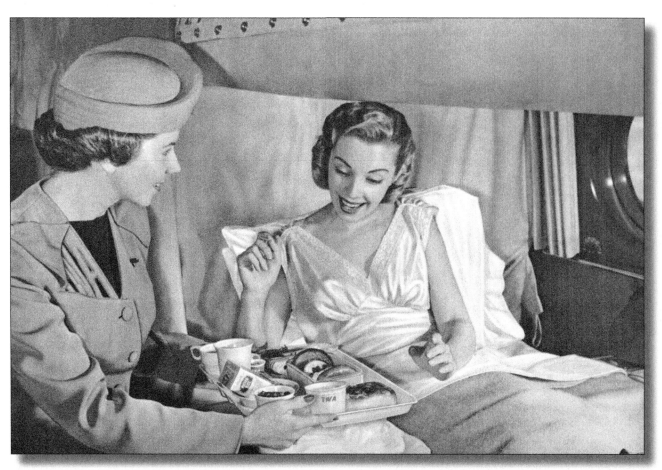

Hostess Lynn Stanton offers breakfast in bed on a Connie.

cocktails for sale. Meanwhile, a limited number of sleeping berths were available for Ambassador customers on night flights. In the more spacious mid-cabin "Mural Lounge," canapés and cocktails were presented from a silver-serving

Chateaubriand carved at your seat, just one feature of Royal Ambassador Service.

tray, followed by a more elaborate meal service with wine and champagne. Trans-Atlantic Super G service began November 1.

The ultimate Ambassador Service was offered aboard TWA's model 1649A Jetstream Starliners, which began replacing the Super Gs two years later. This airplane, often referred to as the "Cadillac" of the Constellation series, entered service with TWA in June 1957 on trans-Atlantic and longer domestic routes.

The Ambassador moniker gave way to TWA's "Royal Ambassador Service" in June 1961, aboard Boeing 707s across the Atlantic. Perhaps the ultimate first-class experience at the time, it was limited to just 20 passengers, attended by three hostesses and the purser. The experience began with hand luggage delivered the passenger's reserved seat. A choice of seven dinner entrees included Chateaubriand carved on an aisle cart, part of a multi-course, 2-1/2-hour

*Twenty first-class passengers were served by three hostesses and a
purser on trans-Atlantic Royal Ambassador flights.*

meal presentation served on Rosenthal china and Steuben crystal glassware. "R/A" Service was later expanded to long-haul domestic flights and became the envy of competing airlines for the rest of the decade.

In April 1970, TWA resurrected the Ambassador Service trademark as part of a complete makeover of its Boeing 707 and Convair 880 cabin interiors to more closely match the 747s that began joining the fleet earlier in the year. The identity, which extended to both first class and coach, later expanded to the airline's 727s as well.

Although the "new" Ambassador Service was well received, it could not match the individualized attention that cabin crews were able to give their customers on the longer flights completed in the pre-Jet Era, when there was time for leisurely meals, making up sleeping berths and offering passengers breakfast in bed.

The Royal Ambassador crest.

Lessons from Tragedy over the Grand Canyon

By Jon Proctor

A different Super Constellation is seen over the Grand Canyon during an early publicity flight. The sequence of pictures was removed from circulation following the accident.

Until Flight 800 went down in 1996, no accident stirred as much press coverage and personal loss for TWA employees as the mid-air collision between one of our Super Constellations and a United DC-7 over the Grand Canyon on June 30, 1956.

This is a condensed version of my original story, published in the August 2006 issue of Wings Magazine.

At the Los Angeles Airport gate on that morning, TWA Flight 2, a 1049 Super Constellation, sat ready to depart at 9:30, bound for Kansas City and St. Louis, then Washington National Airport. At departure time, there was sufficient space for all 25 "non-rev" standbys, consisting of airline employees and family members; one was an infant, technically leaving a single passenger seat vacant.

On the opposite side of the same concourse, United Air Lines DC-7 Flight 718, called "The Hollywood" in the airline's timetable, was readied for its scheduled nonstop flight to Chicago-Midway Airport with continuing service to Newark via Detroit and Philadelphia.

The Super Connie taxied towards its departure runway just ahead of United and lifted off from Runway 25-Left at 10:01, followed in line, only three minutes later, by United 718.

Commanding the Kansas City-bound Constellation was Jack Gandy, a 41-year-old, 17-year TWA veteran with no less than 177 previous flights over this route. First Officer Jim Ritner, a four-year employee, and Flight Engineer Dean Breyfogle, along with with Hostesses Traci Armbruster and Beth Davis, rounded out the working crew. In addition, Flight Engineer Harry Allen hitched a ride on the flight by utilizing the cockpit jumpseat.

As the two airliners climbed through the overcast to their planned altitudes, each was flying on instrument flight rules (IFR) on assigned "airways." The planes took divergent routes that were to cross over Arizona's Painted Desert. United 718 headed to 21,000 feet on a southerly course while TWA 2 was cleared to 19,000 feet.

Jon Proctor

Char Butte, where the United flight fell, is visible in the center of this image. The TWA Connie came to rest almost directly below it, across the confluence of the Colorado and Little Colorado Rivers.

Later, TWA 2's crew contacted its company radio operator to request a flight plan altitude change from 19,000 feet to 21,000 feet, in order to get above a cloud deck. Gandy added that if that altitude was not available, he would like "1,000 on top," an imprecise but routine clearance to fly 1,000 feet higher than the clouds until 21,000 feet became available. The request, forwarded to air traffic controllers, was denied because of its converging flight path with United 718, but 1,000 on top was approved, along with a courtesy advisory that there was traffic in the area – United 718 – at 21,000 feet.

Gandy confirmed his 21,000-feet altitude to a TWA radio operator at Las Vegas and estimated that Flight 2 would reach the Painted Desert checkpoint at 10:31; the information was relayed to the Salt Lake City ARTC. Following their flight plans, both pilots guided their airliners away from the assigned airways as they crossed the California-Arizona border, and began flying more-direct headings to their destinations, another common practice. Once "off airways," the pilots were under VFR conditions and would not receive traffic advisories; they assumed responsibility to avoid other aircraft. In any event, transmitted position reports from the pilots only served to provide a space flow into the next controlled airspace ahead.

Closer to the Grand Canyon, thunderstorms were building, with tops up to 25,000 feet. Both flights probably dodged the clouds and may well have been making turns to give their passengers better views of the scenery below.

At 10:31 Salt Lake City controllers and a few other flights in the area picked up a barely audible radio transmission, but none could hear it clearly. Perhaps an aircraft was experiencing radio trouble. That weak radio transmission, captured on tape, was later deciphered and revealed the chilling words: "Salt Lake, United 718 … ah

… we're going in." In the background, another crewmember could be heard shouting the words, "up … up!"

Shock and Awe

As he came to work at Los Angeles Airport that afternoon, 21-year-old Commissary clerk Ron Green had been with TWA barely two months. A hushed atmosphere greeted him; one of the company's planes was missing and presumed down somewhere in Arizona. Green went about his duties on the ramp as directed by shaken managers, only to come across a United employee who exclaimed, "Hey, we've got a flight missing; it left here this morning." The TWA rookie replied, "We've got one missing too." The ironic coincidence struck them simultaneously: could the two airplanes have hit each other?

At Kansas City, where a crew change was scheduled for TWA Flight 2, hostess Ona Gieschen and her flying partners were rostered to work the continuation of the trip, to St. Louis and Washington National Airport. Instead of receiving

A TWA DC-3 pilot trainer was used to transport remains
from Grand Canyon Airport to Flagstaff.

Jon Proctor

The TWA mass burial plot at the Flagstaff Citizen's Cemetery.

routine crew calls, they were told that the Connie was missing and presumed down, but another Constellation was being readied to operate the flight on its final two segments. Remembering that her parents knew she was working Flight 2, Gieschen got off the plane in St. Louis and called to reassure them that she was safe.

In the fading evening light, Grand Canyon scenic flight operator Palen Hudgin made a low pass over a column of smoke he had reported earlier in the day. The pilot spotted the distinctive, triple-fin tail of the TWA Connie a few hundred feet from a smoldering swath of wreckage near Temple Butte, at the eastern end of Grand Canyon National Park; there was no sign of life. Hudgin also reported the possible sighting of another wreck but by then it was too dark for certain identification. A Sunday morning flight confirmed the location of United's DC-7, on top of and down the slopes of Chuar Butte, a mile from the Connie wreckage and near the confluence of the Colorado and Little Colorado Rivers.

On the same morning, a military helicopter approached the TWA site, landing 500 feet above the canyon floor. An accompanying medic had little to do but confirm what was assumed: there were no survivors. Another 'copter crew, hovering 100 feet above the United wreckage, reported the same observation; the combined 128 fatalities represented the largest death toll in any civil air disaster to date.

Businesses around the country reopened Monday morning, the first workday of a new month. Those large TWA wall calendars given out by company public relations and salesmen needed an update. In barbershops, banks, travel agencies and offices of corporate clients around the country and overseas, merchants flipped over the large-format page, revealing the month of July and a striking color photo … of the Grand Canyon.

Grim Recovery

The Connie's location was on a rock shelf, but helicopters still had a difficult time dealing with winds and heat during the day. During one recovery, pieces of the Connie were found with paint from the DC-7, in addition to small bits of the aircraft itself, confirming a mid-air collision.

A few days later, TWA's vice-president of public relations, Gordon Gilmore, sound asleep in a motel room at the Grand Canyon's South Rim, received a call at 2 a.m. from Howard Hughes. He expressed his concern and sympathy for TWA crewmembers and passengers who had lost their lives, and asked that his regards be extended to TWA people working on the scene.

But he was also upset about a Los Angeles newspaper photo showing a bulldozer preparing a mass grave for the unidentified TWA dead. Gilmore assured Hughes that all possible steps were being taken to meet every standard of respect and dignity. A religious service would include clergy from the Catholic, Jewish and Protestant faiths. "What about Mormon?" asked Hughes, who surrounded him self with members of the Church of Jesus Christ of Latter Day Saints because they neither drank nor smoked. A day later, LDS Elder Delbert Stapley was flown in from Salt Lake City to help officiate at the memorial service.

On July 9, more than 350 people attended a burial service at the Flagstaff Citizen's Cemetery; 1,500 others watched from near by. At a mass gravesite, 67 of those aboard TWA Flight – 63 of them unidentified – lay in three rows of caskets. Three identified remains had been transported to their hometowns for separate burial. At the last minute, the family of one victim had a change of heart and asked that the identified remains be sent home instead of resting with the others. Following completion of the memorial service, the casket was removed, leaving only 66 to be interred. Unaware of this, wire services mistakenly reported the higher figure throughout the media.

Once the human remains were recovered, along with relatively small pieces of the two airliners necessary for the investigation, all work at the crash sites ended. It was decided

to leave the remaining wreckage where it lay. Airline and government officials felt they had been fortunate enough with recovery efforts that involved 76 helicopter trips to the sites; there was no reason to take further risks by trying to extract anything more from the canyon.

The Cause

On April 17, 1957, the CAB released its 53-page report on the probable cause of the accident, which revealed no surprises. The facts in the case were straightforward: these two airliners were flying through uncontrolled airspace in an area where the Civil Aeronautics Administration (CAA) had no responsibility

Jon Proctor
Headstone for United dead at the
Grand Canyon Cemetery.

*Flowers decorated the TWA gravesite plaque to
mark the 50th anniversary of the accident.*

to control traffic. Their pilots were following standard procedures, having violated no rules.

What were the odds of two airliners departing Los Angeles three minutes part and colliding over the Grand Canyon? "If we'd tried our level best to make sure they'd meet," said an airline official, "we couldn't have managed it in a hundred years."

The Fix

A $246-million, five-year plan to modernize air traffic control had been approved earlier in 1956. Following the accident, the government rolled out a formal plan to provide "positive control" of all aircraft flying above 18,000 feet regardless of weather conditions. Expanded use of radar was to be followed by more sophisticated equipment, such as three-dimensional radar displays. Radio transponders on aircraft would eventually transmit their identity to computers that would display the information to the radar screens. In addition, the CAB held hearings on the merits of a crash-survivable "flight recorder" device that would record the airliner's altitude, compass heading and airspeed, among other things.

Longer-range radar systems were ordered to cover larger areas of heavy traffic. Collins Radio Company, a major manufacturer of aircraft radio systems, began work on an instrument that would not only warn pilots of approaching planes but also adjust the plane's flight path to avoid a collision. Similar devices, which only warned of traffic, were envisioned.

Public outcry from the Grand Canyon accident prompted Congress to pass the Federal Aviation Act in 1958. This legislation brought about the Federal Aviation Agency (FAA). With independent authority and funding to modernize and run the country's air traffic control system, it replaced the CAA.

Although progress was made over the four years following the accident, TWA and United were involved in a mid-air collision over Staten Island, New York, on December 16, 1960. Ironically, the identical model 1049 Constellation was involved, this time coming together with a Douglas DC-8. And, like the Grand Canyon accident, there were a total of 128 passengers and crew aboard the two aircraft; all perished, along with five people on the ground. The newer DC-8 was equipped with a flight data recorder, although it only provided altitude, airspeed, heading and vertical acceleration readouts.

Epilogue

In August 1976, TWA Corporate Communications Director Jerry Cosley stood on the floor of the Grand Canyon, near the Connie's final resting place, surveying the wreckage that still remained. Working with Park Service representatives and a company that specialized in recovery of heavy items, Cosley would act as the airline's representative while a substantial amount of the rubble was removed from the canyon. Twenty years had passed since the mid-air collision, and now the Parks Service wanted whatever was left of the airliners, especially the Connie debris, taken away. While the United crash site was all but inaccessible, the area where TWA went down was *too* accessible. Each summer, hundreds of river rafters would tie up at the riverbank and stomp through the grass and wild flowers, looking for souvenirs.

The Arizona Air National Guard assisted private contractors who agreed, in writing, that they would melt down and recycle the metal; none could be resold in another form; recovery photography was also forbidden. There were to be no ghoulish mementoes of this accident.

When NBC-TV's managers learned of the activities, they contacted TWA for a story. Turning a lemon into lemonade, Cosley invited the producers to let one of their reporters from the Today show travel across the country in the cockpit of a Lockheed L-1011 and report on the advances in ATC that had been brought about by the Grand Canyon accident. By doing this, he redirected NBC's focus to the positive developments that resulted from the air disaster, rather than the grim details of the debris extraction.

More wreckage was removed four years later, and as recently as 2004, representatives of the Navajo tribe that live in the canyon requested further cleanup of what they thought might be remaining pieces of the wreckage.

Today, many tourists that come to the Grand Canyon travel on commercial flights that are continuously tracked from takeoff to touchdown

Thomas Donahue

Following designation of the accident site as a National Historic Landmark, the National Park Service posted this tablet at the South Rim.

by air traffic controllers. Although these visitors are probably not aware of it, the enhanced safety of their flights can be traced to lessons learned from a 50-year-old tragedy that ended in this place of natural beauty.

The author wishes to thank those mentioned TWA employees and friends, who shared their memories of events surrounding the accident. In addition, much of the information gathered for this story came various newspaper articles, accident reports and an excellent website: http://www.doney.net/aroundaz/grandcanyoncrash.htm

Fly Me to the Moon

By Craig Kodera

"This is Captain Collins speaking…" came the reassuring baritone voice over the ship's Public Address system. There is our stewardess at the passenger door clad in the customary uniform of our airline, albeit a bit more futuristic. Everything bespeaks a typical passenger flight. Are we sitting aboard another TWA Constellation flight to New York? Hardly. We are comfortably seated in the passenger cabin of the Star Of Polaris at Disneyland in California, Fall 1955, and this craft is about to take us on a flight to the moon!

Not just another "ride" at an amusement park, the TWA Moonliner in Tomorrowland acted as symbol and substance of the unlimited future world approaching us in the middle of the twentieth century in America. There was absolutely no reason to believe we couldn't someday have revenue flights into space, just as we could most certainly count on robotic houses and flying cars in the not too distant times to come. Walt Disney, ever the visionary and (thankfully) optimist, always knew to ask "why not?"

A TWA poster advertises both the airline and Moonliner.

Designed by Disney imaginer John Hench working under the tutelage of rocket scientists Wernher von Braun and Willy Ley, the 76-foot-tall Rocket To the Moon as it was officially known, was actually a one-third scale model of the space craft as envisioned by its creators. The rocket was clad in aluminum sheeting, just like the real thing, although it was structurally like a boiler with a steel skeleton. Early in the planning process as part of Disney's sense of dynamic marketing, TWA President Ralph Damon was brought into the mix so that the red stripes of Trans World Airlines would be seen flying over the park. A nice touch of believability, the advertising was beyond effective. After all, TWA at that time was the official airline of Disneyland. As an added bonus, Disney struck another deal, this time with Strombecker Models to recreate plastic kits of several items from park rides, most notably, the Moonliner. One could purchase one of these

kits a few yards from the real thing, in what was known as Hobbyland.

Inside the actual attraction, passengers who had their "boarding passes" proceeded to the terminal boarding area clad with TWA signage and staging, where they viewed a TWA "agent" explaining the workings of their rocket and the trip into space using a cutaway model, and animated films on the space port viewing screens. All reference to dates was the year 1986. Inside the passenger compartment now, and another two gigantic viewing screens, one above and one below, showed all aspects of our flight. The ever present voice of Captain Collins as he narrated our progress and provided us much scientific knowledge and perspective reassured us that all this spaceflight business was purely routine, and that we would return safely to our launching port unscathed. Passengers on the ride enjoyed the earliest amusement park use of air jackhammers

When Disneyland opened in 1955, this color post card was added to TWA's in-flight stationery folders.

and moving seats to heighten the effects and impart realism to the movement and motion of the rocket. This truly was a realistic look at spaceflight, as far as thinking in 1955 went.

Coincident with this attraction, the Disney television program seen on Sunday nights, featured a three part series inspired by a multipart serial in Collier's magazine, using live actors and plenty of animation. Titled Man In Space, one section of one episode borrowed portions of the thinking and presentation from the Rocket To The Moon ride at the park. In short, everywhere one looked in the mid '50s time period, space exploration was an integral part of our adventure through life. This tugged at the reality of flying a prop-driven airliner to span the country, which therefore became preparatory to understanding why the future MUST include commercial jet transports.

In the meantime however, flying to the moon on TWA was just the most "futuramic" thing a regular person could do.

Born and raised in an aviation family, native Southern Californian Craig Kodera has enjoyed an aviation career of his own. Starting with the United States Air Force, and then being hired by AirCal and merged into American Airlines, Craig finished his flying in 2000 and has since concentrated on his fulltime dual passions of fine art painting and writing.

Memories of "The Irascible Ren Wicks"

By Mike Machat

It was Christmastime 1956 and I was visiting my grandparents in New York City. Sitting on the sofa in their apartment reading *LIFE Magazine*, I was awestruck by a double-page ad showing an artist rendering of TWA's magnificent Lockheed 1649 Starliner. Named *Jetstream*, this giant new airliner was poised to enter service in 1957. Gazing at the ad, however, it was hard to comprehend that an artist created a painting so realistic, so dramatic, and so beautiful. As a nine-year-old kid who loved drawing planes, I could only dream of making such perfectly straight lines and precise lettering, or rendering metal so flawlessly.

I distinctly remember looking at the airplane's wings and thinking they were really, really long, and that the engines were placed too far outboard on the leading edges. Even at that young age, I could tell the artist had exaggerated the airliner's graceful structure for dramatic effect, yet I was totally captivated by that image. I scoured every inch of the ad studying the artist's technique, and found his name written

Mike Machat

Ren Wicks

elegantly in script within the clouds. The name was Ren Wicks.

Years later, as a newly minted member of the Society of Illustrators of Los Angeles, I met

The depiction of lengthened wings on the Jetstream were done at the request of Howard Hughes.

Ren and so began a wonderful friendship based on our mutual love of aviation and history. He was a very stylish gentleman who always wore a dark blue blazer with an ascot. Other Society members used to lovingly joke about Ren's stature in the business, saying "Even God couldn't afford to hire Ren Wicks!" Ren also relished being called irascible, although he had a heart of gold.

Wicks was the personal artist for TWA Chairman, movie mogul, and billionaire industrialist Howard Hughes. In the late 1950s, Hughes sent Ren to Europe and hired a helicopter (I'm guessing a Sikorsky S-55 with its wide side door open) to fly him over major cities served by TWA to take reference photos. That's how Wicks was able to produce those stunning ads of TWA Boeing 707s flying over London, Paris, Rome, Madrid, and Athens.

During lunch at our favorite table at Musso & Frank's in Hollywood one day, I couldn't resist asking Ren about that TWA *Jetstream* Connie ad, and judging by the expression on his face, I could tell there was a good story involved.

"Hughes called and woke me up at 3:00 in the morning," recalled Wicks, "and told me to meet him at a warehouse in Culver City." The two men sat on metal folding chairs cloaked in the secrecy of that vast empty space and discussed the illustration job in great detail. "Hughes specifically asked me to lengthen the wings and exaggerate the distance from the inboard engines to the fuselage," Wicks confided. Then they went to breakfast where Hughes asked to borrow a dime to make a phone call.

The long straight wings of the 1649A were a key selling point for Lockheed, since the increased distance from engines to fuselage

A Wicks masterpiece is this 707 interior painting, showing the dome lighting designed to look like portholes in the cabin ceiling. At night, pinholes of light against a dark background gave the impression of a night sky filled with a galaxy of stars.

significantly reduced noise and vibration inside the airliner's cabin. By complying with Hughes's request to alter the aircraft's wings in the painting, Ren's rendering assumed the proportions of a sailplane, almost resembling the 300-foot wingspan of another airplane closely associated with Howard Hughes – his iconic HK-1 Hercules flying boat, better known as the *Spruce Goose*.

Adding to the feeling of the *Jetstream* gracefully soaring above the clouds was the subtle use of wide-angle distortion Wicks deftly employed in depicting the airliner. The painting is simply a timeless classic, and although the airplane may not be to scale or structurally accurate, you can bet that ad resulted in many ticket sales to TWA passengers who flew aboard one of the most beautiful airliners of all time.

Ren's magnificent ad became forever etched in my memory, and hearing his story finally solved the mystery I'd been wondering about all those years.

While attending the American Society of Aviation Artists' annual forum in San Diego in 1992, my name was called at the banquet as winner of that year's ASAA Founders Award. I saw someone carrying my painting up to the stage to place it on an easel for the award presentation, and that person was none other than Ren Wicks. My painting, entitled *Home for the Holidays*, portrayed a TWA Constellation flying over New York City on Christmas Eve, 1956. It was a surreal moment, as I recalled vivid memories of seeing Ren's *LIFE Magazine* ad in my grandfather's apartment that very same year. Life imitates art, indeed!

Welcome Aboard...

. . . this magnificent jet airplane. When you first know the pleasure of free, effortless flight in the outer atmosphere, your feelings, emotions, and sensations will be something you have never before experienced. Even on the ground, every line of the **TWA BOEING 707** — first of the TWA Jets—inspires confidence... and tells you here is the ultimate in travel speed and comfort. You notice at once the swept back wings...the absence of propellers on the four great pure jet engines. And above all—the majestic size of this totally different plane!

Another classic Wicks rendering shows a family standing in awe as they gaze at a brand-new Boeing 707.

Mike Machat was a staff artist for Douglas Aircraft and established his own aviation art studio in 1984. He was elected first president of the American Society of Aviation Artists and his murals grace the Bob Hope Airport and Museum of Flying in Santa Monica, California. His award-winning paintings hang in the Smithsonian Museum and the Pentagon.

The Longest Day – TWA's Jetstreams
By Jon Proctor

The magnificent 1649A Starliner during a pre-delivery test flight. Pilots called it the "Cadillac of Connies."

While TWA's Model 1049G "Super-G" Constellation had nonstop trans-Atlantic range, prevailing winds and/or winter weather often required fuel stops, especially on westbound segments. Southern European destinations from New York were beyond its capability as well.

In December 1954 Howard Hughes ordered 25 Model 1449 Connies, a turboprop variant still on the drawing board and scuttled by Lockheed only a month later when it was discovered that the T-34 engine was not conducive to the Constellation's wing design. At first, the manufacturer proposed the model 1549 with Allison 501 turboprops, but ultimately, 3,400-horsepower, turbo-compound Wright 3350 EA-2 engines were chosen for what would become the model 1649A Super Star Constellation, a name later shortened to Starliner. Larger, 16-ft, 10-in diameter propellers were incorporated and the 1449's wing was retained. Its 9,728-gallon fuel capacity was sufficient for the airplane to reach any TWA European destination and fly even Europe-to-California polar flights nonstop.

A Ren Wicks depiction includes a look at the Jetstream lounge. Each 1649A had a different lounge mural depicting a TWA destination.

TWA's "Polar Girl," Sarah Pike, poses with officials before the departure of eastbound Inaugural Jetstream Flight 870 on September 30, 1957.

TWA's marketing name, "Jetstream," was adopted for this last of the Constellation series, with Howard Hughes given credit for the idea, although others claimed credit. Of course, the name conjured up visions of a jetliner, but the corporate excuse was that it related to the Starliner's ability to take advantage of jet stream winds.

Following a long delivery delay, TWA was able to introduce its Jetstreams June 1, 1957, on New York (Idlewild)-London-Frankfurt segments. After initially operating all "Sky Tourist" flights mixed, first class/tourist flights began in August. It was not until 1958 that the type dominated TWA's trans-Atlantic flying, barely a year before 707s began replacing them in November 1959.

Until the jets arrived, TWA's 1649As provided the industry's premier service.

Harry Sievers

*Ground staff and crew members stand in the shade under the wing of 1649A
N7307C, after arrival at San Francisco following its record-breaking flight.*

Perhaps the type's greatest asset was it ability to provide reliable nonstop flights across the Atlantic in both directions, even westbound from southern Europe. Its range was even sufficient to allow TWA to begin nonstop flights between the U.S. West Coast and Europe via the Polar route. And while Super G Connies and DC-7s struggled to complete westbound routes across the country against heavy winter winds, the Jetstream completed these segments with ease.

The Jetstreams were furnished with "Siesta Sleeper Seats," perhaps the most comfortable on any airliner at the time. With pullout foot rests and deep seatback recline, the chairs were nearly as comfortable as berths that were also available and provided a competitive edge, both on trans-Atlantic and transcontinental segments. In the Mural Lounges, each 1649A featured a different Maric Zamparelli wall painting representing major cities and nations served by TWA.

On September 29, 1957, twice weekly nonstop Polar service from Los Angeles to London began, flights that took more than 18 hours to complete. Celebrities on the inaugural included actress Donna Reed. On October 1, the first westbound trip, from London to San Francisco, found its way into aviation folklore, having endured the longest time aloft for a scheduled landplane segment.

Flight 801, fully loaded with nearly 10,000 gallons of high-octane fuel, wasted no time after leaving the gate at Heathrow Airport and lumbered off the ground to begin the 5,300-mile trip. The augmented crew included Captain Gordon Granger, TWA's international division director of flying, along with three other pilots, two flight engineers, and two navigators. Purser Gerard Miston and two hostesses looked after 32 passengers, including tennis star Pancho Gonzales. Timetables listed the scheduled time aloft: 22 hours, 5 minutes.

TWA
JETSTREAM*

NEWEST...

FINEST

IN THE

SKIES

*Jetstream is a service mark owned exclusively by TWA.

The trip was subject to a fuel stop, if necessary, at Frobisher Bay (now known as Iqaluit, Nunavut), the principal of three approved alternates in Canada, where a TWA mechanic was permanently based. However, Granger was determined to fly nonstop to California. As a conservation measure,

he filed a flight plan using super-long-range cruise procedures. The intention was an initial, steady climb to 7,000 feet, but two hours after leaving London, over the Irish Sea, the Starliner had reached only 2,000 feet. At 4,000 feet, climb power was reduced, letting the airplane gradually ascend consistent with weight reduction as fuel was burned off. The planned initial altitude was finally attained as the airplane approached the southern tip of Greenland. An airspeed of 200 knots was maintained during most of the flight.

As Flight 801 passed abeam Winnipeg, the crew received a re-release to San Francisco from TWA Flight Dispatch and pressed on. Clearing the Rocky Mountains required a climb to 16,000 feet. Over Pocatello, Idaho, a gradual descent was begun, again conserving fuel as the airplane drifted down. Power was further reduced as the altitude bled off and, according to Flight Engineer Jerry Zerbone, "Our engines were barely turning over."

Following the Humboldt River into the San Francisco Bay Area, descent continued as the airport came into sight. With Oakland Airport visible on the left, just in case, Captain Granger completed the landing on Runway 1 and pulled into the gate 23 hours, 31min after blocking out at Heathrow. The Starliner had been in the air for 23 hours, 19 minutes, a record that stands to this day, although a retired TWA pilot told me he was "pretty sure" that on one of the westbound polar flights, which he flew as first officer, they exceeded 24 hours in the air, but added, "I'm not sure it was completely legal!"

Along with a Lockheed technical representative, an official from the Civil Aeronautics Administration was on hand at San Francisco to check the amount of fuel remaining. Three hundred gallons were required to be "legal," which is exactly what was collectively left in the four main tanks; the other five were empty. Remarkably, the same cockpit crew later re-boarded Flight 801 and flew it on to Los Angeles.

Operating the Jetstream Polar flights nonstop was more a matter of prestige than efficiency. The added weight of full fuel loads prevented cargo carriage and burned more avgas in the process. Using normal cruising speeds with a stop would actually have resulted in less flying time.

While "going direct" may have been popular with customers, these epic journeys did not last for long. TWA's introduction of trans-Atlantic jet service in November 1959 allowed much quicker connections between California and Europe via New York, and the Polar flights were discontinued.

In May 1960, Boeing 707-331s began operating from Los Angeles to Paris with a fuel stop in Montréal, cutting the en route time to 12 hours, 30 minutes. The Canadian stop was eliminated when 707-331B Intercontinental "StarStreams" took over on December 15, 1962; 747s replaced the 707s on October 31, 1971.

Hollywood is depicted in one of the Jetstream murals by Maric Zamparelli.

Flying to Bombay on TWA in 1960

By Marvin G. Goldman

Photos courtesy of the author

Project India 1960 members gathering at rear steps leading to TWA
Boeing 707-131, N731TW, at LAX, prior to publicity photos.

As a young college student at the University of California, Los Angeles (UCLA), I was fortunate to be competitively selected as a member of the 1960 "Project India" team. The program aimed to foster U.S.-India relations during the politically charged atmosphere following India's independence. Each year for 17 years starting in 1952, Project India trained and sent to India up to 14 U.S. college students from UCLA and two sister campuses for a summer of interaction with Indian college students, including presentations on U.S. student life and discussions on current events affecting U.S.-India relations.

Project co-leader Don Hartsock (left), with two team members, Corinne Holman (Rieder) and the author, Marvin G. Goldman, about to board TWA Boeing 707-131 N731TW, at LAX.

The program was sponsored by the University Religious Conference at UCLA and assisted by the U.S. Information Agency. Project India's success contributed to the founding of the U.S. Peace Corps in 1961.

TWA linked up with Project India right at the beginning of the program, in 1952. When one of the Project's founders asked a friend at TWA about the cost of flying to India, the airlines' managers recognized a public relations opportunity to promote its Asian business and offered two free tickets (the maximum allowed by law at the time) if the Project would buy the rest. TWA also offered the help of its representatives at each stop along the flight routes to assure that all went smoothly. The Project raised the needed funds through contributions, and thus began a love affair with TWA that continued during the entire life of the program.

The TWA tickets for my 1960 Project India group were issued on June 23, 1960 for departure from Los Angeles on June 25, with the ultimate destination being Bombay (now Mumbai). Those were not the days of nonstop flights or even one-stop flights to India. Our routing was Los Angeles–

Baltimore/Washington–New York–Paris–Zurich–Milan–Rome–Athens–Cairo–Dhahran–Bombay.

Excitingly for us, TWA had just introduced the pure jet Boeing 707 to its fleet just a little over a year before. TWA used the opportunity to take publicity photos of our group at Los Angeles International Airport (LAX) in front of one of its earliest 707s, N731TW, resplendent in its red and white livery in the morning California sunshine.

On June 25, we boarded our flight at LAX, with bright red-and-white TWA flight bags in hand, compliments of the airline, bound for Baltimore, so we could first meet with U.S. State Department officials in Washington. This was a nonstop night flight (yes, they had 'red eye' night flights from the West Coast to the East Coast even then). Of course, we all dressed up for the flight, coat and tie for the men and stylish dresses for the women, just as most people did those days when flying. There was more comfort in economy class than now, with plenty of legroom and very attentive service.

Then on June 28 we flew on TWA from Washington National Airport to New York's Idlewild Airport (now JFK), where we would connect to our flight across the Atlantic. 1960 was a year of transition in aircraft types for the major airlines. Piston engine prop aircraft still principally operated short flights, such as Washington to New York, so I didn't think much about switching to a "temporary" short flight on a TWA Constellation for that segment.

Upon arrival at New York's Idlewild, we were offered a bus tour of the airport. This seemed strange to us, but as it turned out, this was no ordinary airport. Idlewild was being transformed with newly constructed separate terminals and others under construction. The magnificent TWA Flight Center, designed by Eero Saarinen in the shape of a large bird with spread wings, was partially completed, and we looked with awe on this fantastic architectural gem representing the spirit of flight. That evening we boarded another TWA 707 flight, this time to Paris, with a connection by Constellation for the short hop on to Zurich. In Zurich we would have a two-day rest stay befor proceeding to India.

The arrival at Zurich remains etched in my memory. As we disembarked outdoors on a fresh Swiss morning, and walked on the tarmac to the terminal, I saw hundreds of people on the terminal terrace, looking, waving, taking in all the excitement of passengers arriving and departing, from and to all parts of the world. Other airport visitors were dining outdoors on the terrace while enjoying the aircraft views. The year 1960 was a time of great optimism in the world. New nations in Africa were becoming independent. Jet aircraft travel would bring peoples of the world closer together, hopefully leading to worldwide peace, notwithstanding the West's Cold War with the Soviet Union.

From Zurich we took a short flight by Constellation

via Milan to Rome for an overnight, and the flight to our ultimate destination of Bombay originated the next morning at Rome's Ciampino Airport. Shortly thereafter Leonardo da Vinci-Fiumicino Airport opened and took over that role.

For the long flight from Rome to Bombay, I had expected a return to one of TWA's jets. However, looking out at the tarmac at Rome Ciampino, no TWA 707 could be seen. Instead there rested a TWA Lockheed Constellation propeller aircraft, which was to be our mount to Bombay. At the time I thought this was an old, antiquated aircraft. Yes, the aircraft looked pretty new, but after all, the Jet Age had arrived, so why was TWA flying a "second-tier" aircraft on a long international flight? Little did I realize at the time that this "old" aircraft was freshly minted at Lockheed's factory only two years earlier. It was a Lockheed L1649A 'Starliner' Constellation, registration N8084H. Noted airline historian Ron Davies called this model "the ultimate piston-engined airline flagship." TWA called it the "Jetstream," no doubt trying to give the impression that it was as good as the new pure jet aircraft. (See *The Longest Day*, page 67).

Front of TWA L1649A 'Starliner' Constellation, N8084H, showing TWA fleet number 328 on fuselage to left of the stairs, with Project India 1960 team members boarding, at Ciampino Airport.

Arrival of Project India1960 team at Bombay's Santacruz Airport. The author was last off the plane and had yet to emerge from the exit door.

we took on some additional passengers who were returning to India following the recently completed Hajj pilgrimage.

I had a right-side window seat on the Constellation, near the prop engines. At night I could see flames from the exhaust of each engine, a rather scary sight until assured that this is entirely normal. The drone of the engines actually helped lull me to sleep during the night hours of the flight across the Arabian Sea. Shortly after daybreak we descended to Bombay in a light monsoon rain and landed smoothly at Santacruz Airport on July 4.

Our Project India team had a very productive two-month stay there, giving presentations at some 100 Indian colleges and other organizations, mixing with local students and business groups and meeting with Prime Minister Nehru, many other Indian government representatives and U.S. Ambassador to India Ellsworth Bunker.

The Jetstream indeed performed flawlessly. There was plenty of room in the comfortable seats, two on each side of the aisle. The food was "great," as I wrote home on one of the TWA postcards furnished in the seat pocket and graciously mailed for me by a TWA hostess. The aircraft type had a range of well over 4,000 miles (6,437 km), the longest of any piston propliner ever built, and could easily have made it to Bombay with at most one stop, but our route had three stops; Athens, Cairo and Dhahran, Saudi Arabia. The stop in Dhahran occurred in the middle of the night. There

For our return flight home on TWA, we all expected to again board a Constellation for the initial legs to Europe. However, lo and behold, on the tarmac at Bombay airport rested a TWA 707. That very summer Air India had introduced 707s on its Bombay to Europe route, and to stay competitive TWA did the same. So on TWA we returned to Los Angeles all the way on Boeing 707s.

Years later, as an airline enthusiast, I learned about the fate of TWA's glistening 1649A Starliners. The aircraft I had flown on to Bombay, just two years old at the time, carried passengers for only one more year, until 1961, at which time it was converted to a freighter. TWA withdrew and stored the aircraft in 1964. In 1968, only 10 years young, it was scrapped, a casualty of the jet revolution in air transport.

Nevertheless, TWA's ultimate Constellation, the L1649A 'Starliner', was a proud bird, and I will never forget the beauty and grace of this greatest of piston-powered aircraft. I will also always remember TWA for its contribution to the success of Project India.

For the story of Project India (including its initial contacts with TWA and its connection to the U.S. Peace Corps), see *Project India: How College Students Won Friends for America, 1952-1969* by Judith Kerr Craven, Mill City Press, 416 pages (2014).

Marvin G. Goldman graduated from UCLA law school and practiced corporate and international law at one of New York's large firms for 43 years. His airline memorabilia collection includes more than 280 different TWA postcards, and he writes the Postcard Corner *column of the World Airline Historical Society's publication,* The Captain's Log.

The Convair 880

By Jon Proctor

Terry Waddington photo/Author's Collection

Trailing its signature smoke, Convair 880 N826TW soars into the late-day sun at Los Angeles.

Built at San Diego by the Convair division of General Dynamics, the Convair 880 was the fastest jetliner of its time, although its range was less than the Boeing 707 and Douglas DC-8. It had great passenger appeal, not only for its speed, but also its more comfortable five-abreast coach seating and reduced interior noise level.

Over a 13-year span, Trans World Airlines operated the largest 880 fleet of any carrier, although a plan for TWA to be the first to put the type into service was thwarted by Howard Hughes. As was his practice, Hughes purchased the aircraft, and then leased them to the airline he controlled.

The initial sales contract for the sleek 880 came from joint launch customers Hughes and Delta Air Lines. Forty Convair jets were jointly ordered in 1956, with 30 for TWA and 10 for Delta. But when the first airplanes were ready for delivery in 1960, Howard Hughes could not pay for them without borrowing money from banks, and these institutions declined unless he would put up his TWA stock a collateral. Hughes refused and the airplanes sat in San Diego. Meanwhile, Delta began accepting its fleet and put the type into service on May 15, 1960.

Once Hughes gave up control of TWA on December 30, 1960, new management quickly arranged financing and accepted six 880s, allowing the startup of Convair 880 "SuperJet" service less than two weeks later, on January 12, 1961.

TWA's 880s began service with an 85-passenger capacity, configured with 11 rows of four-abreast first-class seats plus a 12-seat lounge – six available for sale – and seven five-across rows in coach. The initial plan was for an all-first class layout, matching Delta's configuration, but the growing appeal of more economical fares dictated almost token coach capacity. This changed more dramatically over the years.

TWA's Convairs initially began flying short- to medium-length routes, from New York-Idlewild, Chicago-O'Hare, Phoenix, Las Vegas and Los Angeles, followed shortly by Dayton, Kansas City and San Francisco. The longest segments were from Chicago to Los Angeles and San Francisco. Albuquerque and Baltimore followed in April. Eight-eighty operations were initiated at Columbus, Ohio in September.

Speed records began falling immediately. On January 24, an 880, averaging 680 mph, flew from Chicago to New York in 1 hour, 11 minutes. A month later, another Convair SuperJet covered the San Francisco–Chicago segment in 3 hours, 5 minutes. In March, Flight 124 streaked from San Francisco to Los Angeles in only 39 minutes. These feats were accomplished before speed restrictions below 10,000 feet were implemented, but the Convair jets bested even Boeing 707 records.

Twenty 880s were in service by the end of September, a much-needed infusion of jet capacity to TWA's schedules. By then, service to Indianapolis and Oklahoma City had been added, along with Denver, Boston and St. Louis

Awaiting financing, a portion of the TWA Convair fleet sits at San Diego's Lindbergh Field in 1960.

By the end of August 1962, Convair jets were serving 17 TWA cities. A nearly nonstop transcontinental flight had been added, between Pittsburgh and Los Angeles. Although the 880s were flown strictly on domestic routes, TWA managers contemplated basing a limited number overseas to operate intra-European flights from gateway cities. Reportedly, some of the airplanes were pre-wired at the factory for high-frequency radio use, but the plan never came to fruition.

The 12-seat lounge was intended for an all-first class layout.
It was partially removed before complete elimination.

Popular five-across coach seating proved to be a competitive advantage when TW launched "Briefcase Commuter Service," in business travel markets, advertised with emphasis on "roomy, comfortable 2 and 3 seating at low coach fares." When United Air Lines began its new One Class Red Carpet DC-8 service in 1963 with a similar five-across arrangement, TWA countered by placing 880s on most of the routes, while American Airlines did likewise with its newly acquired Convair 990s. Even with only a $6 difference between One Class and coach rates, United was unable to compete and eventually abandoned the arrangement system-wide.

The 880's Achilles heel was its high fuel consumption. It burned the same amount as a non-turbofan 707-331, but carried substantially fewer passengers. Unlike the Boeing jets with adjustable seating, the Convair's seats were bolted to the cabin floor, at a generous 38-inch pitch in both first class and coach. As a result, more rows could not be squeezed in to grow capacity. The only option was to increase the number of coach seats at the expense of first class. From its original 48 first class/35 coach configuration, the mix continually changed until at one point it reached 20/77. Even that

George W. Hamlin

TWA and Delta were co-launch customers for the 880.
Examples of both are seen at Louisville in October 1971.

was not enough to offset the spike in oil prices in the early 1970s.

Plans to gradually replace the Convair fleet were announced on April 25, 1973. TWA ordered seventeen Boeing 727-200s with options on 17 more; deliveries were to begin the following year and stretch through 1975. But when the energy crisis began to take a toll on airline operations, immediate schedule cuts were implemented and the 727 order was deferred. The 880s began leaving during the second half of the year, and all were withdrawn the following summer, Flight 449, from Chicago to Kansas City, closed out Convair 880 service on June 15, 1974, nine years before the 707 disappeared from TWA's schedules.

Author

N821TW, seen at Los Angeles in 1964, was the only TWA 880 involved
in a fatal accident, at Cincinnati three years later.

Growing Up with Ethiopian Airlines
By Fred Reid

I was born in San Francisco in 1950, a few years after my father had returned from the conclusion of World War II, along with his war bride, Heidi. He was pounding the pavements in Alameda in the East Bay in his starter job as a salesman for TWA.

The conclusion of World War II opened up an opportunity for Ethiopia to finally establish a national civilian airline. In June 1945, an Ethiopian delegation dispatched the United Nations to approach the United States Department for Technical Assistance. Uncle Sam arranged a meeting for the Ethiopian government officials to meet with Brigadier General T. B. Wilson, Chairman of Transcontinental and Western Air, predecessor to TWA.

Fred Reid

An Ethiopian DC-3 somewhere in the outback.

Wilson agreed to provide assistance as long as the Ethiopians came up with the money. He believed that Ethiopia's capital, Addis Ababa, could become an important hub in the region, and was later was proven right. By September 1945 details were in place whereby TWA would provide a management team, pilots, accountants, administrators, instructors and technicians to establish Ethiopian Airlines.

Following the successful inaugural flight to Cairo, a regular weekly service was established. Weekly services to Djibouti and Aden followed, as well as a domestic service to Jimma. Demands for additional services were so great that towards the end of 1946, four more C-47 Skytrains were purchased. Since these aircraft were ex-U.S. military, they had few comforts: folding bench-type canvas seats along the sides, with the central aisle kept clear so that cargo, (including sheep and cows) could be lashed to the floor.

Ethiopian Emperor Haile Selassie, as I understand it, had asked our State Department to send "a few good men" over to Addis Ababa for a decade or so to bring Ethiopian from the DC-3 to

Fred Reid

Spartan accommodations were the norm in early DC-3 days.

the (yet unknown) 707 era. As told to me, they got all the technical guys but no one wanted the Head of Sales & Marketing slot. My father, Daniel, was an outdoorsman and fine hunter so he accepted and off we went when I was about a year old.

My earliest recollections were of a beautiful landscape with crystal clear bracing air (Addis is at about 8,000 feet elevation) and the amazingly beautiful chiseled-features of the Ethiopians. Until today, I recognize them unfailingly and stop to say hello.

I recall flying around the country on days when I was not attending the English school, under a corrugated tin roof with no walls whatsoever: I would get entranced with the rain on the roof during class. Short hops were on the vintage DC-3s with no seat belts, frequent-flier points, food, or even WiFi!

The captains were a steely bunch of ex-war pilots with lit cigars clenched in teeth who occasionally came back during the flight to order the tribesmen with goats, sheep and even

Douglas Historical Archives

Factory-delivered DC-6Bs helped to modernize the airline in the 1950s.

Boeing Historical Archives

Ethiopian's first of three new Boeing 720Bs arrived in October 1962.

cows to stop lighting small fires to prepare lunch. The legendary Tex Salyers and Swede Golian were classic examples.

Day trips were a memorable affair: places like Djibouti, Harare, Asmara and dirt fields with wind socks and no terminals. A low pass was required first so that alerted tribesmen could remove cows and livestock.

Long-haul trips to Europe and on to the United States were a different affair: a cozy First Class cabin with men in suits and Fedoras and women in minks and heels. Everyone smoked and drank the whole time.

At the office, Dad had a curved corner office overlooking a busy square. Furnishing were *Mad Men* style with African culture. There was a boy who washed his car almost daily in the parking lot. Later, during the revolution, Dad got him into the United States and I was told he got into MIT on a scholarship and became a great engineer.

Our sociable and gregarious parents held all-night parties that my brother and I watched from the doors of our bedroom: raucous crowds of Italians, Ethiopian Cabinet Ministers, war pilots and some Germans of possibly dubious backgrounds among many others. One morning I awoke to the living room leather chairs resting on the roof.

By 1960 Dad had moved back to New York headquarters, where I sensed he was not so fond of mid-town skyscrapers in a small office versus pre-dawn duck hunts in a souped-up 1929 Ford Model A with his boys tucked under blankets in the rumble seat.

By 1962 he had relocated to San Francisco as Regional Sales Manager for the West and Hawaii. His huge office overlooked Union Square and the large windows were always open to accommodate incessant cigar smoke. In 1964 he was moved back to New York and became Vice President - Sales & Services, then Senior Vice President - Operations, and became a member of the Board. Not bad for a guy who evidently did not finish college.

He rose to airline General Manager during a CEO search and ran TWA on an interim basis, before moving to Kansas City as Executive Vice President - Technical Operations. In January 1978 Dad left TWA after 33 years and joined Lockheed in charge of L-1011 sales.

In addition to its assistance to Ethiopian Airlines, the U.S. government also called on TWA to train pilots from across the world thereby helping to cement partnerships with other countries in an attempt to block the expansion of the Soviet-led communist power. Included in the roster of airlines were Germany's Lufthansa and Saudi Arabian Airlines.

Ethiopian today is fully owned by the Ethiopian government and has become the leader of African airlines in terms of revenues and size of its fleet. Among the carrier's modern jetliners are thirteen 787s with 10 on order. Revenue has grown by an average of 25% per year. In 2015, the airline employed 8,500 and flew to 91 international and 20 domestic destinations with a fleet of 76 aircraft.

The last TWA contract employee left Ethiopia in 1974 and with the invaluable early assistance of TWA, Ethiopians are today managing one of the world's great airlines, ever mindful of how TWAers formed the underpinnings of Africa's finest air transport network.

The airline has transformed itself from a competent regional player to be the continent's leading carrier in just five years. In a region where most airlines are struggling to break even as they deal with the collapse in commodities and political instability, Ethiopian Airlines has recorded a full-year profit of more than all other African carriers combined. Analysts attribute much of the success to the carrier's benevolent owner, which does not demand dividends and, through state policies, helps to keep down labor and financing costs.

Because of my association with Ethiopian through my dad's employment there, I follow the carrier closely and am not surprised that it is Africa's fastest growing airline. It recently launched a three times weekly service from Los Angeles to Dublin, continuing to Addis Ababa and is using the Irish location as the European hub city. With the addition of Dublin, Ethiopian now serves 11 European cities with a network that stretches across 85 destinations on five continents. It has the youngest fleet in Africa, with an average aircraft age of only 7 years. I am proud to know of the role that my father and his TWA colleagues played in laying the foundation for such a successful international air carrier.

I did not plan it this way, but ended up starting early in the airline industry myself, after a stint as a management trainee with the Taj Group of hotels in India. My starter job was writing tickets by hand for Pan American in Saudi Arabia for the princely sum of $14,000 per year!

One thing led to another, and I think I pleased my father by going on to become President of both Lufthansa and Delta over the years, as well as becoming founding CEO of Virgin America, consistently voted No. 1 overall for U.S. Carriers for eight years running. I remember my father Daniel's true devotion to his employees over the years and his uncompromising devotion to stellar TWA style service: hopefully some of that wore off on me.

Fred Reid

Saarinen's Soaring Structure

By George W. Hamlin

Photos: John Pickett/Author's Collection

A 1960 aerial view shows the Flight Center under construction at the top of Idlewild's "Terminal City." Pan Am's elliptical complex is visible below.

In its latter days, it was simply "Terminal 5". Prior to that, it was the TWA Flight Center. For now, it's a lifeless shell at the southeast corner of JFK Airport's terminal complex.

Once upon a time, however, it was new, daring and elegant. In an era when people dressed up for air travel, and many did likewise just to come to the airport, it was unique and beautiful.

The airline was extremely proud of its signature terminal in Idlewild's "Terminal City," as can be discerned by the verbiage accompanying the "double-truck" advertisement that appeared in contemporary magazines, including the oversized *LIFE* Magazine:

This is the new Trans World Flight Center in New York. Architect Saarinen designed it to express the special excitement of jet travel. Its soaring roof and sweep of glass enclose a hundred

new ideas to speed your departure and arrival – like TWA's fast new jet check-in and boarding, and automatic baggage delivery. International shops are here. Comfortable lounges. Glamorous restaurants. One other fact makes the Trans World Flight Center entirely unique: it's the only airline terminal where routes from 70 cities in the U.S. are linked to routes in Europe, Africa, and Asia. One world under one roof.

In its own promotional brochure, the carrier was even more direct and less modest:

TWA is proud of its new Trans World Flight Center at N.Y. International Airport. It is the most beautiful and functional terminal in the world.

There are many who would agree with the characterization of the building's appearance, while quite a few others, including many

By mid-1960 Saarinen's giant bird-like shell has emerged. Behind it TWA jets park at temporary gates, accessed by passengers from the old terminal.

Fortunately, thanks to the late TWA employee John Pickett, we are able to go back to "its day", and actually, before, to see this magnificent edifice's gestation, as a mass of plywood forms for pouring the concrete structure. Upon completion of the basic shell, prior to installation of the glass, it's not hard to see the building as "bird-like".

Even better, John returned with his camera to record what it looked like after it was placed into service. Light filters into nooks and crannies via the enormous expanse of glass; the information counter is busy, while above it the state-of-the-art Solari Board advises travelers and visitors about arrivals and departures. People line up at the

employees that worked there, would have more difficulty with respect to its functionality.

The dust-jacket blurb from Ezra Stoller's book, *The TWA Terminal*, sums it up well:

Eero Saarinen's TWA Terminal stands as the ultimate icon of mid-century modern design. Commissioned in 1956 and completed in 1962, the bird-like terminal at New York's John F. Kennedy Airport was intentionally designed as an eye-catching showpiece that would capture the public's imagination. Its expressionistic concrete exterior and soaring interior spaces did just that, making it one of the most dramatic architectural statements of its day.

The terminal shell as seen from the street.

The Solari Board stands above TWA's information counter.

Floor-to-ceiling windows afforded sweeping views of the tarmac.

window beyond the main waiting area to gaze at the wonders of jet travel, prominently displayed.

Saarinen himself is quoted in TWA's advertising as saying that the building was meant, "to express the excitement of travel." Back when air travel was often viewed as alluring and TWA was one of the best in the airline business, it would have been difficult to prove him wrong.

The Flight Wing gate area is seen from the International Arrivals Building. Despite the modern complex design, underground fueling was not provided.

A Charter to Remember
By Captain Walt Gunn

Jon Proctor

Originally published in TARPA Topics, November 1993, and reproduced with permission.

A most memorable assignment in 39 years of flying would have to be a White House Press Charter in 1966 with President Johnson to Vietnam and the Southeast Asia Conference. The charter left Dulles on October 16, with a 17 day itinerary to Honolulu, Pago Pago, New Zealand, Australia, Manila (conference), Bangkok, Malaysia, Korea, and return to Dulles via Anchorage.

The 707 crew consisted of:

Pilots - Marv Horstman, Billy Williams, Walt Gunn

Flight Engineers - Tony Gatti, Jack Evans

Navigator - Drew Wasson

Pursers - Fred Duss, Bob Strini

Cabin Team - Myrna Encinas, Pat Rellihan, Karen Kiefer, Celeste Mariani,

Julie Knowles

JFK Maintenance Specialists - Carl Yannuzi, Sal Bruno, Tony Ristuccia

Russ Ellis (Station Operations, Washington, D.C.)

Walt Morris (Commissary Specialist)

To describe the ensuing 17 days on a daily basis would be more of a chore than I care to tackle. So, highlights of the tour will be grist for this writing. After ferrying to Dulles from Kennedy, we started our flight planning/briefing in operations.

The purpose of the tour was to solidify the allies of SEATO (Southeast Asia Treaty Organization) in bringing the Vietnam conflict to an acceptable conclusion. The entire tour was met with much pomp and ceremony appropriate to the visiting nations and their leaders.

Air Force One was captained by Col. Jim Cross, LBJ's personal pilot, who had received his 707 training in TWA's initial and recurrent training programs for MAC VIP crews at the Frye Training Center in Kansas City. Jim Cross was a rightful choice for such an important assignment

and a pleasure to work with in coordinating our flight planning and en route communications.

Ceremonies on each arrival and departure smacked of "history-making" importance. The variations in cultural, social, and ethnic expressions left each of us in awe of the events we were witnessing from front-row vantage points.

Arrival in Pago Pago, American Samoa, was greeted by dozens of massively built Samoan chieftains in their regal costumes. Purpose of the stop was to dedicate a grade school for Lady Bird Johnson, the first lady. It was perhaps an event of the century for the natives, to be visited by the President of the United States.

New Zealand greeted us with "minimal limits" landing with ILS and precision approach radar accuracies comfortably guiding us. The country's plush, green, rolling fields were dotted with untold blotches of white sheep, justifying their claim to world leadership in wool and lamb exports.

Our Australia mission took us to Canberra, Melbourne, Sydney, Brisbane, and Townsville. Canberra and Sydney are reminiscent of New Orleans or San Francisco, at least climate wise and local friendliness. Melbourne may compare to Cleveland or Pittsburgh with heavy industry. Strong protests against the Vietnam War met us with paint being splashed on LBJ's limousine. Government officials hastened to have it in prime finish before our departure.

On return to Sydney, Air Force One experienced a brake assembly failure on landing, and with no parts for repair. On that notice, our three maintenance experts took over and spent the night modifying the plane with spare parts we had carried for such an event on our plane. This no small chore since our TWA 707 was a different model than Air Force One. Carl, Sal, and Tony were truly experts in "can-do-fix-it" and each ones expertise complimented the other. As a team, nothing was beyond them.

On leaving Australia, LBJ wanted to "drop in" on a hospital in Townsville, where he had been nurtured to health after a bout with pneumonia during World War II. Prior to our arrival,

George Christopher, assistant press secretary to Bill Moyers, came to the cockpit to talk with Moyers on Air Force One. I contacted Jim Cross on our discrete VHF frequency, asking him to put Moyers on for a chat with Christopher. As Moyers responded, Christopher referred him to the second paragraph of LBJ's welcoming speech, advising him of a change. Moyers read the line and deemed it to be okay. With that, Christopher insisted a change be made where LBJ says, "What a pleasure to return to Townsville — where so many American service men had planted their roots!" Moyers replied that he saw nothing wrong with the wording — to which, Christopher stated, "Believe me Bill, reword it and I'll explain it to you later!"

I never heard his explanation but then, it was quite clear to me, and what with the humor and frank honesty of the Aussies, LBJ might have had a time figuring out the audience's inappropriate laughter at that point of his speech.

Interesting hours were spent with the press staff and secret service agents on our plane. Rufus Youngblood, JFK's guard was along and commented briefly about the tragedy in Dallas and pushing the first lady back in the seat after JFK was shot. CBS news journalist Eric Sevareid really nurtured my interest in world affairs — what a brilliant political writer.

Young Dan Rather portrayed a more exuberant and outspoken image than ever seen as an "anchor person." The secret service agents could only breathe easily while on board en route to the next stop where they were charged with guarding "the old man." One agent, Mike Ditka's kid brother, (not at all built like Mike), often served as lead and after knowing him, I wouldn't dare challenge him. LBJ was in good hands.

A surprise junket was added to the itinerary when LBJ decided to include a stop at Cam Ranh Bay, Vietnam. The area on the coast was frequently an R&R respite for the troops when they couldn't get to Okinawa or Hawaii. Secrecy was still called for in spite of the remoteness from the inland firefight areas.

Manila provided us some four days for shopping and tours during the SEATO conference. The entire crew was catered to in high fashion by the government. We were given discounts on any art crafts and the major department stores otherwise closed their doors, allowing personal shopping and selection of items to be shipped home. Even the San Miguel Brewery delivered two cases of their prized brew to my home (paid for) a month later. Otis Bryan had been president of the brewery before and was well remembered by them.

From Manila to Bangkok, we flew direct published airways, which transited South Vietnam. We maintained radio contact and radar coverage as we could from New York to Los Angeles. Air Force One opted for a circuitous route south of all of the Vietnam area. I had occasion to leave a personal message to my son-in-law, an F-4 pilot, through his base control tower at Chu Lai.

Bangkok proved exceptionally hospitable for the entourage. The Foreign Press Club arranged a banquet, the like of which I have never experienced. The setting was on the massive terrace of our hotel and fronting a major canal. Food was displayed on tables forming a u-shape, which were at least 50 feet long on each of the three sides. A stage was arranged with Thai dancing and kickboxing matches were part of the entertainment.

Leaving Bangkok, we flew to Kuala Lumpur, Malaysia. Our first glance at the airport from a distance, slowly revealed a "miniature Dulles terminal" design as we flew closer. The architecture was identical with cantilevered pillars, glass and marble construction.

Malaysia is an admixture of three cultures – Oriental, Hindu and Moslem. Police are tall, mustachioed Sikhs, with turbans and bamboo shields. As we approached our hotel, a crowd had gathered on the opposite corner of the street, peering at a body lying still. He had been killed in some kind of unexplained dispute. The body was still there as we left for sightseeing and dinner. Brahma cattle roamed the streets freely.

The final stop on the tour was Seoul, South Korea. The 20-mile highway from the airport to town was lined with citizens (mainly school children) estimated at more than two million. Each was waving American and Korean flags. Political leaders received LBJ with encouraging support and appreciation of U.S. aid. The last evening was spent at a newly finished army post, with LBJ and first lady hosting a banquet for all of the White House staff, press, and crewmembers – a fancy and very formal affair.

Departure from Seoul took us within 15 miles of the Russian border and the Kurile Islands. We had U.S. fighters escorted us until we were safely clear and established on our oceanic course to Anchorage. MIG aircraft monitored our flight path and were visible from our cockpit. Landing at Anchorage was arranged for a night's rest and departure early for arrival at Dulles during prime time for LBJ to address the nation on the success of the Summit. The weather on arrival may well have been a more accurate omen of the times. It was cloudy, rainy, with gusty winds, which blew the canopy off the temporary podium where LBJ's message was intended to instill calm and assurance of victory in Vietnam. History belied such optimism.

Great pride remains in the overall operational success and guidance was given to the charter crew by Captain Marv Horstman.

Captain Walt Gunn

A Pilot Class Joins TWA on St. Patrick's Day

By Wayne C. Boyd

To some it was St. Patty's day; for us it was our date of hire: John B. Wickensimer, Ewing P. Goff, David P. Maneilly, John S. Busby, Ron B. Gottshalk, Theodore F. Morrow, Robert L. Gattis, Ronald L. Fox, Charles R. Sebrell, Ralph M. Dykstra, Charles F. Wheeler, Richard S. Saltzman, Larry G. Goetz, William R. Crowe, Charles G. Moorhead, Wayne C. Boyd.

On March 17, 1967 this group of young men began an airline career at 1307 Baltimore in Kansas City, Missouri; that was the address of the Trans World Airlines training center. It became our home away from home for the next several months while our new-hire class was schooled in the complexities of a large jet airplane. In addition, we learned more about the backgrounds of our classmates and assimilated the details of TWA's rich aviation history.

The multi-level brick building was adorned with a huge painted sign occupying much of the south-facing wall, extolling the airline's non-stops between major cities. The large adjacent parking lot adjacent was managed remotely; you simply noted the painted number where you parked your car today, and deposited the fee in the box bearing the same number.

Photo courtesy of the author
Giant billboards adorned the Jack Frye Training Center 1307 Baltimore.

SYSTEM TIMETABLE

EFFECTIVE MAY 1, 1974

Now...TWA...
the only U.S. airline
to Shannon/Dublin,
Ireland.

*A TWA timetable extols new
service to Dublin in May 1974.*

Inside the eight-floor building an elevator made short work of the trip between floors. It was usually "piloted" by a friendly and talkative gentleman named Jim, whose banter livened up the ride. New classes began each week and, depending on airline needs, the type of aircraft type to be taught was decided ahead of time. Our all-important seniority numbers were determined by age, with the oldest in the class being senior. Our class trained to become 727 flight engineers, the same aircraft featured on the building's south wall. The training pace was brisk and we were

soon immersed in mastering the multiple systems on Boeing's "three-holer."

A thick 727 flight handbook and an equally thick *course notes* manual quickly became the daily diet for classroom consumption. We new hires soon purchased nav kits in which to transport the ever-increasing load of publications. Those black bags were stamped with each crewmember's name and the airline logo, and remained a staple throughout our careers.

Large electronic "trainer boards" on wheels enabled classroom instructors to move them from room to room, and to different floors. They colorfully displayed the minutia of a specific system on the airplane: fuel, electrical, hydraulic, pressurization, etc. The classrooms incorporated push-button responders at each student's location. When the instructor asked a question, each student's answer was immediately displayed at the instructor's lectern. The instructor's teaching effectiveness and the student's understanding was thereby immediately revealed. Training not only took place in the classroom, but also continued in the hallways between classes. Electronic quiz boards tested the knowledge of students in various systems. A correct answer produced a green light while an incorrect response produced a red light. The training was nonstop, much like the flights advertised on the training center's south wall.

TWA's cadre of instructors included men like John B. "Buck" Buckmaster and John W. "Mac" McNelley, who brought to the classroom unique blends of subject knowledge, teaching skills, trainer board familiarity and personality. Training quality was a way of life at 1307 Baltimore. In the building's entrance lobby hung a sign...its gold letters presenting a stark contrast to its black background.

PERSISTENT TRAINING IS THE KEY TO TWA EXCELLENCE AND THE FOUNDATION OF PUBLIC TRUST IN ALL OF US.

We had joined an airline, which at that time was one of only two global U.S. carriers.

John B. "Buck" Buckmaster

John W. "Mac" McNelley

Each of us felt a sense of family there, and the goal of becoming a qualified TWA flight deck crewmember was upper-most in our minds. Our focus was on that target.

The accumulation of memories has increased exponentially since March 17, 1967. We settled in different domiciles, trained on different airplanes, and occupied different cockpit seats, but always paused to talk with former classmates.

Each of us had a story to tell; some aeronautical, some financial, some marital. They became stories that are permanent party in our memory bank, special stories because; *to some it was St Patty's day; for us it was our date of hire.*

Captain Wayne C. Boyd

TWA and Hilton International
A Worldwide Travel Juggernaut

By Jeff Kriendler

Photos: Courtesy of Hilton Hotels & Resorts

The Kensington Hilton, London.

For hundreds of TWA crewmembers, the worldwide chain of deluxe Hilton International properties was often their home on the road, offering familiarity and comfort in the highest quality of service. Ask any pilot or hostess to name their favorite and without pausing the names of glamorous world capitals would be offered: Paris, Rome, Athens, London and Hong Kong.

Whether the fond recollections of the Hilton properties triggered memories of crew parties, or menu favorites, it was particularly the friendly staff that welcomed TWA crewmembers who provided a family environment for the travel-weary crews.

Because of the cyclical nature of the airline business, which persists 5 decades later, Charles Tillinghast, TWA's CEO in the mid-1960s, began to seek diversification and first set his target on the contract with the National Aeronautics and Space Administration to provide base support at the Kennedy Space Center in Florida. In 1967, he took a major step by merging TWA with the Hilton International Hotel chain, which became a wholly owned subsidiary of the airline.

In his book *Howard Hughes' Airline: An Informal History of TWA*, Robert Serling wrote that Tillinghast said, "I have no recollection as to when talks first began, except it was about the time Hughes sold his TWA stock. It was Barron Hilton, Conrad's son, who approached us. Barron was anxious to get into the airline business and became controlling stockholder in TWA. It didn't work out that way -- we bought Hilton International, not the other way around."

At that time, Hilton owned or operated 42 hotels in 28 countries with TWA acquiring full ownership of three hotels, 50 percent of a fourth and took over the operation of the remaining 38 under lease or

Mainz Hilton, Germany

Athens Hilton, Greece

management contracts. As part of the agreement, Conrad Hilton, Jr. joined the TWA board.

Serling noted that Tillinghast spread the word around the airline's executive branch: "You guys know how to run an airline and they know how to run a hotel, so stay the hell away from the hotels." Tillinghast pointed out that it was much more financially advantageous to acquire a going concern than to create a new brand on their own and he pointed out that that strategy was vindicated many times over. He said, "The hotels have been a goal of mine. In terms of what we paid for them, we got the purchase price back every year."

TWA continued to chart a course of diversification and brought under the Trans World banner Canteen Corporation, a vending and food service business; Spartan Food Services, a restaurant operation in the southeast and then Century 21 Real Estate Corporation one of North America's biggest franchisers of independently owned brokerage firms.

To learn more about the relationship between TWA and Hilton International one of the founding fathers of Hilton, Curt Strand shared his career highlights spanning more than four decades of international hospitality leadership.

Strand was one of the first employees of Hilton International dating back to the late 1940s until his retirement of as chairman and CEO in 1987. He oversaw this period of tremendous growth with the iconic hotel company watching from the reordering of the global international market following the end of World War II. He also served as a director and vice president of TWA.

"I was one of the first 2 1/2 employees of Hilton International. When we started in 1949 we only had a part-time secretary, my boss and myself. When I retired our portfolio included over

100 hotels in 60 different countries, which massed together employed 35,000 people."

"As often happens in life, it's a question of being in the right place at the right time. We started Hilton International when the door was wide open as the war had ended just a few years before and except for Americans, no one had the means to travel. Therefore, our target markets were where Americans wanted to go, especially in Europe. We were there at the right time; we launched at a time when our founder, Conrad Hilton, had an intuition that we needed to expand abroad."

Strand spoke of the pioneering spirit of the company, similar to TWA: creating something in a place where nobody had done it before. Hilton went and developed hotels in places that never had any 5-star hotel and for Strand, it was a thrilling experience to do it in more remote places like Addis Ababa, Rabat San Juan and Nairobi rather than well established capitals like London or Paris or Hong Kong.

Strand noted that his impression of the airlines today is that people have a negative feeling about what they get when they fly. "There are many reasons for this negative perception, but it is not something that was intended. It was not created by the airlines, but rather a product of the economics of the industry."

"My policy of hiring people was, don't worry so much about their experience; you can train them to do the work. Hire people who are naturally friendly, and who have a propensity to smile. You cannot train people to smile and this goes for all customer-related jobs whether it's an airline or a hotel or some other part of the travel industry, hiring people based on their experience is fine, but it can't guarantee how great an experience customers will receive."

Trans World Corporation was established as a holding company that in addition to Hilton International operated other businesses including Spartan Food Systems, Inc., the Century 21 real estate corporation and the Canteen Corporation.

During Strand's tenure, Hilton International became the business of hotel management, owning only a handful of the far-flung hotels. "The hotels were typically locally owned. We didn't have franchises yet we controlled the standard of operations. We not only managed them but designed them, providing the architects, engineers, interior designers and kitchen planners."

Conrad Hilton's one big mistake, Strand says, was to sell Hilton International. He felt that the market didn't sufficiently show the value of the Hilton company, and that is why he split off Hilton International as a separate company with its own stock. The Hilton family held 25% of that stock after the spin-off and in the deal with TWA exchanged it for $86 million of TWA stock, which became worthless. Strand said, "It turned out to be a better deal for TWA than the Hilton family." He added that Hilton's second biggest mistake was to sell New York's Plaza Hotel. "The Plaza was irreplaceable," he added.

My Career at TWA

By Rod Gaines

ROD GAINES, 29, coordinator of 747 flight services at JFK, is featured in the June issue of *Ebony* as one of the most eligible bachelors for 1972. "Today's *Ebony* bachelor is a doer, a mover," says the magazine. "He looks to the future rather than to the past."

In 1967 I was working as an assistant buyer at Bullock's Department Store in downtown Los Angeles as part of their management-training program. I was also president of a travel club made up of about 30 friends. We were planning a trip to Europe for the first trip there. One of the club members knew a TWA sales representative, David Maxwell, who was invited to attend a meeting and give us information on the steps required for this international adventure.

Dave came with a TWA slide presentation that included photographs of exciting destinations and some of the most beautiful flight attendants who flew for the airline; it motivated me to consider making a move to TWA.

I was told that there was a recruitment campaign for African-Americans and I should visit an office on 85th and Broadway, where HR Representative Tony Ginise was conducting interviews. I met with him and was given an opportunity for a second interview and to take the test for a position as a customer service ticket agent at the Los Angeles International Airport on World Way West. And on April 15, 1968 I was hired and began on-the-job training at the airport.

I did well and became a good ticket agent, learning to work all of the positions including the passenger boarding gates for departing and arriving flights, the Lost and Found office in baggage claim and ticket counter.

Early on, I accidentally drove the Jetway loading bridge into the wingtip of a Boeing 707 that had arrived from overseas and was scheduled to continue on to San Francisco. Extensive wingtip damage resulted in cancellation of that flight and caused disrupted of other flights for several additional days. I expected to be fired, but because the ramp mechanic was at fault for not properly guiding the airplane into the gate, I kept my job.

Then in 1969, I got a call from Director of Employment Cal Filson, asking me to meet with him about a promotional opportunity to become a "two stripe," airfreight supervisor/chief, overseeing a group of IAM union employees working for a super-tough manager named Jim Outersky.

I worked in that department for about a year until a new supervisory position and further promotion was created in 1970. Initially called, simply, 747 supervisor (and later director of customer service) it involved working on board the new jumbos to ensure excellent service from the departure gate, onboard to the flight, all the way to the baggage claim area of the arrival destinations to domestic and international destinations.

From that time, promotional opportunities came almost every year. Late in 1970, I was promoted to the position of the coordinator of 747 in-flight services at the JFK International Airport in New York. Two years later, I was promoted to the position of manager of in-flight customer service, back at Los Angeles International Airport.

In 1973, I became manager of airport services at Friendship International Airport in Baltimore, Maryland, assigned to clean up a poorly managed airport operation that was supposed to take two to three years, a task accomplished in less than one year.

Thanks to my success at Baltimore, we were given the opportunity to manage and improve operations of the TWA passenger reservations office in 1974, at the downtown office staffed with 320 employees. My new title became manager of telephone passenger sales and service.

This assignment was supposed to last for three to five years but I had made the needed changes

and corrections by 1976 was given another promotional opportunity, moving to the corporate offices at 605 Third Avenue in New York City, as the director of personnel and employee relations, with responsibility for 38,000 employees.

In 1977, the senior management of TWA decided to combine two departments into one worldwide department called cabin service programs, with a $120-million budget covering system-wide operations and I became the director of cabin service programs

A year later I became city vice president of sales and service at Washington, D.C., responsible for management operations at Baltimore International, Washington National and Dulles International Airports, along with passenger and cargo sales and service for 19 scheduled airline ticket offices (SATOs).

I made my most stupid mistake and left TWA in 1982 to become a banker and executive for United Virginia/Crestar Bank in Washington, DC, serving as a vice president for First Interstate Bank and Wells Fargo Bank, the Cendant Corporation, retiring in 2005 as the vice president of business development for the J.P. Chase Bank in New York City.

Close to the end of TWA's life, TWA Board member Jewel Lafontant called to ask if she could put my name into nomination to become president of the carrier. What a final chapter that would have been in my life with Trans World Airlines.

*Rod
Gaines*

Flying a MAC Charter
By Arlene Perla Elliott

Jon Proctor

MAC charter aircraft utilized separate ground facilities at Honolulu.

In April 1975, I was walking down a long corridor in the TWA hangar at Los Angeles International Airport when Flight Attendant Domicile Manager Jim Dolin approached me and asked if I had a valid passport. After responding yes, Jim said, "Be here tomorrow morning; you are going to Guam to evacuate Vietnamese refugees."

The next morning, along with my fellow crewmembers, we flew to Honolulu for a layover, then on to Guam for further rest.

The crew:

Captain Don Young
First Officer Hugh Campion
Flight Engineer Jim Riche
Purser Mike Dietel
Flight Attendant Jig Bontrager
Flight Attendant Arlene Perla
Flight Attendant Terry Roundy
Flight Attendant Marilyn Siddall
Flight Attendant Dede Shenk Young

All of us finally reboarded the 707 on Guam to await arrival of the refugees. They had been living in tents on the island since the end of the Vietnam War in 1973. As they boarded it their faces looked tired an anxious. I remember seeing a few of the women wearing lovely jewelry, in stark contrast to the clothing. They didn't have much in the way

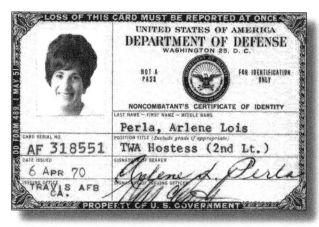

Military identification cards were issued for crewmembers.

of carry-on luggage, probably having left Vietnam with whatever could be carried.

The flight was delightful; these passengers were grateful for the services and amenities provided. There was a movie, stereo music and games for the children. Jig Bontrager pinned junior wings on the kids and an older female passenger, believed to be in her 80s. The tallest gentleman, well over 6 feet, was the only Vietnamese who could see over the seat backs. He carried an American newspaper with the headline, "It's Over."

We flew home, again via Honolulu, and landed at El Toro Marine Base in California, then ferried the airplane back to LAX, exhausted but thankful a wonderful journey and memories to treasure.

Photos: Courtesy of the author except as noted
Arlene on the ground.

Arlene Perla Elliott joined TWA in 1964 as a Los Angeles-based hostess, serving in various positions within the in-flight services department until 1976, when she became an account sales manager at Washington, D.C. and later a field manager of ground operations at Washington National Airport. Arlene's last position was in TWA sales at Indianapolis, before leaving the company in 1983.

Vietnamese children gather for a picture in the forward galley.

Purser Mike Dietel enjoys a conversation with one of his passengers.

Two Summers Behind the Ticket Counter

By George W. Hamlin

The Flight Center as it looked in 1962.

Before there were kiosks for passengers to use to check in at airports if they didn't bother to download their boarding pass on their cellular/mobile phone, there were airline employees – check-in agents – who performed this task. During the summers of 1970 and 1971, and over the Christmas holiday seasons of both years, I had the enjoyable opportunity to don a uniform and perform this task in the TWA Flight Center at New York International Airport (JFK).

In June 1970, after finding out that TWA did in fact hire summer help, I went to Hangar 12 at JFK and inquired about such a possibility. Following an interview, some pre-employment tests, and a medical exam, I was dispatched to a tailor catering to the airline trade and fitted for a uniform. And shortly thereafter, I showed up for

a five-hour duty, 7 a.m. shift and, thereby, became gainfully employed in the airline business.

One of the reasons for the early start was that TWA at JFK had a significant afternoon/evening peak of departures, so becoming initially acclimated was easier during the morning hours. In fact there were no departures between the nonstops to Los Angeles and San Francisco at 9 a.m. and the next set at 11:45. Things were also less organized than might be expected today, and when we part-timers arrived, at first to "shadow" the regular employees, management sent us out for a coffee break until they decided what to do with us.

One miscellaneous task was to assist in the lost baggage office with a planeload of bags disgorged from one of the brand-new 747s, following an engine fire warning indication which proved to be false. At one point in this assignment, I found myself alone, in front of a telephone with all four lines on hold, and having no real idea of which customer was on which line.

Classroom training covered the handling of checked baggage and the rudiments of simple airline ticketing. Prior to regular assignment to the ticket counter, we participated in a tax-collection exercise, for both the newly-launched $3 international departure tax and an increase in the domestic rate, both of which needed to be collected on tickets already issued. And that is how Flight 163, a 727 operating nonstop to Oklahoma City, came to be delayed one afternoon.

It took place at Gate 10, one of two in the older Flight Wing Two that consisted largely of a glass corridor, with floor to ceiling windows. Neither my female co-worker nor I had been issued our uniforms yet, so I was in a business suit, and she in a navy skirt and white blouse, the standard attire for non-uniformed female part-timers.

Per the times, the navy skirt was of the "mini" variety. After we had finished our taxation duties my co-worker was leaning against the glass wall, facing inward. About the time ramp supervision noticed that the baggage wasn't being loaded, the three of us looked down and observed that the entire ramp crew had taken up a position just below us, and were gazing up intently.

When the gate agent pointed this out, my co-worker blushed, no doubt quite a sight from the ramp below, and rushed over to the opposite glass wall, followed by the rampers beneath. Order was restored when the co-worker retreated to the center of the corridor, and Flight 163 eventually departed with bags on board. The two of us weren't charged with the delay but the ramp was. I still wonder how it was described.

After assuming our "permanent" positions a few days later, it became apparent that one of our more significant and revenue-generating functions was the policing of excess-weight baggage, and collecting the fees associated with it.

Economy passengers traveling overseas were allowed 44 pounds free of charge, while first-class and charter customers could take 66 pounds. Although there were limited exceptions, such as reading matter for the flight, small cameras, canes, etc., carry-on baggage other than these items was to be weighed and included in the free allowance. If the total exceeded the limits, a customer would be charged at the tariff rate for the excess weight.

This produced frequent "discussions" with passengers, many of whom stated that their travel agents, who were not there to be consulted, had told them that carry-on didn't get weighed, and therefore, was not part of the allowance. Prominent signs near the scales displayed the rules, which often helped, although what usually carried the day for the agent was the announcement that the checked baggage would be tagged and dealt with once *all* items were on the scale.

Needless to say, many of the passengers disputed some or all of these provisions. Sometimes, the passengers became quite incensed about the process, and called for supervision. In my case, I worked for Ticket Counter Chief Helga Brueser, who was quite supportive of our efforts. After one of these events, the disgruntled passenger warned me that I would hear more about this when he wrote to TWA following his trip and

had to face away from him when I noted him writing down the information from a promotional button I was wearing on my jacket lapel.

One traveler happily paid the $1100 fee required for her quarter-ton (500 pounds) of baggage to go from JFK to South Africa. She was relocating there, and the company was paying for shipment of her personal effects. I suspect that her employer had expected to pay for airfreight rather than checked baggage, but who was I to argue with a person that knew what she was doing, and was willing to pay?

Flights to Athens, Greece produced numerous memorable moments, whether charters or

scheduled services. In any case, many of the passengers were going to visit friends and relatives in Greece for the summer, and they came both in large numbers and with large volumes of luggage.

Flight 880, the nonstop 707 to Athens, was often oversold. On one particularly bad evening, after boarding the 16 people in first class and 129 in the coach seats, plus two more occupying two of the four seats in the first-class lounge, there were still 162 "confirmed" passengers left in the gate hold room. The Port Authority police were called to restore order.

On another night, working an Athens charter, I checked in a family traveling with several trunks, one of which weighed over 200 pounds, followed by a window air conditioner in a battered cardboard box. And when this was tagged for carriage, the luggage was produced. Things were not much better at the gate, with "lap children," supposedly under the age of 2 years, that looked like they might be finishing elementary school in the near future, and an aircraft belly that almost ran out of space once the too-numerous pieces of carry-on had been checked, TWA's 707s had no enclosed overhead bins.

We often worked in conjunction with the skycaps. These gentlemen were quite busy during the afternoon/evening rush, going back and forth between the air-conditioned confines of the terminal, and the hot and sticky curbside area. On occasion, we set up a curbside bag-checking station, which gave me a chance to get to know the skycaps better. One, Gene, was a hard-core New York Mets fan, and typically had a transistor radio on when his team was playing. Another was a college professor in the "off-season." The dignified lead skycap, Leroy Parks, kept things functioning smoothly.

One of the more colorful individuals plying this trade was Leon Scott. He was known to return a tip, when it was overly modest, with the admonition that it was apparent that the passenger needed it more than he. On the other hand, I also saw him graciously refuse tips from passengers that were elderly, or obviously of modest means.

One afternoon, a group of churchwomen was making a long-distance trip; several of them had never flown before, and were nervous. Leon went up to one of them, whispered in her ear, whereupon she clapped her hands and said "Hallelujah," fears assuaged. As soon as they had left the area, I went to find out how he'd done it. "What did you tell her, Scotty?" The answer should have been obvious: "I said that TWA stood for Traveling With Angels," he replied.

The part-time afternoon shifts started typically at 3 or 4 p.m., and were officially over by 8 or 9 o'clock, but late arrivals created the chance to earn overtime almost every night. With the better part of 20 transatlantic flights, including charters on many days, something was generally late, and often, very late. Except for charters, no flights were scheduled to depart after Flight 15 left for Chicago, Los Angeles and San Francisco at 11 p.m., but there were almost always late inbounds from Europe.

Post-midnight late arrivals were not uncommon; meaning whoever was working them often didn't have much to do until they arrived. On occasion, this provided the chance to watch at least a portion of *The Tonight Show* in the VIP lounge, not far from the ticket counter. Meeting a delayed European arrival at 1 or 2 a.m. often bordered on a surreal experience. The FIS (Federal Inspection Services—Immigration/Naturalization and Customs) area under Flight Wing One was quiet as the proverbial tomb, and often as chilly as a meat locker, whereas only a few hours earlier, it had been home to hubbub, with air conditioning struggling to cope with the mass of humanity.

As they came down the escalators, passengers seemed to be zombies, since they had expected to arrive the afternoon before, and it was now 24 hours or more since commencing their journeys. Our job was to get them to their destinations as quickly as possible and provide hotel accommodations and meals as necessary.

One of our allies in these transactions was Delta Air Lines. The Atlanta-based carrier had a flight that departed JFK about 3:30 a.m., for

Atlanta, Dallas and Los Angeles. Surprisingly, many California-bound passengers opted for this rather extreme schedule rather than resting in a JFK-area hotel and proceeding the next morning; they just wanted to get home.

In retrospect, it was a great time to have been in the airport side of the industry. The 747s were brand new and awe-inspiring to many people, both employees and the public. By my second summer, they had sprouted coach lounges, a reflection of the over-capacity situation they had produced in many markets, particularly in the domestic sector of the business.

Working where I did provided an opportunity to meet people from all over the world. Occasionally, I ran into friends from other places

and times that were traveling on TWA. Celebrities could often be seen coming and going. One night actor Kirk Douglas plus singers Johnny Cash and June Carter Cash occupied first-class seats on Flight 900 to Lisbon. On another occasion, actor Sidney Poitier brought traffic in the main lobby to a near standstill when he visited the information counter to inquire about the arrival of an incoming friend's flight.

In reality, while there were stressful moments – and sometimes, many of them, my job was interesting, and, for the most part, fun. History has proven that the functions I was performing in the early 1970s were not something that one could dependably make a career out of, but who knew that then?

George Hamlin began at TWA as a part-time Customer Service Agent in June 1970. In 1972 he joined the Finance staff at 605 Third Avenue, and became Manager Cargo Market Planning in the summer of 1974. In April 1978, he became Director-Schedule Planning at Texas International. Subsequently, he worked for Lockheed, Airbus North America, and has been in airline consulting since 1996.

TWA's First Widebody Jets

By Jon Proctor

Named City of San Francisco *for the inaugural 747 service to New York, the airplane was christened by Shirley Temple Black shortly before the paper name banner was removed.*

In 1996, TWA celebrated the 25th anniversary of its Boeing 747 inaugural flight, giving it, at the time, the distinction of having operated them longer than any airline in the world.

As the second airline to place the 747 into service, TWA equipped the jumbo with the latest support equipment to provide the ultimate in-flight service. Litton microwave ovens and electric beverage blenders were installed in the first-class galleys. Larger convection ovens allowed for increased-size entrée plates in coach. Seating 58 in first class and 284 in the back, an upstairs lounge contained 16 seats not offered for sale.

Twelve 747s were ordered in September 1966. Originally, three were to be convertible cargo models, but the contract was later modified and all were produced as passenger versions. Four delivery positions held by Eastern Air Lines were later taken over, and an additional three airplanes ordered, for a total of 19 747-131s. All were delivered between December 1969 and October 1971.

After introducing 747s between Los Angeles and New York on February 25, 1971, TWA began New York–London service on March 18 and then concentrated on expanding trans-Atlantic widebody flights, as well as on selected transcontinental routes, plus Chicago to Los Angeles, San Francisco and Las Vegas, and later Los Angeles–St Louis.

Early improvements to the fleet included engine upgrades and landing gear modifications, which allowed an increase in maximum gross takeoff weight. These changes enabled longer segments, including flights from New York nonstop to Athens, Tel Aviv and Cairo, plus the Los Angeles–London polar route. New York–Honolulu nonstops were flown briefly in 1986, and Caribbean service briefly featured 747s.

TWA purchased three long-range 747SPs in 1980. When expected routes to Saudi Arabia that did not come to fruition, the trio was sold.

Thirteen second-hand 747s were operated between 1981 and 1996. Earlier, nine 747-131s had been sold to the Imperial Iranian Air Force, although one – N93119 – was bought back.

The 747s were originally configured with 58 first-class seats.

Ironically, it was lost in the tragic crash of TWA Flight 800 in 1996. Towards the end of their careers, the remaining factory delivery airplanes racked up almost 4,000 hours per year on trans-Atlantic duty. Three exceeded 100,000 hours before retirement, including N93108, which operated TWA's last 747 service in February 1998, from Tel Aviv to New York via Shannon.

The L-1011 TriStar

Nearly 18 months after TWA ordered Boeing 747s, a joint announcement was made, on March 29, 1968, between Eastern Airlines, Air Holdings, Ltd. and TWA for 144 Lockheed L-1011s. The Trans World portion was for 44 airplanes (33 firm orders and 11 options), with 22 deliveries scheduled for 1972 and the balance spread over the following two years. This multi-company contract officially launched the Lockheed widebody tri-jet, considered to be the most advanced commercial jet of its era. Following a tradition of assigning stellar designations to its aircraft, the L-1011 was named "TriStar" following a contest among Lockheed employees.

For TWA, the L-1011 order renewed an old relationship with the manufacturer that began in 1931 with the Lockheed Vega and stretched to the propeller-driven Constellation. TWA planners envisioned that the L-1011 would be its flagship on medium- and long-haul flights within the United States while the earlier-delivered 747s were to be concentrated on the trans-Atlantic market and remain on selected transcontinental nonstops until the new tri-jets were available.

TWA's first L-1011 was handed over on May 9, 1972, and the airline began regular service with its single TriStar (a trade name the airline didn't use in its advertising) on June 25, from St Louis to Los Angeles. Nonstops from the Chicago hub to Los Angeles, Las Vegas and San Francisco followed.

Mechanically, the L-1011 was advertised by TWA as "the most advanced airliner in the sky," capable of flying itself from takeoff to landing. Its Category 111-a, all-weather auto-land system permitted touchdowns with ceiling visibility reduced to zero and 700 feet of forward visibility. Pilots liked the airplane's handling characteristics and ability to take off and land on shorter runways such as those at New York's La Guardia Airport.

The TriStar was the first type TWA acquired with a factory-installed coach lounge, which seated 10. Waist-high carry-on luggage compartments helped to compensate for a lack of centerline overhead bins, a feature Lockheed

George W. Hamlin

Although Boeing 707s were replaced by the 747, many still remained in trans-Atlantic service through the 1970s.

Imre Quastler

London-bound 747 polar flights needed the full runway length to become airborne at Los Angeles, as this dramatic February 1979 photo testifies.

Author

*The L-1011 that operated TWA's inaugural TriStar flight
taxis to the gate at St. Louis on June 25, 1972.*

Author

Lightly loaded, this L-1011 executes a steep climbout at St. Louis in July 1985.

ignored in favor of a more open cabin design. Thirty first-class seats and a four-place lounge made up the forward-most portion of the front cabin, with 176 in coach.

The TriStar featured an under-floor galley, reached via a pair of lifts that accommodated serving carts or cabin crew. The L-1011's comfortable seating was immediately popular with TWA passengers. In first class, seats in the center row swiveled to allow groups of four to face each other. Small cocktail tables could be raised up to accept a larger, foldout top for the meal service.

The first batch of six TWA L-1011s were in service by October 1972, allowing schedule expansion that included a second Los Angeles–Chicago flight and two Chicago–Phoenix sectors with one sequence continuing to Los Angeles. Chicago–Las Vegas and Los Angeles–St Louis flights reverted to 747s for the winter while a Los Angeles–Chicago TriStar service was extended to Philadelphia in December.

Eastern Air Lines and TWA began reciprocal leasing of TriStars from to bolster capacity during the carriers' opposite peak travel periods. The first TWA L-1011 to join Eastern arrived in November and was returned the following spring, when Eastern sent two to TWA for its summer schedule. The agreement ran through the 1974-75 winter season.

With increased passenger load factors, managers at American, United and TWA successfully convinced Civil Aeronautics Board (CAB) to effectively mandate removal of aircraft coach lounges. TWA began tearing them out of its 747s and L-1011s in March 1973. Meanwhile, the first TriStar transcontinental nonstops began in April. As aircraft deliveries continued, service was added to other domestic cities.

Following a study begun two years earlier, a decision was made in early 1978 to begin conversion of six TWA TriStars for trans-Atlantic use. The resulting L-1011-100 featured center fuel tank capacity and increased takeoff weight. Lockheed undertook basic structural changes with most of the additional work done in house at

considerable financial savings. TWA inaugurated "Dash 100" service on April 30, 1978, between New York and London. Boston–Paris TriStar flights were added a year later and eventually spread to nearly all of TWA's European destinations, and as far east as Bombay..

Conversion of the overwater aircraft coincided with the refurbishment of the entire TriStar fleet, including replacing 8-across coach seating with a 9-abreast layout. First-class capacity on the -100s was reduced.

TWA launched a major Florida schedule expansion at the end of 1979, adding Ft Lauderdale, West Palm Beach, Fort Myers and Orlando to existing Tampa and Miami service. Initially a pair of TriStar flights were scheduled between New York-JFK and Miami, followed by Ft Lauderdale–New York-JFK and Miami–St Louis.

Five more TWA L-1011s were converted for overseas use in time for the 1981 summer season, including two returning to TWA after 30-month leases to Gulf Air. Having exercised attractively priced options, TWA accepted five newly built L-1011-100s from Lockheed beginning in 1981.

It was announced in February 1996 that TWA would acquire 20 Boeing 757s, with three scheduled for delivery that year, followed by 12 in 1997, two in 1998 and three in 1999. The new Boeing twins were to gradually replace TWA's last fourteen L-1011s still in service.

Gradual withdrawal of TriStar service culminated on the final day of L-1011 revenue flying, September 3, 1997. TWA operated three flights, from Boston and Orlando to St Louis and a Los Angeles–New York-JFK nonstop, which was the last to land.

Despite two L-1011 hull losses, there were no fatalities or serious injuries to passengers or crewmembers. The fleet more than earned its keep, providing dependable service while carrying the lion's share of domestic capacity on TWA's routes for 25 years.

Traveling the World Around

By George W. Hamlin

Flight 840 was one of several evening European departures from New York.

Airlines have long found the prospect of 'round the world (RTW) service fascinating, although apparently it has not been terribly remunerative. Pan Am, of course was famous for it, with Flights 1 and 2 girdling the globe for years. Others tried it as well; BOAC at one point crossed the Pacific on both northerly (U.S.-Tokyo) and southern Pacific routings, the latter, of course via Australia.

Japan Air Lines achieved its membership in the club via DC-8s routed London-New York (JFK)-San Francisco, which overnighted in New York in one direction. More exotic was Qantas' "Fiesta" route, which was unique in its inclusion of both Mexico and Bermuda, while omitting the U.S. More recently, United scheduled RTW flights, on a Los Angeles-Washington (Dulles)-London (Heathrow)-Delhi-Hong Kong-Los Angeles routing.

And, as of 1969, TWA joined this relatively exclusive club. Using newly won trans-Pacific authority, it completed the airline version of baseball's home run by bridging the gap between its historic service to India and Thailand (via Europe) and California, via Hong Kong, Taiwan, Okinawa (still under U.S. jurisdiction at this point), Guam and Honolulu, on the way ultimately to Los Angeles and San Francisco.

TWAers were very proud of the new service, although the financial analysts soon learned of at least one fatal flaw. While a routing from Hong Kong to Los Angeles via Guam and Honolulu looks fine on a flat map, the reality is that it involves considerable extra distance versus the "great circle" routing via Tokyo. Unfortunately, it wasn't possible to charge more for the additional sightseeing, so that profitability remained elusive

Jon Proctor

A Boeing 707 awaits onward customers at Rome.

throughout the relatively brief career of TWA's Pacific operations.

As an employee with free and reduced rate travel privileges, the round-the-world service had a siren lure, especially after the 1973 fuel shortage/price run-up. Rumors swirled around 605 Third Avenue (TWA's headquarters in New York) that its Pacific Division was not long for the world, scuttlebutt that would prove to be true before long.

Thus, choosing a vacation destination for 1974 became an easy proposition, leading to a May 10 departure, on Flight 844 for Rome (FCO). As of 1974, the RTW service (Flights 810/742, eastbound) actually originated in Boston, and operated via Paris to the Eternal City. Accordingly, it was easier to fly the JFK-FCO segment via 747, and join the 707 headed east in the Italian capital.

Hard to believe today, not only did TWA's 747s still have original 9-abreast interiors, but on our flight there were few enough passengers aboard that an enterprising non-rev could stretch out across an entire four-seat row in the center section of economy. Arrival in Rome showed evidence of heightened security, in the wake of the destruction of a Pan Am 707 at FCO on December 17, 1973 by terrorists. Guards greeted passengers with drawn weapons when going up into the transit lounge, and bullet holes were visible in the glass.

Since Flight 810's next stop was Tel Aviv, security was much in evidence, including a thorough search of the carry-on luggage, and an attempt to persuade us to check these items. Since we were making this journey with only one bag (plus camera equipment), we had no intention of letting them out of our sight. Production of a TWA ID card seemed to matter little, but a final tug at the end of the search table gave me the prize, while the defeated bag screener went back to try his luck again.

As has been the case for many years, security was much in evidence at TLV, heightened by the fact that we were parked next to the aircraft being used by then-Secretary of State Henry Kissinger for his "Shuttle Diplomacy" between Israel and Syria. We were told that following arrival we should remain in our seats until the aircraft was inspected by Israeli security. After this task was performed, by several individuals in fatigues bearing automatic weapons and accompanied by a dog, those disembarking in Tel Aviv were permitted to deplane. We managed a peek out the forward boarding door at the USAF "shuttle" vehicle, but were encouraged to return to the aircraft's interior almost immediately.

Resuming the trip, and headed for Bombay (BOM), India, it would have been logical to assume the aircraft would have headed east shortly after takeoff. However, that would have caused us to fly over territory where the inhabitants were not friendly towards Israel. Thus, after departing, we headed west, back out over the Mediterranean, thence north to Turkey, and east over

that country and Iran, which in those days had a friendly relationship with Israel. Needless to say, this routing, which added about an hour versus a theoretically direct routing, did nothing to enhance the economics of TWA's RTW service, either.

What often occurs when a meal is being served on an airliner? Turbulence, of course. We were in the vicinity of Mt. Ararat, the final resting place of the Biblical Ark, and although it was dark, could see clearly, with the aid of spectacular lightning flashes, there was nothing other than what appeared to be rocks as far as could be viewed. In a message meant to reassure, the purser advised the passengers that the captain wanted everyone to know that he was trying to eat his dinner, also; several on board expressed the wish that he had his hands on the controls, rather than his eating utensils.

The episode of uncomfortable flying proved to be brief, and the rest of the flight to BOM was uneventful, with the exception of an approach that seemed to take us halfway to Bangkok prior to landing to the west. Unlike most other airports, Bombay's Santa Cruz was bustling at 4 o'clock in the morning. Aircraft with the range of the 747-400 were a futuristic dream in 1974, so nearly all

Author

This former TWA 707-131, seen at Hong Kong, found a new career with Air Siam.

Date	Routing	Miles	Equipment	Aircraft
May 10-11, 1974	JFK-FCO	4,277	747-131	N53116
May 11-12, 1974	FCO-TLV-BOM-BKK	5,808	707-331B	N8730
May 15, 1974	BKK-HKG	1,063	707-331B	N8730
May 18, 1974	HKG-GUM-HNL	5,896	707-331B	N8730
May 18, 1974	HNL-OGG	101	DC-9-30F	N94454
May 20, 1974	OGG-HNL	101	737-297	N73712
May 20, 1974	HNL-LAX	2,556	707-331B	N18712
May 21, 1974	LAX-JFK	2,475	747-131	N93119
	Total:	22,277		

flights between Europe and eastern Asia stopped in India. The result was a flotilla of aircraft from major European carriers, as the provision of reasonable departure and arrival times in Europe and Asia meant that India (both Bombay and Delhi) typically were served in the middle of the night. We were able to deplane and stand briefly, onto the ramp. The scene was different than in the U.S., with what appeared to be a farm tractor pulling the bag carts, and barefoot personnel servicing the aircraft.

With a 5 a.m. departure, breakfast was served on the Bombay-Bangkok (BKK) leg. The entrée was an omelet that appeared to have been concocted from powdered eggs. Dawn came relatively early as we proceeded across eastern India, and then on to Thailand.

After several days of hot and humid sightseeing in the Thai capital (good preparation, climate-wise, for later living in Houston), we returned to Don Muang Airport to catch Flight 742 on the relatively short hop to Hong Kong (HKG). BKK's observation deck provided the chance to shoot an aircraft or two, and then it was off to board the same aircraft that brought us into town.

Apparently, after depositing us in Bangkok, the 707 continued to HKG and on across the Pacific to LAX and SFO, via Taipei, Okinawa, Guam and Honolulu. After resting overnight in San Francisco, it had flown to Boston the next morning, and then immediately commenced the 810/742 sequence again, twice around the world, in succession.

Ira Ward/Author's Collection

707-331B N8730, ridden all the way from Rome to Honolulu.

Even though we hadn't paid extra, everyone was treated to the classic curved approach to runway 13 at Kai Tak, including flying between buildings and directly over a neighborhood basketball game. Arrival festivities paled in comparison to Bangkok, and we were in the hotel shortly afterwards.

Sightseeing in Hong Kong completed, it was time to depart for Honolulu (HNL), on Flight 744. Since we were traveling space available, we had chosen to take the "express" flight to Honolulu (HNL), which stopped only in Guam, and thus avoided the chance of being "bumped" in both Taipei and Okinawa. Arriving at the airport early enough to visit the observation deck, we were able to witness the departure of one of Cathay Pacific's few remaining Convair 880s, plus 707s from the likes of Singapore, Air Siam and Cathay, where the type was then the premier equipment prior to arrival of its L-1011s. By the way, don't look for flocks of widebodies in the accompanying shots taken at HKG. The massive expansion of Asian/Pacific markets, which took place in the latter 1970s and beyond was still in the future!

Since our aircraft was parked in the distance, it was not possible to identify which of TWA's numerous fleet of 707s was going to transport us across the Pacific that afternoon and evening. Soon, however, the bus brought us alongside the same airplane again. Having completed two back-to-back global circuits, this time the aircraft had "only" been dispatched across the Pacific after its SFO overnight. By now it was an old friend, which we boarded eagerly. Another "seasoned" element on this sector was the cabin crew, all women, none of whom appeared to be less than 50 years old.

At one point, it was "30 and out" (or grounded) for airline hostesses. By the early 1970s, this was no longer true, and the U.S. carriers were also beginning to hire male cabin attendants in significant numbers. Lest the foregoing comments imply that well-experienced airline hostesses were not something to look forward to, it should be noted that we received some of the most gracious onboard service experienced anywhere from the ladies who deplaned in Guam.

The cabin crew from Guam to Honolulu was somewhat younger, on average, but featured a female purser with an interesting dry wit. On approach to HNL, she announced the federally required spraying of the cabin with insecticide, and noted in a droll manner that "nursing mothers should cover the nipple… (inserting a pregnant pause here) of the bottle they are using."

Following arrival in Hawaii, a brief side trip to Maui was undertaken, sampling the only non-TWA flights of our journey. On the way to Kahalui, we took Hawaiian Airlines, traveling on a DC-9-30, which was equipped for conversion to all-cargo service, as evidenced by the palletized seating and raised floor. Our return to HNL was via one of Aloha's colorful 737s.

TWA's afternoon flight from HNL to LAX was as close as we came to not getting on a flight due to flying standby, but all of the non-revs trying to get back to the mainland were accommodated. Unlike today, other ocean-crossing single-aisle aircraft were prevalent at Honolulu, as well.

After a night in Los Angeles, it was back home the next day on TWA's last "original" 747. A modest amount of turbulence was the only noteworthy item on an otherwise routine flight. A year later, and the journey couldn't be replicated, after TWA swapped its Pacific route authority with Pan Am in early 1975. Lots of good memories, some now-vintage photos, but also a nagging question: how did we manage to travel from New York to Honolulu via Europe and Asia, on four flights on different days, and only log two aircraft registrations?

The Hijacking of TWA Flight 840
By Thomas D. Boyatt

Flight 840 originated at Los Angeles, where the hijacked 707 was photographed earlier.

Seizure of Aircraft

The first hint of trouble occurred on August 29, 1969, when TWA flight 840 was over Brindisi, Italy. A hostess came rushing down the aisle to the rear of the plane with a very worried expression and held a flustered conversation with the senior cabin crew. Several minutes later, when the plane was overflying the Corinth Canal, the captain broke in on the public address system, stating there was an emergency but "no need to worry." The female commando (the second was a young male and both were armed with grenades and pistols) next came on the loudspeaker to announce the "Che Guevera Brigade of the Palestinian Liberation Movement" had seized the plane because a Zionist assassin was on board. Passengers were told to fasten their seat belts and put their hands on their heads. For the next several minutes as we headed east, the female and male commandos took turns on the loudspeaker assuring us that we were in no danger, that their enemies were only the Israeli aggressors, Zionists, and Imperialists and that their "demands" would be "heard" when we got on the ground.

After crossing land, the plane made a pass over a city (later identified as Tel Aviv) and circled the airport there. At this point we picked up at least two fighter escorts with Star of David markings. The plane left its landing pattern over Tel Aviv, regained altitude and headed north over the desert. We soon lost our fighter escort. The woman commando instructed the hostesses to run through emergency landing procedures with passengers twice, which she did. The woman then announced that we were about to land under emergency conditions and that the plane would explode shortly thereafter.

Meanwhile, the pilot seemed to be coming down over the desert. After maneuvering, we spotted a landing strip, which looked much too small. Passengers all took emergency seat positions and the pilot brought the ship in for a beautifully smooth landing on a concrete airstrip that appeared to be in the middle of nowhere. Actually, we landed at the newly completed Damascus International Airport. The impact of the landing did not cause any explosions.

```
FOLLOWING FOR IMMEDIATE RELEASE-ALL NEWS MEDIA AND ALL EMPLOYEES
                    SUBJECT HIJACKING
     /PRESIDENT NIXON-S CONDEMNATION OF AERIAL PIRACY
IN HIS SPEECH TODAY BEFORE THE GENERAL ASSEMBLY OF THE UNITED
NATIONS PUTS THE ISSUE BEFORE THE WORLD-S HIGHEST DIPLOMATIC
TRIBUNAL AND ENCOURAGES US TO HOPE THAT SPEEDY ACTION WILL BE
TAKEN TO ELIMINATE THE UNSPEAKABLE CRIME OF HIJACKING-/ F.C. WISER
PRESIDENT OF TRANS WORLD AIRLINES COMMENTED TODAY.
     MR. WISER PRAISED THE EFFORTS OF PRESIDENT NIXON-S STATE
DEPARTMENT TO DATE IN WORKING TOWARD THE RELEASE OF TWO ISRAELI
CITIZENS WHO HAVE BEEN DETAINED IN DAMASCUS SINCE A TWA AIRCRAFT
WAS HIJACKED THERE ON AUGUST 29.
     /ALTHOUGH THE UNITED STATES DOES NOT HAVE DIPLOMATIC
RELATIONS WITH SYRIA- THE STATE DEPARTMENT WAS ABLE TO WORK THROUGH
THE ITALIAN EMBASSY IN DAMASCUS TO HELP EFFECT THE RELEASE OF
FOUR ISRAELI WOMEN PASSENGERS WHOM TWA RETURNED TO TEL AVIV
ON SEPTEMBER 1-/ MR. WISER SAID.
     MR. WISER SAID TWA HAS BEEN WORKING THROUGH AND WITH THE
INTERNATIONAL AIR TRANSPORT ASSOCIATION- AND HAVE HAD THEIR
FULLEST COOPERATION.
     /THE GROWING MOVEMENTS IN THE UNITED NATIONS AND ALL
OTHER ORGANIZATIONS DEVOTED TO INTERNATIONAL COOPERATION
ENCOURAGE US TO BELIEVE THAT THE ISSUE WILL BE SETTLED BY
DEALING WITH BASIC PRINCIPLES- FIRST- TO INSURE THE PROMPT
REPATRIATION OF ALL PASSENGERS INVOLVED IN AN INTERNATIONAL
HIJACKING- AND- SECOND- TO PROVIDE SWIFT EXTRADITION AND
APPROPRIATE PUNISHMENT FOR THE HIJACKERS./
     MR. WISER SAID THAT IN VIEW OF THIS ENCOURAGING
DEVELOPMENT- TWA HAS DECIDED TO REPAIR THE AIRCRAFT WHICH
WAS DAMAGED BY AN EXPLOSION IN THE COCKPIT AFTER THE
PASSENGERS AND CREW HAD BEEN EVACUATED IN DAMASCUS ON AUGUST 29.
     TWA MAINTENANCE PERSONNEL AND THE BOEING CO. OF SEATTLE
WILL MAKE THE REPAIRS AT A COST OF APPROXIMATELY DLRS 3/000/000
IN AN ESTIMATED TIME OF THREE MONTHS.  A BRAND NEW NOSE
SECTION WILL BE MANUFACTURED BY THE BOEING CO. AND WILL
BE FLOWN FROM SEATTLE IN A /PREGNANT GUPPY/ TYPE AIRPLANE
AND INSTALLED AT DAMASCUS.  FOLLOWING THOROUGH TESTING BY TWA
PERSONNEL- THE AIRCRAFT WILL BE FLOWN FROM DAMASCUS TO TWA-S
OVERHAUL BASE IN KKANSAS CITY WHERE A NEW INTERIOR WILL BE
INSTALLED AND ADDITIONAL TESTING COMPLETED.  FINAL INSPECTIONS
WILL BE MADE BY SPECIALLY QUALIFIED ENGINEERS OF TWA AND THE
FEDERAL AVIATION ADMINISTRATION.
     /THIS IS ONE WAY FOR TWA TO DEMONSTRATE THE WORLD-S
ABHORRENCE FOR THE CONTEMPTIBLE CRIME OF HIJACKING-/ MR. WISER
SAID.  /IF ABANDONED IN SYRIA THE AIRCRAFT COULD BECOME A
PERPETUAL MONUMENT TO PIRACY AND LAWLESSNESS./
GILMORE 181650Z
;AVS
```

Evacuation of Plane

As soon as the plane stopped, the cabin crew popped open doors and emergency chutes. Those at the front and rear of the aircraft began evacuating in an orderly manner through normal doors and using chutes. Other passengers in the middle of the aircraft opened emergency doors and went out over the wings. I evacuated through the rear portside door. A young lady in front of me froze at the door but a swift blow to the middle of her anatomy sent her rapidly down the chute.

In loose group formation we started across an open field to put as much distance between ourselves and the plane as possible. Unfortunately, the ground was covered by a thick growth of thorns and prickly pears, which made it rough going since we had taken off our shoes in accordance with emergency landing procedures. When we were about half way across the field, I noticed that one or two passengers, who had left via the center emergency exits and slid off the port wing, had crumpled to the ground. Some got up but two did not. I started back across "Prickly Pear Alley" to help an American soldier carry an injured woman back across the field. Another male passenger had also hurt himself but was able to hobble along with us for the most part under his own steam. We continued away from the aircraft as fast as possible but because of the thorns, all were hobbling. Other passengers and crew came out to meet us and we dived into a sandbagged slit trench, apparently a part of the Syrian Airport defense setup, to rest.

When moving away from the aircraft we heard the popping of small arms fire and a small explosion. At one point I noticed a thin young man running around the aircraft firing at it with a pistol. Apparently he was trying to hit the gasoline supply in order to blow up the plane. Had he been successful he would have been blown up himself, I think. This was a prospect many of us viewed with less than normal concern. Shortly after we got into the slit trench, the front end of the airplane disintegrated in a puff of smoke followed by a loud explosion. The amount of damage and the force of the explosion made me think the commandos had some sort of nitrogen plastic with them.

After the debris settled (and none of it got too close to our slit trench), our small group was able to join the rest of the passengers who were now strung out over a quarter mile area. With the help of crewmembers, I assembled these people in a small depression in the ground and we sat there while troops with World War II vintage Bren guns ran up and stood around eyeing us. At the same time airport personnel began to arrive with trucks and buses and we were driven to the airport, with the injured and ladies going first.

Roundup and Interrogation --- We were taken to an airport waiting room and after all groups of passengers had straggled in, the crew began the slow process of a head count. Following several false starts, we were called over to the control point and asked to identify ourselves by name and nationality. Within a very short time the only two male Israelis in the group were led off for questioning.

Shortly thereafter, all families with children were taken into Damascus by bus. The rest of us sat around for several more hours with four female Israeli passengers kept in a special corner. The crewmembers were led off for questioning and some 30 of us remained. About midnight a bus came for us and upon leaving we picked up the four Israeli women and were all taken to a school that had been set up as an interrogation center. As soon as we got to the school, Syrian authorities tried to take the Israeli women into a separate room. I protested and insisted that an American passenger be with them at all times. My position was that the Israelis had been flying in good faith toward a destination other than Damascus in an American flag carrier.

Syrian officials agreed that an American schoolteacher, Miss Perry, and I could be present.

The Syrians gave us plenty of food and then began their interrogation around 2 a.m. The Israeli ladies were taken first. Questioning was quiet and neither force nor intimidation was employed. As soon as the Syrians were through with the Israeli women, I sent them off to bed in Miss Perry's company.

For the next few hours the Syrians continued to interrogate everyone else in our group and agreed that I could be present during all questioning. I was particularly worried about the fate of some American Jews but the Syrians made no move against anyone with a claim to any nationality other than Israeli. Questioning continued until 5 a.m. After everyone was bedded down, I was allowed to draft one cable (a brief summary to Ambassador Popper in Nicosia) but I don't know whether it was actually sent. The Syrians then took me to a hotel where I was kept in a single room all night with a guard outside the door.

Return to Airport and Departure

On the next morning (August 30), guards allowed me to circulate throughout the hotel and I found the entire crew. We had breakfast and lunch in the hotel.

Shortly after noon we again boarded a bus, which went around Damascus collecting various groups of passengers. TWA officials from Beirut had arrived earlier that morning and I attempted to persuade the Syrian officials to send the Israeli women with us, but we were unable to see the ranking officer. Meanwhile some Americans in

my group had decided not to move unless the Israeli women were permitted to stay with us. Outside of the bus a large crowd of Syrians had gathered and the noise level was soon in the mega-decibel range. Although emotionally inclined to a sit-down strike, I decided student activist tactics simply would not impress the Syrians and that such action would only worsen the situation. Everyone in our group decided we should go along. The bus slowly began to move through the crowd and we continued on to the airport. But everyone felt defeated, having been forced in the end to leave the Israeli women behind. We spent the rest of the afternoon at the airport collecting belongings from the damaged plane and waiting around for an Alitalia relief flight, which finally came.

Final Comment

Throughout the entire experience, including the emergency landing, evacuation of aircraft, interrogation and futile effort to obtain release of the Israelis, crew and passengers conducted themselves in unbelievably good fashion. There was no panic at any time and almost no hysteria. The description which I think, best fits this group —which was basically an American group—is that currently in use by the younger generation. People on TWA 840 were "very beautiful people" indeed.

The newly manufactured 707 nose is ready for loading onto a Pregnant Guppy cargo aircraft and transport from Seattle to Damascus.

Foreign Service officer Thomas D. Boyatt was a passenger on TWA Flight 840, which was hijacked on August 29, 1969, by two members of the Popular Front for the Liberation of Palestine. The preceding is his eyewitness account cabled from Athens on August 31, after his evacuation from Damascus. No attempt has been made to be exact with specific times or names. The purpose is simply to "tell it like it was" from the viewpoint of a single participant. Mr. Boyatt retired from the Foreign Service in 1985.

TWA Gave Me the World

By Erminia Gigante

Jon Proctor

Free travel gave Erminia the World.

I would like to start with a little story about how I joined TWA. The daughter of Italian immigrants, I was living in Long Island outside of New York City and at 18 years of age had just graduated from high school.

My goal was to become an artist/commercial illustrator and I mentioned to a friend my interest in pursuing the art world. She suggested that I go to a type setting school in New York City.

After a 6-month course I actively went out and hit the pavement, looking for a job with all the New York based airlines and left my name and résumé on file. After nine patient years working at different art jobs, my wish came true when TWA called and asked me to join the family.

It was such a thrill to work for and represent the airline and I enjoyed great travel benefits, exploring the glamorous and exciting destinations that I had dreamed about. Taking advantage of the wonderful flight opportunities, I not only enjoyed my travels but certainly the experience of flying the great TWA first-class product.

I was fortunate to sit next to many celebrities through the years including Warren Beatty, the American actor, Vincente Minnelli, Liza Minnelli's father and husband to Judy Garland, and Barbara Rush, the great American stage, film and television actress.

Among my most memorable experiences was escorting the late, great Mohammad Ali, generally considered among the great heavyweights in the history of boxing, to the first-class lounge; he was a delight, so much fun to be around.

I was very proud to have worked with other staff members in the art department to develop the design of his menu when in 1979 Pope John Paul II visited the United States. All the work was done at our corporate office at 605 Third Avenue in Manhattan.

TWA was my second home and in many ways was like a family with many of my co-workers becoming great friends for life. It was an honor to work for TWA in so many ways. It showed me the world including countries like Italy, Denmark, Germany, France, China, Japan, Spain, the United

Author

The author's parents, Mr. and Mrs. Gigante.

Kingdom, Greece, Morocco and Africa plus many exotic Mediterranean islands.

Travelling as we did, airline employees got to know the culture of the people and the way they dressed, the different foods they ate and their special customs. It was also a pleasure to travel with my family members and other TWA employees who shared my fondness for our airline.

TWA employees who worked at 605 Third Avenue were truly like a family. We would try to meet every Friday night at the "Kitty Hawk" restaurant near our headquarters building. We chose Kitty Hawk because it was close to the office and had a connection to the airline industry.

The entire restaurant was decorated with different items from many airplanes covering the history of aviation the Wright brothers' historic

1903 flight to the present, with items hanging on the walls and ceiling and aircraft seats placed around the restaurant and the bar. Aircraft engines, landing gear and other artifacts created the perfect environment for a group of happy TWA people. Ironically, the Kitty Hawk, North Carolina reference became the state I reside in at this point in my life.

Looking back at employee pass travel in the 1960s and '70s, I often talk with my friends about the travails of flying standby. Also at TWA, employees and family members were required to follow a dress code in keeping with the image of the airline and to always be respectful of revenue passengers.

We had to adapt to the rules or face the prospect of being denied boarding, and it happened we were flying first class to Las Vegas and my dad forgot a tie. I think I set a record on running to the gift shop to buy him one, not unlike O.J. Simpson running through a crowded airport banging into people along the way. Fortunately, I got back to the boarding gate just as our names cleared to board.

Daydreaming is a short-term detachment from one's immediate surroundings when one's contact with reality is blurred and partially substituted by a visionary fantasy especially of happy pleasant thoughts. I often remember daydreaming when I attended elementary school in Brooklyn and my old-fashioned teacher never smiled. Actually she was my penmanship teacher and to this day I thank her for what she taught me in class.

This is where my first thoughts of flying around the world originated and I would often look out the window and dream of doing something nice for my mother and father. It would turn out to be giving them the opportunity to fly around the world. After joining TWA I went to meet my paternal grandparents on my father's side, in Sicily. TWA made my dreams come true and though it might be gone these will always remain my fondest of memories. Thank you, TWA, for showing me the world.

Erminia Gigante

Flying as a DCS

By Jon Proctor

Recently delivered 747 N93118 about to depart from San Francisco.

The DCS (Director of Customer Service) position at TWA dates back before the widebody era, and can probably be credited to the Director – Passenger Service (DPS) at Continental Airlines, which began with that carrier's Boeing 707 "Golden Jet" service in 1959. TWA looked at the concept and tested it briefly on 707 flights, but decided against implementation. In the late 1960s, Pan Am also tinkered with the idea, in preparation for the 747s then on order.

TWA entered the widebody era as the second carrier to begin 747 service, following Pan Am by only a few months. With this huge airliner nearly tripling passenger capacity over that of the 707, a decision was made to add a new cabin attendant position; enter the Flight Service Manager. On international flights, the Purser position remained as well. Still, 747 flights were, to put it kindly, a bit disorganized. It became obvious that the transition from narrow to widebody needed even more to pull it all together. Enter the DCS.

My class was the second in 1971, following six the year earlier. It was made up of 15 "candidates," another way of saying that our jobs were dependent on successfully completing the 6-week training course at TWA's Breech Training Academy in Overland Park, Kansas. It included furloughed pilots, pursers and ground employees. The days were long and crammed with subject matter.

Instruction first concentrated on the flight attendant job. We become emergency-qualified in order to occupy cabin jumpseats, and learned all about meal services, galley layouts and procedures, as well as union contracts, and even got into grooming. Everyone had to jump down the 747 evacuation slide, out of the cabin mockup and into the adjacent parking lot. In the pool, we inflated rafts and erected canopies.

Another week involved becoming familiar with tariffs, multiple-destination fares, ticket writing, reservation follow-up and all the other things that our ground people dealt with on a daily basis.

For us each trip began with a visit to the dining unit or food caterer, inspecting every piece of dining and commissary equipment including food and drink. After participating in a crew briefing, we met the gate agents, their supervisors and even the station mangers when necessary. Diplomacy was required in order to develop good working relationships with these people, not easy when we had to give them negative feedback about earlier flight problems.

Once aloft, we oversaw the cabin crew and offered passengers assistance with future airline, hotel and car rental bookings in addition to cabin service oversight. After arrival at destination, the DCS accompanied passengers to the baggage claim, or helped staff service counters in Customs to help out as necessary. Various reports were to be filed at the end of trips, rounding out long days.

My entire class was assigned to the New York domicile and I began flying the line on September 1, 1971. During the first month I drew London trips, then Madrid. The best part this job was the schedule, usually

Jim Dolin, seen in a 707 cabin trainer, flew in the DCS test program.

three days on, three days off, although there were occasional domicile meetings in between.

A few months later I was suddenly reassigned to work Flight 840, a five-day trip to Rome, Athens and Tel Aviv. Affectionately called the "Ravioli Rocket" or "Bagel Bomber," it was quite a challenge for the DCS. After a layover in Italy, we continued with a Rome-based cabin crew to Israel, endured a minimal layover and returned the next day. Twenty-five hours later it was home to New York with yet another cabin team.

Flight 840 was notoriously late. If it wasn't delayed while transiting JFK in rush hour traffic, there were multiple opportunities for problems at Rome, where labor strife was almost constant. My logbook tells me the first trip was typical, delayed 1 hour, 30 minutes leaving JFK. From Rome we were more than 7 hours late thanks to a mechanical problem, mandating a 1-hour delay the next morning to allow for minimum crew rest. Incidentally, DCSs had no minimum rest rules! Finally, on Day 5, we returned to JFK, this time 2 hours, 30 minutes late with yet another mechanical problem. This meant the majority of our connecting passengers would miss their onward flights and thus overwhelming the service desk in Customs and adding more duty time for one tuckered-out DCS.

But there were plenty of good times, like an extra day in London over Christmas, with dinner at the Columbia Officers Club, accessed thanks to our sky marshals who happened to be military veterans.

Leaving New York

I transferred to Chicago in April 1972, where all initial L-1011 flying was to be based starting in June. Until then,

Author

Roy Kral and Bob Anderson were in the first DCS class. They are pictured in the 747 upper-deck lounge early in the program, before receiving their uniforms.

there was an ad hoc DCS base in place to cover a daily Las Vegas turnaround, plus overnight trips to Los Angeles and San Francisco.

I left on my first ORD-based trip April 21, a two-day 747 pattern to San Francisco with a nice downtown layover. All went well on the westward flight until a flight attendant with a serious look

George W. Hamlin

The mighty 747 became our airborne office.

of fear on her face reported, "There's a passenger back there who says he's going to blow up the airplane!" Oh, swell.

It seems a German merchant seaman had apparently over-indulged in drink and decided to make a name for himself, telling the flight attendant that the airplane would "blow up like a crescent," and that he had the bomb in his travel alarm clock, which he showed to her. By the time I got back to confront this man, he had passed out and the very common, small clock lay on a seat next to him. I removed it and consulted with Captain Jim Lydic, who said we would take the threat seriously while proceeding to our destination. The authorities were alerted and the "bomb" was stowed deep within a galley storage compartment.

On arrival at San Francisco, an FBI agent, fluent in German, was standing on the steps, along with two other law officers. I identified the emerging offender and he was promptly handcuffed and taken into custody. Several of us on the crew were interviewed briefly and gave written statements. The seaman was promptly deported back to Germany.

The daily O'Hare–Las Vegas 747, appropriately numbered 711 westbound, returned from Glitter Gulch after a 90-minute layover, just enough time for crewmembers to run a roll of quarters through slot machines in the lobby. The flight carried heavy loads and was a big moneymaker, even over these relatively short segments for a jumbo jet. We still had coach lounges and two flight attendants were assigned duty behind the standup bar. I vividly recall $300 receipts from the lounge alone, and this was when drinks were a dollar and beer was 50 cents. Of course the return portion brought in considerably less revenue and dispensed considerably more black coffee.

TWA's first L-1011 was accepted on May 9, 1972. Early the next morning, the delivery flight departed from Palmdale with a number of Lockheed instructors and technicians headed for Kansas City to provide TWAers with familiarization training. I was one of eight management personnel serving as a flight attendant. A Lockheed cabin crew instructor signed each of us off as having completed our "qualification flight."

We served breakfast to the Lockheed folks and later offered complimentary drinks from the fully stocked coach lounge bar, receiving thanks from our "passengers." Several commented that they were on the delivery of Eastern's first Tri-Star and received only box meals and no adult beverages.

It was fun getting in on the ground floor with the L-1011 introduction and I was aboard the inaugural flight as an instructor. At the beginning, the airplane was spacious, with first-class and coach lounges and only 206 seats. Food and beverage carts were stationary for the service and kept out of the aisles. Eight flight attendants could offer a separate cocktail service and choice of three entrees in coach.

DCS Jim Tucker and his Chicago-based cabin team.

German Held For Airport Bomb Hoax

A 28-year-old German merchant seaman aboard a Trans-World Airlines 747 flight from Chicago was arrested Friday night when the flight landed at San Francisco International Airport after he allegedly pointed to an alarm clock and told a stewardess "This clock is a bomb . . . the whole plane is going to go up in a crescent."

Taken into custody by FBI agents and San Mateo County sheriff's deputies was Klaus Coch, a German national scheduled to sail aboard a freighter out of San Francisco, according to Sheriff's Deputy Robert Cancilla.

Cancilla reported that an unidentified stewardess passed Coch, seated in the rear of the plane, and heard him say "My clock has a bomb in it." She asked him to repeat what he said, and the man told her the plane was going to "go up in a crescent," Cancilla said.

The threat occured at about 7:45 p.m., he added, but the flight's 100 passengers were apparently unaware of the threat until after the plane had landed in San Francisco at 9 p.m.

Author

Aboard the polar flight.

There were some early problems with the L-1011's Rolls-Royce engines, including one incident when one of the powerplants literally came apart in flight. Not long after we began a San Francisco morning departure from O'Hare, I was assigned to that pairing. We served breakfast and were abeam Kansas City when the captain

called me up front to advise that we were losing oil pressure in the No. 3 engine and he was about to shut it down.

I remember him telling the co-pilot to get clearance to 25,000 feet from 33,000. He replied, "they can't give it to us." Captain: "Tell them we've GOT to have it!" About that time I left the cockpit to give our passengers the bad news. Planning had us fly all the way back to ORD; total time in the air was nearly three hours. One lady had a bit of a panic attack after the captain announced that emergency equipment would be standing by on our arrival. It all worked out but we canceled on arrival at O'Hare.

I was assigned to temporary duty at Los Angeles for a month, flying the six-day, 747 polar flight, nonstop to London, then Chicago, back to London and finally returning to the West Coast, crossing 28 time zones in the process. On one trip the Osmond family occupied the entire first-class cabin. Actor Roger Moore was aboard another flight, along with Peter Lawford. On another

Author

The L-1011 inaugural flight cabin team. Left to right: Janet McAnnally,
Carol Graham, Janis Hawkins, Patty Donahue, Hank Krueger, Jon Proctor,
Lin Migliore, Mary MyLanski, Caroline Abbot and Carol Valenta.

segment, comedian Henny Youngman, traveling Economy, offered to do his shtick in the upper deck lounge if I would upgrade him to first class!

At midnight on November 4, 1973, TWA's flight attendants went on strike, a work stoppage that lasted 45 days. I was on a layover in Phoenix and returned to O'Hare via two different "sweep" flights dispatched to carry crewmembers and a few non-revs home, via LAX, San Francisco and Kansas City.

During the work stoppage, a variety of jobs were placed upon the DCS corps to keep us busy, including "guarding" the airplanes at night, in vehicles on the ramp. We were paired up for this exercise, thank goodness, or most of us would have fallen asleep. Roy Davis, the legendary general manager of maintenance at O'Hare, assigned us the tasks aircraft cleaning and polishing. On those days, he stood at the coffee machine in the break room as we filed in, inserting coins to provide us with java. One day, Roy told us to bring our cars into the hangar and we washed and waxed them instead of airplanes.

As the strike dragged on, it was decided to check the DCS cadre out on all of TWA's narrowbody aircraft. An instructor came up from Breech to give us the required classroom time. Instead of the obligatory door and exit operations in the training center mockups, we simply climbed on board our idled jets and performed the same tasks. The only problem: we didn't have a DC-9 at O'Hare, so could not complete the drill for that aircraft type.

They were going to send us to Kanas City to operate the DC-9 doors but it was going to be difficult getting us there as Ozark and Braniff, which flew the route, were full because of the strike. While Ralph Wilson, our boss, was scratching his head, contemplating the logistics of sending 30 or so of us to MCI, I pointed out to him that Ozark's hangar was right behind ours and there always seemed to be a DC-9 parked there.

Sure enough, a couple of phone calls later a single instructor was shuttled back up from Breech to sign each of us off as we operated Ozark's

passenger doors and over-wing exits. Ralph gave me a gold star for that one.

The strike was settled just a week before Christmas, hardly enough time to regain all of our customers for the holiday rush, but it was a welcome relief. We had been working on reduced pay for nearly a month and were happy give those the polishing rags back to Roy Davis. Incidentally, I worked an L-1011 trip out to Los Angeles on Christmas Eve, spent the evening with family, then came back Christmas Day on an afternoon flight, with 11 passengers and 12 crew.

Following a two-year assignment in our corporate offices, I returned to the DCS position in 1976 and remained until the program ended late that year. By then the position was essentially redundant. Too bad, as I would gladly have retired in that job.

Today, members of the TWA DCS Alumni Association gather at annual reunions to relive the memories. The group maintains a website at *www.twdcs.org.*

Author

Aboard the polar flight.

TWA Runway Overrun During Rejected Takeoff

By John Bruno

Clint Groves/Proctor Collection

N15712 rests in San Francisco Bay.

I was a Lead System Technician (LST) for TWA at San Francisco, working the graveyard shift on September 13, 1972, when Cargo Flight 604 overran the departure runway and crashed into San Francisco Bay at 10:43 p.m.

Bound for New York-JFK, Boeing 707 331C N15712 had just passed V1, on its departure roll when the crew experienced an airframe vibration and a reduction in aircraft acceleration. This prompted the captain to abort the takeoff but he was unable to stop short of the departure end of the Runway 01-Right. The aircraft came to rest in San Francisco Bay, 50 feet from the shoreline.

It was determined that the right-hand landing gear No. 4 tire assembly had burst due to sidewall failure, and the right-hand No. 3 tire failed from the resulting overload. Dual rim marks from these wheels was evident along the runway.

Dean Slaybaugh/Proctor Collection

*The broken wreckage was moved onto airport pavement
for inspection and eventual scrapping.*

us who service aircraft, airplanes become special entities rather than inanimate objects.

Unfortunately, Fred Hersey contracted hepatitis from his ordeal in San Francisco Bay, but the project was otherwise a success.

The next morning I was directed to remove fuel from the Boeing as required by the Environmental Protection Agency (EPA) before we were allowed to lift the aircraft from the water.

Working out of a rowboat, TWA Service Engineer Vern Johnson, Mechanic Fred Hersey and I surveyed damage and installed the necessary defueling equipment to transfer JP-4 to awaiting fuel trucks. The wings were submerged and required de-fuel hoses to be installed underwater, which became the job of Fred and Vern, who were certified divers and volunteered their services. With the wings under water we had to modify over-wing fueling caps with lengths of hydraulic tubing to allow venting above the water line, a job assigned to another TWA Service Engineer, the late Dick Born.

With the fuel tanks empty, N15712 was lifted by Bigge Crane and Rigging Company and loaded onto a flatbed truck for transport to the "Super Bay" hangar.

The wrecked cargo jet was shored for inspection and salvageable parts were removed. Salt water damaged the aluminum and titanium structure and components. As result those component began disintegrating and parts began falling off the aircraft. This was very sad to witness. For those of

John Bruno began his TWA career in 1966 as an A&P mechanic and became a lead system technician before leaving the company in 1980 to form Aviation Consulting Corporation, becoming the company's president. He is currently serving as the heavy maintenance project manager for Atlas Air, based in Taiwan.

President Richard Nixon Opens Up China

By Captain Bill Dixon

Journey to Peking

TWA 707 on the ramp at Peking. Operations Control Building is in background.

TWA Today

In 1972, I had the good fortune to be the co-pilot with Captain Marv Horstman on a special White House charter carrying 80 CBS, NBC, and ABC TV technicians to Peking (now Beijing), when President Nixon, at the height of his popularity, visited Peking to meet with Mao Tse-tung, leader of the Chinese Communist Party. Jim Hackett was the flight engineer.

We flew in a couple of weeks ahead of Nixon, and returned for the passengers a week after Nixon left China. This time I was the captain with an all San Francisco cockpit crew consisting of Captain

TWA Today

The charter pilot crew: Captain Marvin C. Horstman, Flight Engineer James E. Hackett and Captain William Dixon.

Chuck Thompson as co-pilot and Gail Howell as flight engineer.

A convertible Boeing 707-331C was reconfigured for both cargo and passengers to carry the network experts assigned to help China construct the satellite station that would broadcast the details of the meeting worldwide. N794TW, fully loaded, left Los Angeles on January 28, 1972, and after a refueling stop in Honolulu continued to Guam for a four-day layover and crew briefing.

Special navigation and airport charts were required for the Guam-Shanghai-Peking route. Key White House personnel told the crew and passengers what to expect on arrival. They explained Chinese are very patient, meticulous and principle is everything to them; we should not touch men or women, even a pat on the shoulder, as it is not there custom. They do shake hands with Westerners since this is our custom.

We departed from Guam on February 1 for a nonstop flight to Shanghai. The aircraft was loaded to maximum takeoff weight, 334,000 pounds. Passing over Okinawa and turning towards China, we were a bit nervous when handed over to Shanghai traffic controllers, although they spoke perfect English. After an instrument approach (the ceiling was reported at 400 feet) we landed at Shanghai. It was the first time a commercial U.S. aircraft had visited the People's Republic of China in 23 years.

A group of about 25 smiling people met the flight. All dressed essentially alike, in black or dark brown Mao-designed jackets and trousers. In 1972, it was hard to tell men from women.

Our crew was served an elaborate late lunch and given a weather briefing while the aircraft was topped off with an additional 55,000 pounds of fuel. We departed after a couple of hours for Peking, with a Chinese radio operator and a navigator, neither of which were really needed, but were required to carry on flights within the country. We were not permitted to take pictures from the air, but could on the ground.

Our landing at Peking in relatively clear weather was uneventful. There were two concrete runways, each 10,500 feet long. The terminal lobby, virtually empty, was dominated by a huge statue of Mao Tse-tung. Passengers were taken to a hotel downtown, and the crew to a small hotel near the airport. We slept for about 5 hours, had a light snack, and took off about 2 a.m., returning to Guam. The 10 hours spent at Peking were longer than planned because, much to their chagrin, the Chinese had trouble unloading the equipment.

The crew returned home but N794TW sat at Guam for a month, awaiting the return flight to Peking.

By far the most interesting part of the China experience, in spite of the excitement of the original entry, was returning on March 1 to pick up the passengers we had left behind. This time the crew was scheduled to remain in Peking for approximately 24 hours. We were housed downtown at the Friendship Hotel and and taken on a tour of the Forbidden City, the Ming Dynasty Tombs and the Great Wall. Our drivers honked their horns almost continuously. There were bicycles and buses in great number; also many trucks, but practically no automobiles – much different than today. Our cars carried a special sign in the windshield that obviously carried a lot of clout. All traffic, from horse carts to trucks to pedestrians, scurried out of our way.

Arriving at the Great Wall – the main area where natives and tourists visit – we were struck by the spectacle it presents. The wall here was rebuilt during the Ming Dynasty and was in magnificent repair. "It is Chinese legend," our guide leader, Mr. Lee, joked, "that no man can be a hero unless he has seen he Great Wall. You can go home now," he laughed, "and be a hero!"

We saw no golf courses, tennis courts, green lawns, swimming pools, or suburban towns. Houses grouped together and surrounded by walls, which blended into the dreary landscape. Windbreaks of cornstalks were in wide use, largely to protect garden plots.

We witnessed many workers walking home from fields, men and women carrying spades, rakes and hoes over their shoulders. All the women wore pants and jackets, never saw a skirt or dress. Most surprising to us, and an example of the total control of the Communist regime, was that law forbade women in large cities to marry until age 28. It was difficult for young men and women to meet socially, an interpreter revealed, except at universities. For entertainment couples went to plays, movies and took walks. Public affection was discouraged.

"Can you change jobs?" I asked. "Oh, yes," was the proud answer, "with approval of the authorities."

That evening the crew was taken to The Peking Duck Restaurant for dinner. We sat 10 at a table, along with the two U.S. Air Force crews still there, plus our crew of three pilots and four flight attendants. Regular silverware plus chopsticks were beside each plate. As pilot in command of the TWA plane, I was seated next to the top official, a constant smoker and typical bureaucrat. I think I surprised him by using the chopsticks, which I had learned to do during layovers at Hong Kong.

Toasts of Mau Tai were offered and the feast was on. "In China," one of the men at our table said, "we eat everything but the feathers." We applauded as beautifully bronzed roast duck were brought in for ceremonial showing before being placed on the tables. The servings included even a tidbit of duck brains. Eggs and vegetables also were served. Cold hors d'oeuvres and soup had opened the dinner. Duck-bone soup was served as part of the finale. We were told it was made by boiling the ground-up duck bones and straining the liquid.

Mr. Lee paid my room a visit at the Friendship Hotel after the dinner. First though, we stopped en route at a store, which was kept open for us to shop. We all bought a few things. For very little, I purchased an acupuncture set. Mr. Lee was dressed in a nice-looking striped dress shirt open at the throat. I had seen the shirts at the airport shop and wondered who wore them. He was the first man I had seen in China without his Mao jacket and had obviously had worn his black jacket over the shirt at the restaurant.

He had presents with him, which he said "were gifts from my government for you and your crew as mementos of your visit." Each of us received two bottles of Mau Tai, two cans of jasmine tea, a framed picture of a ceramic bird and tree in Chinese design, and an embroidered tablecloth, plus large Chinese wall calendars.

Our wakeup call came at 6 a.m. the following day, just two rings; no one was on the line. I took a quick bath in the huge tub before retiring; there was plenty of hot water. Two packages of cigarettes and a thermos of water were on the bedside table. Forty to 50 Chinese, mostly men, saw us off. I was able to persuade Mr. Lee, as we always addressed him, to accept several boxes of cigars and cartons of American cigarettes, and some TWA fountain pens and flight bags as token gifts. He at first demurred, but I told him it would hurt our feelings if he turned us down. He was about age 30, spoke excellent English, told us he was married, no children, and worked for the diplomatic corps.

Before departure, a large bag of pears and tangerines was placed in the cockpit as a final gesture of hospitality. As we headed back for the U.S. from Peking, our cabin attendants began defrosting hamburgers and hot dogs as a surprise for our passengers. The announcement was greeted with loud applause. We were happy to be heading for home.

Originally published in TARPA Topics, March 2001, and reproduced with permission.

Thomas Livesey

*The China charter aircraft, N794TW. It was only time a TWA
707 was operated in a combi configuration.*

A Pilot's Remembrances of Ozark Air Lines
By Captain Greg Pochapsky

The author's new office, Fairchild-Hiller's turboprop FH-227B.

My first encounter with Ozark was entirely unplanned. In 1974, I arrived at Scott Air Force Base, Illinois to pre-position for a two day Air Force Reserve flight in the C-9A Nightingale. I checked in with the 375th Aeromedical Airlift Wing command post only to be advised my trip was downgraded to a one-day event and I was free of duty for the ensuing 48 hours. I called a squadron mate, Dennis Lucido, and arranged to meet for dinner.

Dennis was also an Ozark Air Lines pilot and, hearing of my free time, invited me to visit the airline's facility while he ran some errands. Shortly after our arrival, Dennis came over to me and suggested we speak to the personnel folks about a possible job. He spoke to the person in charge and she summoned me to her desk. It seems they couldn't find my application.

The young lady apologized for misplacing the application form and requested I complete another. All of this was no surprise to me, as I had never applied. In any event, Dennis and I walked down the street and found a typewriter in a vacant office of the Missouri Air National Guard complex. I quickly filled in the required blank spaces including a paragraph describing why it had been my life's desire to become an Ozark Air Lines pilot.

Returning to the personnel department, I was asked if I had time to take several written tests and complete an interview or two. Apparently, in speaking with Dennis, the personnel department got the impression that the chief pilot personally wanted me interviewed. Dennis knew he was on a cruise with naval reserved and not contactable.

I arrived at the interview that afternoon. Captain Dick Bradin, principal check airman for the Fairchild-Hiller FH-227B program and a true gentleman, invited me into his office conducted the most professional interview I have ever witnessed. Besides being a former Marine pilot, Dick was ever the optimist and always gracious and positive.

At the end of the working day, I met with Captain Peter Sherwin, Director of Flight Training and Standards and the "man" with final say regarding a new hire's fate. I left the interview with Captain Sherwin feeling positive, but hardly expecting a class date in the near future and headed toward the first floor lobby while mentally resigning myself to having had an interesting, albeit unfruitful day.

Pushing on the exit door I heard my name called and turned to see Captain Sherwin standing at the top of the staircase. To this day, I can see him looking down at me and asking, "Are you sure you are at least 5 feet, 7 inches tall?" It seems Ozark had been embroiled in a lawsuit over pilot height requirements and Peter was the main company witness.

Reporting for Duty

Our new-hire Ozark pilot training class began in April 1974. Every member of the class had made a point of being early that day for fear of being identified as one who might in the future, oversleep and delay a flight. There were, in total, 13 of us, each eyeing the other and wondering who would have the highest seniority number, which, after all, governs everything in a pilot's life from schedules and equipment to vacations.

Mr. Bill Bourne, Manager of Ground Training for pilots, soon greeted us. The avuncular Mr. Bourne was the right man to assuage the fears of a new hire. It was immediately evident he took great pride in getting his students through training. In addition to his training duties, Bill was Ozark's unofficial resident historian and an experienced aviator in his own right. His wife, Peggy, was the Director of Flight Attendants, whose duties included the selection, training and management of one of the finest groups of attendants in the industry. The Ozark route system was foreign to many in the pilot class. Most knew little of stations like Clarksville, Tennessee or Clinton, Iowa. Mr. Bourne's lectures kept us spellbound with concepts like operation specifications, flag stopping, ramp radios, in-range calls and flight crew pay forms. We wondered what any of it had

David H. Stringer Collection

to a manual or note, he lectured us 8 hours a day about such subjects as the pneumatic system, the Rolls Royce Dart engine and the enigmatic Dowty-Rotol propeller.

At last, we thought we were going fly the airplane, but first had to travel to the freight hangar area of the Greater Pittsburgh airport to train in a Fairchild flight simulator belonging to Allegheny Air Lines. The visual system consisted of a camera hovering above a model train-type landscape and was time-shared between the various equipment types in the Allegheny fleet. After some 32 hours in the "sim" we were off to St. Louis for a final check ride in the actual airplane and then a year of probationary line flying.

All along the way at Ozark, new friends were made. As flight crews, we were privileged to meet fellow employees in all the stations and, more often than not, became first-name friends. That professional camaraderie went a long way in getting the mission completed. Crews were sensitive to the stations' commitment to schedule and the stations were equally sensitive to the needs of the crew. It was not uncommon for a crew to call the station with a meal request and an agent would be sure it was ready for the crew on arrival. Mattoon, Illinois was famous for taking crews orders for pork tenderloin sandwiches. Station agents would invite crews to their homes for holiday meals and local restaurants would drive four-wheel drive vehicles through heavy snow and gather the crews for dinner. Those who had initially been disappointed in not flying to exotic ports-of-call, soon realized flying the Midwest brought with it its own special rewards.

For me personally, what started out as an off-handed visit to Ozark Air Lines would be the beginning of a most wonderful 34-year career as an airline pilot and a very close lifelong friendship with Peter Sherwin.

Ozark: The Name

It certainly was not unusual for airlines to choose a company name associated with their

to do with flying, but were damn sure going to learn all of it. And we did.

The next event consisted of two weeks of aircraft systems training on the Fairchild-Hiller FH-227B, a steroidal relative to the venerable Fairchild F-27. Mr. David "Dave" Jones was the principal "FH" instructor. Without ever referring route system. Allegheny, Piedmont, Eastern and even Delta are just a few. Pan Am started as Pan American, reflective of its geographical footprint.

The name Ozark was derived from the French "Bois aux Arc" meaning "Woods of Bows." Bois d'Arc (bow wood) refers to the name of the wood known as Osage orange, which grew throughout the Mississippi River region and was used for bows. Later, English settlers changed the name to Ozark. Ozark Air Line's original route system transited stations in the Ozark highlands and was a logical appellation for the nascent airline. Unfortunately, those unaware of the name's etymology were more inclined to associate it with barefoot, bib overall-wearing characters from Al Capp's comic strip, *Lil Abner*. This was unfortunate as the employees at Ozark Air Lines were as diverse, experienced and worldly as those of any air carrier and represented nearly every state in the nation.

Employee Philosophy:

Employees at Ozark were, with some exceptions, extremely nationalistic about their employer. Prior to U.S. Deregulation, very few airline employees, especially flight crews bound by a seniority system, ever changed companies. There was a vested interested in the success of one's carrier as a lateral move between organizations was not likely. Employees protected the company and the company protected the employees. At Ozark, termination of an employee was a rare event and reserved for the most serious infractions. The result was an intensely loyal and dedicated family of workers. Some 30 years after being merged with TWA, members of this Ozark family still gather annually for an all-day picnic and reunion.

Greg Pochapsky enjoyed 34 years as an airline pilot with the opportunity to fly for Ozark, TWA and American Airlines. He retired in 2001 as a Boeing 767 international captain. Since retirement, Greg has served as Director of Safety and Chief Accident Investigator for a major regional airline. He resides in St Louis with his wife, two married children and granddaughter and enjoys spending off moments flying his Cessna 180.

On Assignment with Saudia

By Jon Proctor

Author's photos except as noted

Riyadh Airport was not equipped with Jetways, presenting challenges on full Saudia 747 flights.

When President Franklin Roosevelt gave the Kingdom of Saudi Arabia a C-47 (DC-3) in 1945, TWA was selected to provide management assistance to the newly formed Saudi Arabian Airlines, later known as Saudia. Over the years, TWA helped to build it into a proud flag carrier, providing training and personnel, especially in the areas of maintenance and flight crews. Thousands of TWAers completed temporary assignments, mainly at the Jeddah base.

The airline's first widebody L-1011 jets were about to arrive in 1975 when the airline requested help training cabin crews that would include an In Flight Supervisor (IFS), to be modeled after

Two TWA L-1011s were sold to Saudia. The first is shown at
Kansas City upon rollout from the paint hangar.

TWA's DCS program. Six TWA employees from that position were recruited to serve six-month assignments that would include training the initial Saudia crews at Breech Academy, visiting the Lockheed factory at Palmdale, California and on-the-job training from the Jeddah base. Saudia's rapid growth brought additional Tri-Stars into the fleet and the call was put out for more TWAers to assist.

Saudia initiated Boeing 747 flights in June 1977, wet-leasing a pair from Beirut-headquartered Middle East Airlines (MEA), to be operated by MEA cockpit and cabin crews, plus two London-based Saudia hostesses and a Jeddah-based Saudi purser, along an American IFS. It brought about a regular potpourri of nationalities and diplomatic challenges.

While Saudia for some time had maintained a hostess domicile at London, the IFS group was Jeddah-based until the 747s were introduced.

Twelve of us were accepted for the 18-month U.K. assignment, and officially belonged to Saudia as of May 1. We received an informational briefing by our industrial relations people at Kansas City, covering Saudi Arabian laws and the airline's policies.

One of the challenges was a different tax code in the U.K., requiring that we spend at least one month per year in country. To meet the standard, each of us would complete 30 days on office duty annually.

We were paid an amount equivalent to that of a TWA in-flight supervisor plus a premium, and were considered management employees. Paychecks came from TWA and were direct-deposited into U.S. bank accounts. Expense money came in the form of a check payable in Saudi Riyals, to be cashed during our layover time in the Kingdom. Unlimited travel on Saudia was granted, something I never had occasion to take advantage of; back then the carrier did not fly to the United States.

Ten days of classroom training commenced at the Heathrow Hotel, where we were provided housing through the end of May. Most of the instruction involved serving procedures. Except for the absence of alcoholic beverages, first class was to be nearly identical to what we were used to at TWA. In the back there were to be no serving carts in the aisle. Instead, soft drinks and juices would be offered from serving trays, followed by the meals, hand-delivered from the galleys. This simplified service was in stark contrast to MEA's procedures, and everyone wondered why 17 or 18 people were needed to carry it out, but we didn't ask.

Safety instruction consisted of differences training between MEA and TWA 747s and license certification according to Lebanese government rules. We were able to get Heathrow Airport ID badges and obtain United Kingdom multiple-entry work visas relatively easily.

The 747s would fly daily between Riyadh (RUH) and Jeddah (JED) via Cairo (CAI) plus four times weekly between Riyadh and London. Patterns were typically five and eight day's duration.

The two 747s were configured with 48 first-class seats on the main deck plus 16 in the upper deck, and 322 in economy. Although wearing exterior Saudia paint, the airplanes' interiors were vintage MEA and quite attractive. We did not have "no smoking" sections in either class.

In contrast to Jeddah, the city of Riyadh is inland, at an altitude of 2,000 feet, making it less humid but usually warmer. Our crew layover hotel was the Elkherji, where Spartan accommodations varied. It was not uncommon to enter a sweltering room before the A/C gave limited relief. Hot

Author's Collection

water, when we had it, often came from the cold-water spigot.

An added challenge in the Kingdom was the Islamic calls to prayer, loudly recited five times daily over public address systems. At Riyadh a loudspeaker was attached to the outside of the hotel and close to our rooms, depending on which ones we occupied. Calls in the middle of the night were common.

Saudia was growing exponentially and all departments struggled to keep up with its rapid expansion even before 747 operations began. The jumbos were an added challenge for ground crews, especially at Riyadh and Jeddah. Both airports

The first Saudia uniforms were rather generic. Jackets were optional in the Middle East; ties were not!

had painfully inadequate terminal buildings and relatively small ramp areas with no Jetways. To compound the problem, both 747s were often on the ground simultaneously at Riyadh.

On flights within the Middle East, there were numerous examples of more passengers boarded than seats available. Small children – and there could be as many as 100 on a single flight – were on occasion counted as infants, referred to as "lap babies." We would have too many in seat rows without sufficient drop-down oxygen mask capacity, producing "musical chairs" to meet those restrictions, plus remove the customers still standing. Lack of seat assignments exacerbated the problem.

MEA maintenance engineers assigned to Riyadh, Cairo and Jeddah met every flight and made repairs, usually at night when the airplanes were on the ground for more than a few minutes. I rode in the cockpit several times and was impressed with the professionalism displayed by the pilots.

With London–Riyadh service only operated five days a week, we flew some five-day pairings while others were eight days long, with two of the circuitous, Riyadh–Jeddah roundtrips. A once-weekly Riyadh–Beirut (BEY) pairing gave the 747s brief visits to MEA's maintenance headquarters.

We endured 30-hour stays as part of the eight-day pairings. With no restaurants in the immediate vicinity of the hotel, little shopping and no sightseeing to speak it became challenging it became to occupy one's time. Much of it was spent writing letters and reading; I averaged more than one book a week. Some of the rooms had black & white televisions with a single channel and a once-daily, 30-minute news program in English. Cartoons with Arabic subtitles quickly grew old. Full-length films were shown on the main floor utilizing a Betamax video system that produced a fuzzy picture and often broke down.

Men and women on the crew were always assigned rooms on different floors and we were not allowed on those occupied by the opposite sex. Other than gathering in the lobby or the dining room, there was little opportunity for socializing.

The situation at Jeddah was marginally better. The Saudia hostesses were at a different hotel, but we often met up and went out for dinner. The IFS was not permitted in the hotel and the hostesses were restricted by curfews. They had to wear pants and dress conservatively. After dinner we usually went to the souk, where I cashed my expense checks for Saudi Riyals, British Pounds and U.S. dollars.

Crew meals were not very appetizing within the Middle East, where pigeon was considered a delicacy. About the only time I ate any of the inflight food was out of London. Arabic bread (also called Pita bread) and humus could be relied upon for safe consumption in restaurants. With pork products forbidden, the Saudis consumed large amounts of lamb and other beef products.

My first Beirut visit began on June 28, 1977. The flight from Riyadh was packed, with every seat taken in addition to 39 lap babies and 24 crew. Adding to the drama was Sheikh Pierre Gemayel, founder and head of the Lebanese Phalangist Party, who rode in the upper deck lounge. Our captain was so concerned about his safety that he ordered the search of everyone who came upstairs before departure. On arrival at BEY, two military tanks pulled right up to the airplane with soldiers manning their gun turrets. Welcome to war-torn Lebanon.

An appreciated relief from Saudi lodging was Beirut's Coral Beach Hotel on the shores of the Red Sea. It featured large rooms with balconies, a swimming pool and the Beachcomber Bar. Getting there from the airport required passage through numerous security checkpoints staffed by armed militia from the Arab peacekeeping force.

In early July, we began operating the first of several "teacher flights." Most schoolteachers in the Kingdom were Egyptian and flown home, with their families, to Cairo from Riyadh for summer holidays. The only large-capacity aircraft available was one of our 747s normally scheduled for an overnight layover. So after a long day and evening, one of us would be stuck with this unique charter, operating to CAI and ferrying back to RUH. On-duty periods stretched to 16 hours or more. But it wasn't a whole lot worse than sitting or sleeping at the Elkherji. In the fall we instead ferried to CAI brought full loads back. My logbook says that on two September segments we carried a total of 810 passengers including lap babies.

On a regular flight in August, Palestinian leader Yasser Arafat and his party of six were booked to fly from Cairo to Riyadh. We had already gone through individual bag identification when Arafat and his group were driven to the foot of the boarding stairs. Then, as quickly as they arrived, the group left and we were given clearance to depart. The captain told me this part of Arafat's own security measures; he would book on one flight then take another. It was a quiet but unnerving ride over to Riyadh.

New uniforms were issued in 1978. Roommate Allan Johnson photographed me as I was about to depart for the airport.

With implementation of the fall 1977 schedules, three of the five weekly LHR–RUH flights included an en route stop at either Geneva (GVA) or Rome (FCO). The time adjustments meant shorter layovers at RUH off the southbound flights and later LHR arrivals northbound; flights between RUH, CAI and JED were not affected.

Coming back from RUH to LHR on October 13, we were to operate nonstop until, at the last minute, an operations agent came out to tell us a ground vehicle had damaged an L-1011 at JED. We were to divert there and pick up the passengers. I went to the cockpit and told the captain who said, "That would put us 32,000 pounds overweight for landing at Jeddah. Tell them we can't do it." I passed along the information, only to be advised, "Tell the captain to dump fuel on the way." I was astounded and the captain was angry. But we did just that, jettisoning more than 5,000 gallons of kerosene over the Saudi desert.

I was scheduled for just two five-day trips in December, both with Rome stops in each direction. Having only three days off in between, I couldn't head back home until December 26. The first pairing went fine until the last day, when London was socked in with heavy fog. We circled over Dover for nearly an hour, and then diverted to Manchester, England, becoming the first ever Saudia jumbo to land there. The front door was opened an hour later, followed by another 2-1/2 hours before the bags were unloaded. The passengers and cabin crew were transported to London by train.

The Middle East weather cooled off by January and was quite pleasant, even in Jeddah, although we knew it would be short-lived. My trips were routine except for a diversion when a sandstorm, with 55-mph winds, arrived at Riyadh shortly before we were due in from Cairo. Our alternate was Dhahran but that airport became saturated with other flights so we instead landed a Bahrain and sat two hours before returning to Riyadh.

In March, fighting in Lebanon escalated. I was about to depart for Beirut when the captain urged me to get off the airplane and take the two Saudia hostesses and Saudi purser with me. "We live there. It is not worth the risk for you," he said. I took the captain's advice and told the others to get off, but the purser insisted on taking the flight. I did not object.

Our contracts called for 30 vacation days that were not accrued, meaning we had to take them within the first year. I gleefully headed home with for a month away from the Middle East.

The rest of spring and summer became somewhat of a boring ritual, back and forth on the same two jumbos, flying the same patterns over and over. We had been offered a 10% bonus to extend our contracts by a year. It was tempting, but I declined.

By fall I was due another 30 days of vacation and had the month of September off, then returned to London and flew two more trips, completing the final pairing on October 16. The next morning TWA Flight 709 carried me home from this great adventure.

The Saudia contract was probably my greatest test of self-control. While a rewarding and memorable experience, I was most happy to be back in the States for good, especially with the approaching Thanksgiving and Christmas holidays. It was wonderful to be home.

An expanded version of this story can be found at *www.jonproctor.net.*

Pretty MEA hostess Dalai Sinno posed with me at the R-5 door, en route from Riyadh to London on my last Saudia trip.

OPINION: Why Deregulation?

By Floyd D. Hall

The Airline Deregulation Act of 1978 brought the greatest turmoil to the airline industry since the cancellation of the airmail contracts in 1934. Flight delays at major cities, bad passenger service at over-crowded terminals, and greater-than-ever baggage losses became common. Large fines for maintenance irregularities and some tragic accidents that have cast doubt about pilot proficiency have caused frequent users of air transportation, including some members of Congress, to question the wisdom of deregulation. Much of the travelling public is asking, "Why deregulation in the first place?"

It had its roots in economics, but it became a political ploy, then a campaign and then almost a crusade.

The travelling public had not demanded deregulation, or even regulatory reform. In fact, public opinion polls taken in the early 1970s indicated that the public was well satisfied with the airlines. The system of trunk and regional carriers developed by the Civil Aeronautics Board (CAB) provided good service to most parts of the country, even to some areas where traffic was hardly sufficient to warrant air service at all. Perhaps because the public had no real way to compare and evaluate ticket prices, and because the CAB set fares in the United States, passengers seldom complained, except to wonder why there weren't more excursion fares like those offered by the non-skeds. But competitive pricing by the airlines under CAB regulation was rare, for most airlines were so far below a satisfactory level of profits that cutting fares was not even considered as a way to improve earnings. The elasticity theory (i.e., lower fares bring added new business to offset the cuts) had never been proved to the satisfaction of the airlines.

The movement for regulatory reform was much broader than complaints about the value of fares, however. The question of big government regulating the private sector caused serious debate even before the Civil Aeronautics Act of 1938 was finally passed. There was strong belief that no business should be controlled by an omnipotent government, but must be allowed to compete in "the free market place."

Laissez faire, even in the air, had been the guiding rule of government up to the coming of the New Deal in 1934. The question of a free, unhampered, private sector versus government regulation "in the public interest" remained a disputed political issue until World War II put an end to such discussions.

But after World War II, the subject arose again. Many new airlines were formed by flyers that had flown in the War, but the CAB denied most of them certificates to operate as scheduled passenger carriers, although they authorized some new cargo carriers. They lumped the rest together as "non-skeds," and called them supplemental carriers. They were supposed to provide excursion-type fares to excess passengers that could not be accommodated by the scheduled airlines in peak travel periods.

Right or wrong, the CAB appeared to protect the scheduled carriers from price competition in the passenger business, while also protecting their routes from new, unconventional, carriers.

To some students of transportation, the CAB and the airlines formed a "legal cartel," which the airlines controlled. Supporters of the free enterprise system found this very distasteful, even if it were legal.

By the mid-1960s, most airlines were equipped with jet-powered airplanes, and the industry enjoyed the best record in its history. Service was good, there were frequent schedules, flying was safe and reliable, and profits, while still modest, seemed assured for the foreseeable future. To some students of transportation in America, the airlines had, at last, reached maturity and the "Golden Age" of air transportation had arrived. But, in analyzing the financial effects the jets would have, the economics of airline operations was examined in much greater depth than ever before, and students of transportation began questioning the efficiency of continuing regulation.

Other economists focused specifically on the airline industry and agreed that reform was necessary, and some even suggested that the Civil Aeronautics Board had outlived its usefulness. They believed that both the airlines and the travelling public would profit if the CAB was abolished and the airlines permitted to operate without restraint in the competitive market place.

Richard Caves, a prominent and respected student of air transportation, concluded that the industry could, in the American tradition, go from regulated to free competition without serious difficulty. Because of the nature of air transportation, it should be possible for unregulated airlines to "move their assets" from one market to another, and this flexibility would improve profits while competition from other carriers, which would be free to enter any market they chose, would keep prices low and the quality of the service good. From the point of view of theoretical economics, the resulting situation could be a near "text-book perfect" competitive environment.

Although they strongly believed in it, the economists and transportation specialists knew that there was little likelihood of achieving regulatory reform unless they could win over some influential government leaders. They would need broad legislative and public support to be successful and it is likely that deregulation would never have come about had not some important men in government been persuaded to agree with them.

Stephen G. Breyer, formerly a Professor of Administration and Antitrust Law at Harvard and now a Supreme Court Justice, served as a special counsel to Senator Ted Kennedy's Committee on Administrative Practice and Procedure of the Judiciary. He also served in the Antitrust Division of the Department of Justice in the late 1960s, and was a special counsel in the Watergate investigations. He knew his way around Washington and was sensitive to programs with potentially high public visibility. Fortuitously, some new, even more important forces would join the movement for regulatory reform.

Around the time of the Watergate investigations, inflation was a critical problem and big government as believed to contribute substantially to inflation through outdated controls over industry. The time had come to "get big government off the back of the public."

Deregulation was so widely discussed in Washington that some Congressmen said "... deregulation is the new religion in this town." Regulation in basic industries such as public utilities, communications, trucking and air transportation was believed to contribute substantially to inflation by perpetuating obsolete regulations that protected inefficient companies. Many airlines seemed to fit the description.

Breyer argued for reform in his speeches and named a special counsel to specialize in the matter. He held meetings with members of Congress and urged the Domestic Council Review Group (DCRG, formed by President Ford when Congress failed to appoint the special commission he had requested) to make recommendations to promote reform. The group met weekly at The White House and their enthusiasm grew as it became evident that the President, even in an election year, was willing to challenge large, powerful forces that might oppose regulatory reform. They expected strong opposition from the CAB, the airline companies, and organized labor.

Regulatory reform (getting big government off the back of the people) became a popular election year theme. Both Presidents Ford and Carter agreed on reform, each trying to out-do the other in their fight against inflation. Reducing the size of big government was essential, and regulatory reform was a good place to start.

One of the early appointments of President Carter's administration was Alfred E. Kahn to be Chairman of the Civil Aeronautics Board. A Professor of Economics at Cornell University, (head of the Department of Economics) he was unusually bright, dynamic, and an eloquent and persuasive speaker. He was experienced in New York State regulatory matters, and had served on the staff of the Antitrust Division of the Department of Justice, as Breyer had done, and he was also a senior staff member of the U. S. Council of Economic Advisors.

When appointed as Chairman of the CAB, Professor Kahn was well aware of the President's goal of freeing American business from excessive regulation, but as a scholar and an educator, he was inclined to take some time to study the matter. He soon found, however, that the decision to reform had already been made and he undertook to change CAB controls by deregulating the airline industry as rapidly and as extensively as possible, under already-existing law. In the CAB staff, he found some bright young people who were upwardly mobile professionals. They acted with enthusiasm in carrying out his policies. He brought in Philip J. Bakes, who had been Chief Counsel to Kennedy's investigation of the CAB, to be his Chief Counsel; and a brilliant, young, aggressive (and abrasive) Yale law professor, Michael E. Levine, who had challenged airline regulation and criticized the CAB in the Yale Law Journal as early as 1965. He put him in charge of a new consolidated department that effectively bypassed the old staff of the CAB and Levine responded by aggressively pushing deregulation to the limit. Kahn soon found that he had considerable latitude and he made full use of it.

Proponents of deregulation had expected the airlines to oppose it. In the beginning they did, except for United Airlines, but the resistance was not very vigorous. At the end of the Ford administration, and before serious talk of deregulation had begun, several airlines considered drafting their own proposals, leading to regulatory reforms. Their aim was to speed up fare increases when they were critically needed, as in the fuel crisis of 1974. But in the end, it became impossible for the Air Transport Association, which would normally prepare an industry position on such an important matter, to find a consensus among the carriers. Organized airline opposition to deregulation collapsed.

It is interesting to note that almost no one had expected full deregulation and complete elimination of the CAB until Senator Cannon's bill was nearing completion. When the opposition of the airlines collapsed, and even the CAB voted to eliminate itself, the sense of the developing legislation was changed from "regulatory reform" to complete deregulation and "sunset" for a major, well-entrenched government agency, the CAB.

To gain support for deregulation, its advocates promised lower fares and better service for the travelling public, with no loss of air service to the cities and towns; and greater profits for the airline companies. After 10 years, the jury is still out on whether these expectations can be met.

Over-scheduling of the big travel centers, which quickly became airline hubs, should have been foreseen, for it was obvious that the airlines would move to concentrate their flights in the cities where the most business could be found. Excessive congestion of the airways around the hub cities can only be attributed to a lack of adequate management of the air traffic control system, although there were billions in a special federal fund to overhaul and improve it.

As an indication of things to come, it is interesting to note that only seven large air carriers now carry 90% of the domestic passengers and their number may yet be reduced.

There have been some important gains from deregulation that will help achieve those adjustments. America's free enterprise system has produced the highest standard of living in the entire world, and it is worth keeping. There is great value in setting your own fares based on costs and marketing considerations. And the value of choosing your own routes cannot be overestimated, either. It permits airlines to balance their route systems to maximize the productivity of their airplanes. Freedom to acquire or merge with another carrier, with no restraints other than the stockholders and the Department of Justice, in the long run will produce better, financially stronger airlines. Now that the labor pains of a radically new industry are passing, there is much to look forward to.

Floyd Hall joined TWA in 1940 as a co-pilot and worked his way up the ranks. He was appointed Vice President and General Transportation Manager in 1959 and System General Manager in 1961. Hall left TWA to become President of Eastern Air Lines in January 1964.

Originally published in TARPA Topics, May 1988, and reproduced with permission.

The Father and Son Nason

By Merton D. Nason III

TWA Skyliner
Son and father on the ramp at JFK Airport.

My father, TWA executive Mert Nason, Jr., was born in Boston and grew up in Philadelphia, Pennsylvania. He attended Germantown High School, Staunton Military Academy and the University of Villanova. He married his high school classmate and sweetheart, Helen McCluskey in 1938.

Dad's career spanned the booming days of commercial aviation and the headier days of hotel expansion and was inspirational in my own personal professional development.

After a stint in sales with Paramount Pictures, he joined TWA in Philadelphia reservations in 1941. Two years later TWA placed him in charge of its Boston operations with responsibility for the airline's wartime military air transport activities as well as its domestic civilian service.

This was the period when the Douglas DC-3 was establishing itself as the first passenger plane to pay its own way in the air. At this time the much larger Lockheed Constellation, conceived and promoted by TWA's majority shareowner, Howard Hughes, was in initial production.

Author

Mert at his 605 Third Avenue office desk in New York City.

During his tenure in Boston, both the TWA DC-3s and Boeing 307 Stratoliners, along with fresh off-the-assembly-line Lockheed Constellations were enlisted in the war effort, carrying high priority military and civilian passengers to the European theater. His dedication to Country clearly influenced my decision to "Go Navy."

At the end of World War II, Dad was promoted to district traffic manager in Philadelphia, eventually to be developed into the position of district and regional general sales manager. In the decade that followed, he was a leader in commercial air transportation in the region.

In 1952 TWA and my father were significant contributors to the opening of one of the first modern air terminals in the United States along the Delaware in Philadelphia. He employed a Lockheed Constellation for the terminal's grand opening, conducting flying tours of the area for many citizens who had never flown in an airplane, much less the grand passenger aircraft of its day.

It was a spectacular aviation adventure at the time and, not surprisingly, TWA was fast becoming Philadelphia's number one air carrier; Dad was "Mr. TWA" in Philadelphia. He was a pioneer in the promotion of new nonstop coast-to-coast services aboard new Lockheed Super Constellations, offering, in this area, nonstop service from Philadelphia to Los Angeles and San Francisco.

Dad's success catapulted him to district sales manager for the massive New York district and, finally, senior director of sales at TWA headquarters, located then at 380 Madison Avenue, where he organized the airline's rapidly expanding international sales activities.

After 20 years with TWA, in 1962, he retired and moved to Hilton International Hotels, where, as corporate director of sales, he oversaw worldwide sales management as the company expanded from 23 to 50 hotels in foreign countries around the world, supporting Hilton International's growth and global expansion.

Like father, the apple didn't fall far from the tree. I was born and raised in the Philadelphia and Princeton, New Jersey area and attended Germantown Academy in Philadelphia, Colgate University and graduated from the University of Arizona.

I grew up under the wings of DC-3s, Boeing Stratoliners, Lockheed Constellations and Boeing 707s when my dad was integrally involved in the advancement of commercial aviation as a TWA sales pioneer and executive in Philadelphia and New York.

My first job with TWA came in 1961 as a fulltime seasonal employee where, for four years during summer college break, I served as a telephone representative in one of TWA's major reservations facilities. At the same time, during the school year, I worked as a ramp and customer service agent at Tucson Airport.

After active duty service with destroyers in the US Navy I returned to Arizona to pursue graduate studies at the Arizona State University's school of business in Tempe. While studying I rejoined TWA as a Passenger Service Agent at Phoenix Sky Harbor Airport.

In 1970, as TWA introduced the first giant jumbo jet, the Boeing 747, I was selected to join a newly created position in the air, designed to coordinate the challenges of a passenger plane nearly triple the capacity of the Boeing 707. The new management position was designed to function as flying facilities manager, public relations liaison to the large passenger load as well as crew supervisor of the 15 flight attendants now required to serve these passengers. Dubbed the Director of Customer Service (DCS), the roster expanded to cover the 747 and the equally remarkable jumbo, the Lockheed L-1011.

I joined this new management crew, assigned to TWA's JFK domicile, flying 747s, primarily across the Atlantic, five times per month for two years, supervising passenger service, public relations and cabin services related to the departure and arrival of each flight.

My next move was to join TWA's Eastern Region Quality Control department, based in Philadelphia and also covering Washington and

Baltimore. I then advanced to TWA headquarters at 605 Third Avenue, New York City, managing the worldwide service quality assessment program.

During my time at NYC headquarters I held the positions of Manager—Quality Assurance,

Manager—Passenger Service Automation, Director—Ground Service Programs, and Director—In-flight Service Planning. These positions were responsible for establishing corporate operations and service policies, advancing equipment, amenities and service improvements and providing day-to-day standards guidance for airport and in-flight service crews.

I was instrumental in the development, advancement and implementation of the airline's industry's first early boarding pass program, designated "Airport Express." This major computer expansion was developed to provide, for the first time, boarding passes to passengers at remote city and airport locations days before flight. For this unprecedented introduction, TWA, in 1978, won the coveted passenger service award from industry's major trade magazine, Air Transport World.

TWA was the only airline offering both early and round trip check-in for all domestic flights. Airport Express allowed passengers the opportunity to receive their out-and-back seat assignments and boarding passes with only a one-stop check-in. As an added incentive, passengers were also allowed to check in at a downtown City Ticket Office (CTO) or at the airport as early as 28 days before their departure.

The program allowed passengers to complete all ticketing and seat assignment formalities in only one step, eliminating bothersome lines. The seat selection was instantly available at any TWA airport or city ticket office for all flights regardless of the point of origin or destination.

In 1985 I was posted to the position of General Sales Manager for the Rocky Mountain Region and, subsequently, Southwest Area Director. I retired in 1998.

I also retired as a captain in the United States Navy after nearly 28 years in the active and reserve fleet, substantially aboard destroyers, ending my naval career as Commanding Officer, Naval Forces Command Korea, the reserve unit designated to provide the naval defenses in the event of an attack from North Korea.

I am married to Juanita Schiess of Cali, Colombia. We have two sons, Derek and Craig, and five grandchildren who reside in Littleton, Colorado where I try to instill on the family that special spirit of camaraderie that epitomized TWA.

Our neighborhood's high school in suburban Denver is Columbine. Our younger son, Craig, a junior, was trapped in the choir room of the school for nearly three hours in 1999. He escaped safely, but not without the loss of friends and grief and puzzlement that followed, much like the loss of colleagues and customers in an aviation mishap. Nonetheless, we fly on, with three generations of happy memories, spanning the nation and world on Trans World Airlines.

Merton D. Nason III

Traveling with the Pope

By Sally McElwreath

Harry Sievers

Shown at the Kansas City Overhaul Base in a fresh coat of paint,
Shepherd I *wears the Papal crest next to the forward door.*

I started my new job as director of marketing communications for TWA in September 1979. One month later, I was travelling with Pope John Paul II on his first visit to America.

Previously, I spent nine years with United Airlines. United was largely a domestic airline at that time, with a few international routes handled administratively through United's Eastern division, where I was assistant director of communications. In 1979, U.S Airline Deregulation was in its early days and competition in the airline business was a very different business.

Moving from a largely domestic carrier to an international airline was a little daunting. And at the airline's world headquarters! What did I know about all of the countries to which TWA flew, what were the airline codes for those cities? I had some learning to do.

No sooner did I report to my office, fresh from United, when I was called into my boss's office.

Pope John Paul II, the leader of the Roman Catholic Church, was going to be making his first trip to America, and much of it was going to be on TWA. There would be three aircraft travelling to six cities in the United States. The Pope's plane was dubbed Shepard I; he was to occupy the first-class cabin, with Italian press in the main cabin. Shepard II and Shepard III were to carry non-Italian press, mainly Americans. I was TWA's representative to rotate travelling with the press on the three aircraft. What an honor and a privilege, what a job.

Shepherd I is Christened

Charles Douglas, aircraft painter at MCI, affixes the papal emblem on the side of the TWA Boeing 727 which carried Pope John Paul II on his visit in the U.S.

TWA Skyliner

The Pope was to fly from Rome to Boston on Alitalia, then TWA on to New York, Philadelphia, Des Moines, Chicago and then Washington D.C. for a visit to The White House.

TWA had a very close relationship with the Vatican and its clergy, including Popes, had travelled on TWA when they weren't on Alitalia, Italy's national airline. The relationship was so close that many in the industry said that TWA stood for "Traveling With Angels."

At every city, the Pope was received like a rock star, as admirers lined the streets and highways as his motorcade proceeded from the airport into the city. In New York City, he filled Yankee Stadium, Shea Stadium and Madison Square Garden.

Some vignettes I remember:

• One of the natural concerns was the weather, be it at the airport on arrival where there were well-wishers congregated, or those lining the streets and roadways. At almost every stop, it rained, but when the Pope's plane arrived, and the aircraft door opened, the sun would break out. Some said it was a miracle. What wasn't a miracle was that in those cities where the Pope caught a few raindrops, his clothing had to dry overnight. Picture a TWA 727 at the airport looking majestic against the sky. What the public didn't see was a clothesline on the other side, with the Pope's damp clothing hanging out to dry. Once he returned from the visit to the city, laundry was collected through the cockpit window.

• As a public relations professional, one of the things one wants to do is to make sure that TWA gets full exposure in the media showing the world that TWA is the Pope's transport on this historic tour. A typical photo would show the Pope at the

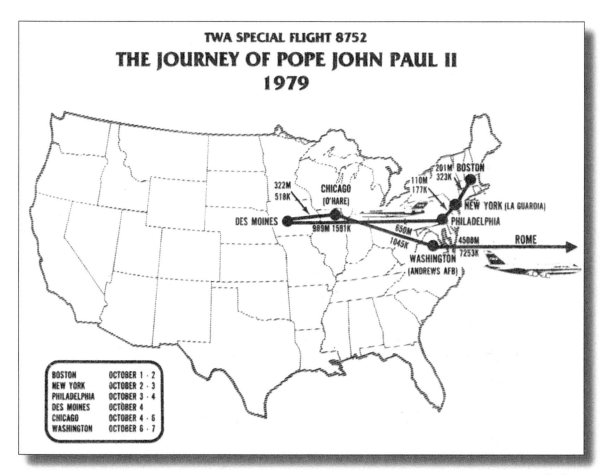

TWA SPECIAL FLIGHT 8752
THE JOURNEY OF POPE JOHN PAUL II
1979

BOSTON	OCTOBER 1 - 2
NEW YORK	OCTOBER 2 - 3
PHILADELPHIA	OCTOBER 3 - 4
DES MOINES	OCTOBER 4
CHICAGO	OCTOBER 4 - 5
WASHINGTON	OCTOBER 6 - 7

TWA Skyliner

aircraft's open doorway bearing the Papal crest of the aircraft, deplaning via the stairs rolled up to the aircraft. Gone were the days when airlines used the stairs that were rolled up to airliners. For the most part, eople now deplaned via Jetways. We managed to find stairs at each city to roll up to the forward door. We affixed TWA logos on each step so that as the Pope descended, the cameras could see TWA with each step the Pope took. The photo was shown worldwide as he arrived at each city. But there was a problem: the media wasn't going to give us "free advertising" and airbrushed the TWA logo out of each step. As the Pope descended the aircraft, each step on the stairway was shiny white…and blank. Foiled again!

• Security was of course very tight during the Pope's six-city tour. Because he is considered a head of state through his leadership of Vatican City, the Holy Father is entitled to Secret Service protection. When I met the battery of agents attached to the tour, I took care to be very serious and official. What I found was a corps of men and women who were almost giddy at their assignment. "Wait until I tell my grandmother that I'm protecting the Pope" was overheard. It was a joyful assignment. Don't' get me wrong, they still maintained their professionalism.

• My great opportunity for personal contact with the Pontiff was when I finally rotated onto Shepard I to travel with the press in the main cabin. The first-class cabin in the Boeing 727 had been reconfigured as a comfortable parlor for the Pope. It was there that he met with his aides, kept up with briefings and had refreshments and lunch specially prepared by the TWA catering director. (Yes, the Pope had a food checker.) The media were boarded through the rear cabin doors so they wouldn't be passing through the Pope's quarters. I positioned myself just inside the first class cabin door. I had been taking random photos for our TWA's company newspaper and had my camera (single lens reflex Nikon with film) ready. As the Pope reached the entrance, and I was 3 feet from him, and asked, "Your Holiness, may I take your picture as you enter the aircraft?" He signaled

yes, and my big moment was at hand. I took aim, and heard the click. What I didn't hear was the film advancing. I was out of film! What to do? I couldn't say "Your Holiness, would you please stand there until I re-load my camera?" My big moment was gone. No close up of the Pope in my camera. I could only let him pass in front of me and sit down in his special compartment.

• Everyone involved with the Pope's TWA flight wanted to have some documentation or souvenir that they worked with or on the Pope's airplane. As the 727 stopped at each city, I'd briefly examine what was being done with the aircraft, particularly any mechanical work in progress, just to make sure there were no potential problems. When I examined the check lists, I was alarmed that there were many entries and so many checks, possibly reflecting that there was an inordinate amount of potential problems. I found that the mechanics, baggage handlers and fuelers all wanted to have in writing that they were part of the Pope's trip. They all wanted to find a reason to sign the check off list. There were no mechanical problems.

On the final 727 flight, those who had worked on the Pope's aircraft signed their names Shepard I's fuselage. And on one of the flights, Captain Salvatore Farrugio brought his bible on board and the Pontiff came forward into the cockpit and signed it.

When the 747 was being prepared for the Pope's return trip to Rome, the upper deck of the aircraft was configured like a bedroom suite. A bed was built atop a covered wood pedestal, with a bedspread bearing the Papal Seal. The bed itself was tested for stability but when the inspectors shook the bed, they could hear a strange rattling sound. Was the bed's underpinning loose? That would not do! When the mattress was lifted, underneath were many, many rosaries, holy cards, crucifixes, and other memorabilia, each with name tags. The idea was that these pieces would be blessed by the fact that the Pope slept over them, and that the items would be re-claimed or sent back on a return flight to the person whose tag was attached to the holy item. I cannot say whether the mission was accomplished or if the items were removed to stop the rattling.

There were many more stories. All bring back sometimes amusing, sometimes inspiring memories.

Pope John Paul II was recently declared a Saint by the Roman Catholic Church. I feel blessed at the privilege of having been in his presence.

Author

Sally Chin McElwreath, center, pictured at a Navy League dinner. To her right is Admiral William Gortney, U.S. Navy Commander – Fleet Forces Command. Sally was not in uniform but wearing her medals in miniature as is customary in civilian garb.

Make it a Triple

By Angus McClure

John Strege – *Golf Digest*

It was in Spain on October 14, 1977 when "the blue of the night met the gold of the day" and Bing Crosby, the famous crooner, sang his final song. "Der Bingle" had just finished playing in a golf tournament when he collapsed and died.

It was a couple of days later, and there I was on the ramp at the JFK International Arrivals Building, awaiting the TWA flight returning Mr. Crosby to the U.S. With me were his wife, Kathryn Crosby (a beauty-and-a-half as I recall), and son Harry, who

FINAL ★★★★

DAILY ⊚ NEWS

Partly sunny, 50s. A 20% chance of showers tomorrow. Details page 39.

Vol. 59. No. 96   New York, Saturday, October 15, 1977   Price: 20 cc

BING CROSBY DIES AT 73

Stricken After Golfing in Spain

New York Daily News

was about thirteen. Also on hand were about 25 members of the Fourth Estate including television and print media types. I had spent several moments expressing my condolences to the Crosbys, and as we chatted the aircraft appeared on the taxiway, loudly making its way towards us.

Moments before I had met with the ground crew foreman that would be off-loading Bing's casket via the nearby conveyor belt, standing at the ready. We had a considerable audience on hand and I hoped all would go smoothly.

As the engines of the 707 wound down, the ground crew sprang into action and swung open the cargo hold door. Nervous moments passed all too long, and I began to find small talk more and more difficult as the foreman rode the conveyor to the ground and strode towards me making little motions for me to join him half-way.

I excused myself to the Crosbys and anxiously made my way to his foreman's side, only to hear a whispered, "There's a bit of a problem. Mr. Crosby's casket must have broken loose during the flight and he wasn't in it when we opened the door!"

Without hesitation I replied, "No, it didn't .... it's not ... he's in it and he'd better be coming off

the aircraft in the next five minutes!" With that I spun on my heels, returned to the family, noted some concern on Mrs. Crosby's face, but assured her that all was well.

Thus commenced the longest five minutes in my 16-year career with TWA. I was babbling inanely, I'm sure, about the weather, etc., when suddenly the conveyor belt began to move and off came the casket looking (to me), surprisingly shipshape. It was placed on a cart, and the army of television and still cameras rolled and chattered, as Der Bingle continued the journey to his final resting place.

I wish I could remember the name of the foreman for I owe him, big time! As for me, I bid the Crosby family adieu and headed for the Ambassador Club where, if memory serves, my first words were, "Make it a triple!"

Angus McClure, who was with TWA from 1965 until 1986, served in Public Relations/Corporate Communications.

This story was originally published April 21, 2004, on the TWA Seniors website (www.twaseniors.org)

An Airline Career Fills a Travel Lust

By Michael Patrizio

Jon Proctor

A 747 touches down at JFK, the author's homeport.

I grew up in Brooklyn, New York, of Italian Immigrant parents and started travelling to Italy when I was three years old. And yes, my love of travel and flying started at such a young age. I was fascinated with airplanes and luckily we lived near the JFK flight path. I would spend hours staring into the sky above and watching all the wonderful airplanes flying off to far off destinations. In those days there was no Internet, so as a child, I would call each airline that served JFK and request a timetable. With all of them in hand, I would best guess where these big birds were going or coming from. The 747s always got my attention, especially Trans World Airlines and Pan American World Airways.

Once an adventurous traveller, I would often fly alone to just fully experience a new culture and force myself to meet new people. One memorable TWA trip occurred when I was 25 years old. I was working in finance at a pharmaceutical company and planning my annual two-week vacation, to Italy for sightseeing and then visiting with family; grandmother, aunts, uncles and cousins. But in planning the trip, I realized it was possible to fly first to Tel Aviv and then backtrack to Rome for the same fare. So why not visit a new destination? As fate would have it, the Italian ship, *Achille Lauro* hijacking occurred on the day I left New York, but even terrorism didn't stop me. The first leg of my journey took me from JFK to Paris. I was too tired to get off the plane in Paris and woke up after we took off for Tel Aviv. Unbeknownst to me, while I slept, a comfy TWA blanket was placed over me, along with a pillow at my headrest. I will never forget the kindness and superb TWA service on that flight. TWA flight attendants always had that Midwest warmth that made you feel at home, no matter where you were.

After finishing graduate school, I responded to an ad in the *New York Times* for the position of strategic planning analyst at TWA. A few weeks later, I was called in for a round of interviews and then offered the position. My excitement was beyond words. I was able to go to work for TWA, talk about flight schedules and airplanes all day and get paid for it. All this plus the ability to take off for Rome, Paris, London, Cairo and many more destinations, even on weekends. Although with TWA just three years, I consider those to have been some of the best of my life. What 27-year-old could say he going to Paris to buy shoes! I once went to Rome to pick up my parents on a Friday night and did a quick turn around and flew right back to JFK, all for free.

I loved working at TWA's corporate headquarters, 605 Third Avenue. It was centrally located in Midtown and close to airport transportation. The most interesting aspect of working there was the people. Everyone seemed to have a passion for airplanes and travel, coupled with the excitement of working in Manhattan. We all loved our airline and our jobs, along with the ability to travel the globe. During the summer months, I often ran in the corporate challenge in Central Park and proudly wore the TWA T-shirt during the race. I always felt special having people know that I worked for TWA because in and of itself showed that I didn't have an "ordinary life."

George W. Hamlin

Along with JFK, St. Louis became a TWA hub.

The strategic planning department evaluated the best possible routes for TWA. We analyzed internal data and came up with projections on passenger demand. For example JFK–Rome summer rotations were compared with competitive flight schedules, aircraft availability and pricing. Once analysis demonstrated the additional demand for during the summer months, we added a second daily 747 on the route. This type of analysis increased our revenue share on a market-per-market basis, creating greater passenger convenience and satisfaction.

The Airline Deregulation Act of 1978 removed government control over fares, routes and market entry. Given the new legislation and falling oil prices prices, we were able to do more with routes and pricing. Hub-and-spoke systems then became the norm for most major domestic airlines. JFK and St Louis became TWA's hubs. Until then, airlines were required to fly point to point and many flights were half-full. The European flights would also have traffic from hubs plus "feeder" revenue traffic originating in smaller U.S. cities, flying on to Europe and beyond. Deregulation became a double edged sword, positive in that it gave carte blanche to the airlines, but negative because it resulted in competition so fierce that it became unwieldy to manage competition and costs.

Unfortunately, Carl Icahn took the company private and saddled it with hundreds of millions of dollars in debt. This was the beginning of the end for TWA. After he moved to corporate office to Mt Kisco, New York, I was unable to do that commute on a daily basis and knew I would have to leave the company. My airline career didn't end with TWA. Luckily, I found another position with Pan Am in finance, and worked there until its demise in December 1991.

I am so grateful to have been able to work for these two iconic airlines and realize my childhood dreams of travel, beyond my wildest imagination. Sadly, I found myself at the foot of the North Tower on September 11, 2001. I voted in the New York City primaries that day and was running late for work and thankfully never made it up to my

office in the American Express Tower, directly adjacent to the Twin Towers. Witnessing the horror and devastation of that day somehow changed me to the core. I was so lucky to have been able to physically "run away" from that event but so many were not, and I will forever be praying for those souls and their loved ones. Looking back on that TWA trip to Israel on the day the *Achille Lauro* was hijacked seems a distant memory, yet terrorism has increasingly become a critical fear of air travellers. These days travel much less but feel fortunate to have so many memories of my worldwide travels; for now, they are enough to fill my travel lust.

Michael Patrizio

TWA and Me

By Jonathan Kriebel

TWA flew me from Denver into Kansas City for a two-day interview at Breech Training Academy in Overland Park, Kansas. A year later in February 1979 I was in training there with 19 other selectees where we went through several weeks of intense Safety and Service training. I always said if I had studied that hard in college I would be a doctor now. Several of my classmates are still close friends. We studied, learned and lived in Beach Training Academy's "L & Ls"—Living and Learning centers. We learned how to carve chateaubriand in first class, jump out of a 747 and down a slide, how to serve passenger their dinner "wet" (with a drink), and the list goes on.

After graduation, we flew from Kansas City to St Louis in a McDonald Douglas DC-9. Fire trucks and emergency vehicles met

Breech Training Academy in Overland Park, Kansas.

our arrival and beginning of our Flight Attendant Career, after the No. 1 engine failed en route. Quite an exciting beginning to a wonderful career with a wonderful airline!

During my 20-year career I was based and flew out of St. Louis, Boston and New York. I was on reserve for most of my

Jon Proctor

Reporting to domicile was a memorable DC-9 experience.

20 years as those hired in the '60s and '70s never wanted to leave this awesome career. My very first trip was to San Francisco where I spent my layover in the Mark Hopkins Hotel. I had never stayed in such beautiful hotel. That evening when I returned to my room, I found my light on and bed turned down. I called the front desk to say that someone had been in my room. They asked me if there was a chocolate on the pillow, which there was. "That's what we do here at the Mark" was the answer.

My career took me to city cities such as Athens, Paris, London, Brussels, Rome, Milan, Venice, Florence, Cairo, Tel Aviv, Frankfurt, Vienna, Berlin, Stockholm, Amsterdam, Istanbul, Lisbon, Madrid, Barcelona, Nice, Zurich and Geneva. I am sure there were others—but I get jet lag thinking about it. Most of the time we would arrive in a city in the morning, sleep for a couple hours, have some Espresso and hit the streets running to see the sights, eat the food and drink the spirits (not necessarily in that order). In London at the Kensington Hilton, we would arrive just as the outbound crew was having breakfast. We would join them, waiting for

Intercontinental Hotels of San Francisco
The Magnificent Mark Hopkins Hotel.

our rooms to be ready and drink "crew tea" … beer or wine in teapots. The hotels we stayed in were almost always 5-star.

I remember having celebrities on board such as Mohamed Ali, whose bodyguard was bigger yet, and didn't listen to me until Mohamed told him to. Barry Manilow, Julia Child (I still have a signed Ambassador Class Menu signed by her with "Bon Appetite"), Bob Newhart (Scotch at 10 a.m.), Connie Francis, Grace Slick and Jefferson Starship, Connie Stevens, Tommy Smothers, Truman Capote, Pelé and Farrah Fawcett, who was eating nuts and reading Gorky Park in first class. I told her that if I hadn't been involved with another woman I would chase her to Hollywood! She smiled, wrote on a menu –"I would love for you to follow me to Hollywood. Love, Farrah."

The Bee Gees, during a New York to Miami flight, invited the crew to their home in Miami Beach. It was a sight to see and tough getting up the next morning. Flying from St Louis to JFK the Dalai Lama was on board with 20 monks and his personal assistant. I was instructed not to speak directly to him; his assistant would handle all such communication. At the end of the fight I thanked the Dali Lama for flying on TWA—he had not acknowledged me the entire flight—he turned his head and winked at me.

We would always eat at "Kelly Badger's sister's restaurant" in Rome… Kelly was a Boston Flight Attendant whose sister travelled aboard and never came home after she fell in love with an Italian chef.

The downing of Flight 800 to Paris did us all in. Fifty-four crewmembers died, including a deadheading and working 747 Crew. We lost part of our family that evening.

Waylon Jennings was flying from Omaha to St Louis with us one time. Merv Conover and I were working the flight. We had blocked out when the Captain called for us to lower the 727 aft ventral staircase. Up came Waylon. He had been in Omaha for a concert and was heading back to Nashville. He asked us if we would join him for a drink at the St Louis Airport before his flight to Nashville. We were done upon arrival in STL, and did so.

TWA employees played hard, worked hard, worked as a team and took care of each other. Safety was ingrained in all of us. It was fun being a part of such a wonderful airline. What was most enjoyable were all those friendships that still exist.

Tenzin Choejor
The Dalai Lama.

Around The World Luxury Charter

By Jon Proctor

At Mahé, Seychelles, our 707 rests against a dramatic background.

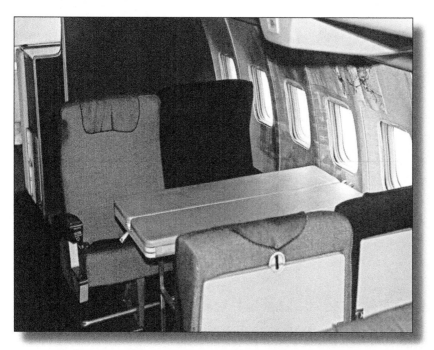

A four-seat lounge was installed aft, complete with he same table used on an earlier Papal flight.

For 20 years TWA operated 707 globe-circling charters for various tour companies, over various routings. Some were completed with all-coach charter layouts and a few in 92-seat, all first-class configurations; the same arrangement used on White House press flights and special charters flown on behalf of ARAMCO, the Arabia-American Oil Company. I was fortunate to be on what wound up to be the last of these adventures.

I was flying a regular line of time as a flight attendant in early 1980, based at New York, when JFK In-Flight Service domicile manager Bill Borden asked if I would be interested in a temporary assignment, as charter coordinator on a trip the following month. Always an adventurer, I replied yes without hesitation, and was assigned a 35-day, around-the-world charter flight, scheduled to depart from New York on February 20.

I was formally placed on temporary assignment February 14 and spent long days completing paperwork and outlining needed supplies. On the trip I'd be reprovisioning liquor, wine, champagne, soda, juices, glass and chinaware, bar supplies, plus cleaning items. This load of 3,500 pounds, my private pantry, was to be transported in the forward cargo hold. With so few passengers and no freight to carry, there was plenty of room in the belly and it was much cheaper and more efficient than trying to buy everything en route.

Described as a "The Great World Air Cruise," our tour was organized and managed by Travel Corporation of America, a.k.a. Travcoa, a

Changing a turbocompressor in the heat and humidity at Lomé, Togo.

California-based company specializing in luxury travel. It is still in business.

The per-person cost was $16,000 ($49,000 today). In addition, surcharges were levied up until departure date, based on rapidly increasing fuel costs. Except for gratuities, everything was included: airfare, meals, hotels and transfers. Each couple was allowed 300 pounds of luggage, with suitcases designated for warm or cold weather visits.

Once through customs, luggage was transferred to the hotels and delivered to the guest's room. Likewise, on departure from a hotel, they had only to leave their suitcases in the room for retrieval and transfer to the airplane cargo compartment.

The manifest listed 81 guests, four tour guides and the Travcoa president, plus a crew of 11. Passengers were divided into four groups, each assigned to a tour director. This and the tour owner brought the revenue payload to 86. Maintenance Supervisor Gino Galli and I were assigned the final two regular seats on the airplane, in the last row and across from the lounge.

I joined most of the crew for a pre-departure briefing Tuesday, February 19, at the International Hotel on the airport. It included Captain Norman Schaefer, First officer Claude Rothe, Flight Engineer Chuck Frederick, Purser Joe Bouadana

Gino Galli and I got most of our rest and relaxation in flight.

and Flight Attendants Gerry Victor, Bonnie Brooks, Tommie Hurston, Ann Gerardo and Beverly Jorda. Earlier in the day Captain Norm and I signed for $25,000 at the airport bank, for expenditures at locations where the only accepted form of payment was cold hard cash. All of our stopovers were to be at non-TWA locations.

Our flight originated at Kansas City on February 20, where about 40 passengers boarded. A domestic crew operated the segment to JFK. It was there that I met and developed a bond with Rome-based Maintenance Supervisor Gino Galli, who became responsible for the airplane's upkeep.

The first TWA jet to call on Shanghai since the Nixon charter, N18712 sits at the lone terminal building on a cold, overcast day.

Our crew on the Great Wall, clad in TWA parkas. Top: Joe Bouadana, Ann Gerardo, Tommie Hurston, Captain Norm Schaeffer, First Officer Claude Rothe and the author. Bottom: Flight Engineer Chuck Frederick, Maintenance Foreman Gino Galli, Bonnie Brooks, Beverly Jorda and Gerry Victor.

With everything in a high state of readiness, Flight 8510 lifted off from JFK for an overnight, 8-hour, 10-minute journey to our first stop. T-minus 35 days and counting. After a sumptuous rack of lamb dinner and inflight movie, a light breakfast snack was served as our 707 passed high over Gibraltar, followed by a gradual descent for landing at Marrakesh, Morocco.

Following a (very) good night's sleep we departed at mid-morning for Lomé, Togo, in West Africa, among the smallest countries on the continent. Numerous overfly restrictions resulted in a nearly 5-hour flight. An extra day there allowed time to change out the No. 2 engine turbocompressor, an especially tedious job in sweltering heat.

From the hot and humid weather in Togo, we headed across the African continent February 24,

on a 4-hour, 2,300-mile flight to Kigali for three-day stay. Located in the center of Rwanda, this capital city sits at an elevation of 5,100 feet.

Servicing the lavatories there presented a challenge. With none of the appropriate equipment available, ground handlers simply opened the dump chutes, letting the contents fall to the ground. Men from the airport fire department provided two 50-gallon drums of water and we formed a bucket brigade to refill the tanks.

I set up the menu that afternoon. The only beef entrée available was Zebra steak, tasty but tough. As I recall we didn't tell the passengers what they were eating until later.

From the moderate temperatures in Rwanda, Flight 8510 headed to more tropical weather February 28. Our 1,700-mile, 4-hour flight plan took us over Tanzania with a view of 19,341-foot

Mount Kilimanjaro, and then the Indian Ocean to Mahé, largest island of the Seychelles.

We arrived in mid-afternoon with another technical problem: the HF (high-frequency) radio was intermittently malfunctioning. Gino began a six-step part-replacement process to locate the source of this malfunction. Meanwhile I tidied the cabin, restocked items and met with the airport caterer.

On March 1, Flight 8510 departed in mid-afternoon for a 4-hour trip to the next destination, Sri Lanka, about 1,800 miles distant. Upon landing at Colombo, the 707's No. 1 engine reverser refused to reset, necessitating its replacement. Air Lanka loaned us the part. It involved removal and reinstallation of 200 support bolts.

Meanwhile, the HF radio replacement part did not solve the problem. Gino had to go back up to pull a different component from the tail compartment, requiring use of a cherry picker crane that didn't quite reach, so an 8-foot ladder was pressed into service.

The next segment, on March 4, was 2,278 miles, nearly a transcon flight, to begin a 6-day

stay in the People's Republic of China. We proceeded to Shanghai, arriving after sunset. Ours was the first US airliner allowed to land in China since 1972, when Pan Am and TWA 707s brought the press during President Nixon's historic visit.

Desmond Yee, TWA's district sales manager for the Central Pacific, was on hand to break down language barriers for us. As I recall, his fluency in Mandarin did not completely meet the challenge of local dialects but it certainly helped. Desmond also replenished our cash supply. Passengers and crew were accommodated at the Ching Chiang Hotel, where President Nixon had stayed during his visit.

While passengers and the rest of the crew toured Shanghai on Wednesday, Gino and I were back with the airplane, cleaning, reprovisioning and completing a 50-hour maintenance inspection.

That afternoon Desmond Yee and I arranged for onward catering with a local restaurant, thanks to a lack of catering companies on the airport.

Owing to flight restrictions for non-Chinese airlines, passengers and crew flew on CAAC to Peking (now Beijing) for two days of sightseeing

This Lockheed C-130 Hercules transported our passengers
and a few lucky crewmembers to Antarctica.

The mighty Moreno Glacier.

on March 6. We enjoyed a traditional, multi-course Peking duck dinner, visited typical Chinese residences, a school and farm, the 2,500-year-old Great Wall, the Palace Museum, Tiananmen Square and The Forbidden City, returning to Shanghai March 8.

The next morning we looked forward to the warm weather at Bali, Indonesia, our next stop, 2,777 miles to the south, for a three-night stay. The 6-hour flight reached Denpasar International Airport at Bali, Indonesia, soon after sunset. During taxi to the terminal came an announcement: "Gino to the cockpit!" The No. 3 engine oil pressure had dropped to near zero as we rolled out on the runway.

After extensive trouble shooting, it was decided to change the engine. A plan was developed to ship a spare powerplant on Thai Airways, from Paris via Jakarta, for arrival the following day. A replacement JT3-D finally arrived on Tuesday, March 11, but everything ground to a halt when Indonesian officers refused access to the powerplant until Customs clearance "formalities" were completed. Customs formalities lasted

another day. The flight was scheduled to leave Wednesday night; it wasn't going to.

Our people in New York were able to charter an Air Niugini 707 for the leg to, Port Moresby, Papua New Guinea. Our airplane ferried a day later to catch up with the group.

I flew ahead on the charter trip to get a head start on catering. The Air Niugini ground people were friendly and efficient. However, there were some tense moments at the hotel. The coalition government had been overthrown a day earlier and some frightened party members took refuge in the hotel; rooms were in short supply. I spent time in the lobby awaiting my accommodations.

Flight 8510 departed the morning of March 14, on its longest segment, 3,724 miles, en route to Rarotonga in the Cook Islands, during which time we passed the International Date Line. Suddenly, it was March 14 again, even though we departed on the 15th.

The Rarotongan Hotel was not large enough to house both passengers and crew so we were billeted in what amounted to dormitory living at a nearby hostel. The next morning we checked out and were driven to the Rarotongan for the balance of the day, enjoying the adjacent beach and catnapping for the overnight flight ahead.

Owing to Rarotonga's relatively short runway, a fuel stop was required at Pape'ete, Tahiti, 670 miles to the east-northeast, en route *Isla de Pascua* (Easter Island in Spanish). Known as *Rapa Nui* in the Polynesian tongue, this Chilean territory located in the southeastern Pacific Ocean, nearly mid-way between Tahiti and Chile. Described as one of the most isolated populated islands in the world, famous for its mysterious statues, called *moai*.

A major portion of the island's 3,000 population turned out to meet our flight, the first non-Chilean airliner to ever land there. Gino and I took care of the airplane, cleaning and inspecting, then buttoning it up. On St Patrick's Day we had time to tour this fascinating island. That evening, our passengers treated the crew to an outdoor cocktail party, a reflection of their character and generosity.

On March 19, Flight 8410 departed on another transcon equivalent, 2,692 miles to Rio Gallegos, Argentina, nearly all of it over water. Only as small amount of additional fuel was added, thanks to the quantity tankered in. It was going for more than $3 per gallon, an outrageous amount back then but necessary based on the cost of transporting it from Chile by ship.

During the three-night stay in southern Argentina, passengers were taken on a day-trip excursion to Tierra del Fuego, the world's southernmost city. Then came a visit to Antarctica, reached by an Argentine Air Force C-130 from Rio Gallegos, landing at the Marambio scientific research base.

There were a few extra seats on the two flights and the crew drew numbers. Naturally Captain Norm was exempt and got to go. But others, including me, did not win the lottery. Instead, we visited the majestic Moreno Glacier, 200 miles north.

The March 22, 3-hour flight was entirely over land, a 1,294-mile segment north to Buenos Aires. It afforded a late-morning departure with lunch served en route. All was well until we approached the Argentine capital just as a cold front came roaring through after five days of record heat. The turbulence exceeded anything I had ever experienced, and it continued a missed approach required another 10 minutes in the air. Some china and glassware was dislodged from the galleys and came crashing to the floor.

A city bus tour for the crew was arranged, to see this beautiful city and enjoy lunch at a local eatery. Travcoa hosted a farewell banquet party for passengers and crew.

Most of us rested up on the last day, for our overnight flight to Miami. Owing to closure of the longest runway at Buenos Aires Airport a "pit stop" was required, at Curacao, and the departure time was moved up an hour so as to arrive at Miami in time for connecting flights.

The sight of TWA ground equipment and personnel on the morning of March 25 were most welcomed as we pulled into the gate at Miami International Airport, our U.S. re-entry port. A domestic crew was waiting to take over for the final leg back to Kansas City.

Ninety-seven travel-weary souls filed off N18712, and into Customs to declare their many acquisitions from more than 40,000 miles of travel. I closed up my bags and packed away my passport, contemplating the expression, "It's a small world."

There were a lot of good-byes, hugs and exchanges of addresses between passengers and crew. By then we knew them all by first name and it seemed as though a family were breaking up after a month-long reunion. But the memories would be kept for a lifetime by those of us who were lucky enough to cross the equator four times, span three oceans, and circle the globe on The Great World Air Cruise of 1980.

Our beloved Gino Galli passed away suddenly in 1988. His son sent me this picture of him at Rome (on the left) a year earlier, with fellow workers who took care of the 747 that brought John Paul II home from a United States visit. By then, Gino was head of maintenance for Italy.

Epilogue

Sadly, three of our crew are gone.

Captain Norman Schaeffer, with his 1944 seniority date, could have been flying the 747 in 1980 but chose to remain with his favorite airplane, the 707. He retired shortly after our charter flight and passed away in 1989

Joe Bouadana left us on January 23, 2010, at age 70. The attached eulogy says it all about this true TWA legend.

Gino Galli was taken far too early in his life, suffering a fatal heart attack in 1988; he was not yet 50.

On a positive note, I still keep in touch with Gerry, Bonnie, Ann, Tommie, Chuck and Claude. All are, of course, retired but in good spirits. Hopefully we can all get together once more to celebrate our adventure that took place more than 35 years ago.

An expanded version of this story, with additional images, appears on my website, at: http://jonproctor.net/around-the-world-i/

Flight 847

By Peter T. McHugh

Jon Proctor

N64339, the hijacked 727, is seen at St Louis two years later.

Captain John Testrake, answering questions of journalists at Beirut. Next to him in the cockpit is one of the terrorists.

TWA Skyliner

Memory is a funny thing. There are experiences in your life so searing, so intense that you think you could never forget them. But, you are wrong if you believe that. Memory is selective—you remember specific moments vividly, but not the entire chronology of the experience. For me, that is the case with the hijacking of flight 847— moments that are still so present and alive it's as though they happened yesterday, and blanks where I don't remember certain specific actions at all.

This is what I remember: On June 14, 1985, I had gone to my office in London where I was vice-president of TWA's international division, responsible for operations outside the United States. As soon as I arrived, I got a call telling me that flight 847, which originated in Cairo and had just departed Athens for Rome, had been hijacked and was now en route to Beirut. Immediately, senior executives in New York, including Dick Pearson, President of TWA, were on what we called an "open" line with us in London. We were told that the plane had landed in Beirut and 19 passengers, all women and children, had been allowed to leave in exchange for fuel. There was also a list of demands, including the release of about 700 prisoners held by Israel, as well as the threat of executing hostages. When we learned that the plane was headed to Algiers next, arrangements were quickly made for me to fly to Algiers with a couple of colleagues.

As our chartered plane neared Algiers we were denied permission to land, so we detoured to

Mallorca. But once on the ground, it was quickly decided that we had to land in Algiers, permission or not. So, we headed there and arrived in the early evening. We could see the terminal and were walking toward it when soldiers, fortunately not hostile, intercepted us and escorted us to the customs area. While the officials were surprised, they processed our passports quickly—and we were in. Flight 847 had already left for Beirut again but 21 more passengers, mostly American women and children, had been released and taken to the American ambassador's residence. I went there immediately and, as this was in the days before cell phones, what the passengers wanted most was access to a phone to call home and report that they were safe. I quickly arranged that and then we took the passengers to a hotel for the night. First on our way to the ambassador's house, and then again as we drove towards the hotel, I realized that

we were being followed by Algerian security— silent, and, at the time, slightly menacing.

June 15, 1985. Early that morning—I know it was early as I was sound asleep—the phone rang and I was told to get to the airport immediately as the plane was returning to Algiers. We learned that one hostage had been shot in the head in Beirut and thrown on the tarmac and a dozen or so heavily armed hijackers had boarded the plane. With the loss of life, a tense situation was now considerably more so. Colleague Dave Wookey, and I got to the airport, followed again by security forces. When we were denied entrance to the tower and the roof, they intervened and got us where we needed to be. We had been told to look at the plane as it landed to see if the pilot was signaling with his lights. While we didn't know what the signaling code was, there was hope that there would be patterned flashing which we could

At Rome, Captain Dick Vaux and crew descend from the 727 upon return from Beirut, via Cyprus.

have reported, had decoded, and that would have given us a view of what was happening on board. Unfortunately, no such luck. But, from this point on, I realized that the silent security guys were there to help and they continued to make access easier the whole time we were in Algiers. There was more good news: the release of 65 more passengers, including all the flight attendants.

We had vans, we had wonderful help from the people at Air France, and we managed to get all the passengers and the five female crewmembers to the hotel. All the women were now off the plane. Two of the young women passengers shared the disturbing news people had been taken off the plane in Beirut. They were desperately worried.

The flight attendants wanted to return to London immediately. While CIA people wanted to interview them in Algiers, I said they could do that in London and had our chartered plane take them to England that same night.

June 16: The hijackers released three more hostages and then flew to Beirut once again, for the third and final time. All the passengers released thus far were flown on a chartered Air France flight to Paris. We stayed in Algiers, waiting for our next instructions.

June 17: Most of the hostages were taken off the plane and held in various locations in Beirut to discourage a U.S. rescue attempt. I decided to go to Athens to begin the investigation of the security lapse that allowed the hijacking to occur in the first place. There was redundant security at Athens; one level run by the Greek government officials, and another level of screening at the TWA gate, mandated by the FAA. On June 14, as it turned out, the FAA was auditing the security at Athens airport and observed the boarding of flight 847. The normal process would have been for approximately 25 to 50 bags to be searched, after screening, but because the FAA was there, 100 plus bags were searched. There are a lot of theories about how the hand grenades and the gun got on board, but nothing definitive was ever discovered.

For the peak summer months, a number of family members (largely wives and children) of 727 flight crews stayed just outside Athens while their spouses flew in and out of Athens. Dale Landers, TWA's general manager in Greece, and I updated these very distressed family members. It was a difficult and sad day as the situation was still quite dangerous.

June 18—June 29: Negotiations for the hostage release went forward. There are many accounts of this, documenting the bravery and endurance of the flight crew, the work of U.S. diplomats, and the cooperation of the international community.

June 30—July 1: All the ex-hostages were flown to Frankfurt, Germany and then taken by bus to Wiesbaden, Germany where the U.S. Air Force has a large base and hospital. I arrived there the day before the hostages and went directly to the base where I met with a couple of colonels and Robert Oakley, then the director of the State Department office of combating terrorism. I was "told" that when the ex-passengers arrived they would be put in the hospital, kept away from their families and debriefed. The families would be housed in the barracks. Having spent the previous night in those same barracks, I immediately objected, knowing that we would have a near riot! So, negotiations began. We (TWA) had reserved a wing of a luxury hotel for the families who were beginning to arrive and we wanted the ex-hostages reunited with them as soon as possible. We thought that it was reasonable to have the passengers at the hospital for a couple of hours, but then we insisted that they must be allowed to see their relatives and leave. They were, after all, citizens, not military or government personnel. We won this one, and after a few hours at the hospital, all the hostages were taken to the elegant Nassauer Hof, a hotel next to Wiesbaden's casino and thermal baths.

July 2: The next morning the ex-hostages and their families were flown to Andrews Air Force base. I flew with them. About an hour out, the pilot told me that they had already been cleared to Andrews Air Force base—the earliest he'd ever been given clearance. I remember the mood as upbeat, but frankly, I was exhausted and fell asleep for much of the flight. As we landed, you could see the helicopter taking off from the White House with President and Mrs. Reagan. Shortly after landing, the President and Mrs. Reagan came on board and met everyone. There was a brief ceremony at Andrews Air Force Base and then all of us gratefully headed home.

Peter McHugh began his TWA career in 1965 as a part-time reservationist, continued working through college and, over the next twenty years, served in various sales and marketing positions. He was Vice-President of the International Division from 1984 to 1986, later rising to Senior Vice-President of Marketing and Sales. Peter joined Pan Am in 1988 where he served as Chief Operating Officer. Peter is married and lives in Charlottesville, VA and New York, New York.

President Reagan's Welcome Home

By Sally McElwreath

Bill Fitz-Patrick – White House via CNP

The hijacking of TWA Flight 847 in 1985, sometimes referred to as the Beirut hijacking has many, many sidebar stories, some of which cannot be told. My story has to do with President Ronald Reagan and his extraordinary sensitivity in how he handled the homecoming of the American hostages. Here's what I mean:

It was July 2, 1985 at Andrews Air Force Base in Maryland, near Washington, DC. The L-1011 was bringing the final American hostages home.

The ordeal that had begun 18 days earlier when TWA Flight 847 was hijacked on a Rome bound Boeing 727 aircraft with 139 mostly American passengers and eight crew members on board was over and 30 of those that had been held and who had endured three days of captivity in the aircraft and 17 days in Beirut were coming home.

During the long ordeal while the hijacked aircraft flew back and forth between Algiers and Beirut for three days while the hijackers made their demands, passengers were tortured, and one man, U.S. Navy Seabee SW2 Robert Stethem,* was murdered. After the third day of captivity, all but forty of the male passengers and crew were released. The forty remaining hostages were flown to Beirut to remain in captivity in various parts of Beirut for 17 days.

After successful negotiations in which the President of the United States exhibited steadfast resolve, 30 of the released American hostages were to be welcomed home by President Ronald Reagan. (The other ten chose to fly directly home from Germany rather than on the charter to Andrews.)

Behind the scenes at TWA headquarters in New York City there was the great relief, coupled with sorrow at the death of one brave sailor. The next important task was how to get the remaining hostages back home. All of those previously released had been flown from their release point to an Air Force base in Germany for medical check up, The bulk of the earlier released passengers had flown home on commercial aircraft. Now the remaining 40 that had been held captive in Beirut were being transported to Germany for medical aid, examination and de-briefing.

In the meantime, while certainly not to be compared to the ordeal of the hijacked, my colleagues and I in the corporate communications department thought: no more tense moments, no more killing, while at the same time marveling at the brave actions of crew and passengers alike. For me, no more sleeping on two office chairs put together in my office so I could be there 24/7 to follow the event, verify details and answer calls from media in different time zones all over the

world. (And this was before texting and common use of emails.) My colleague Dave Venz and our boss Jerry Cosley, took turns taking (maximum) four hours of sleep on office couches or on the floor.

Arrangements for returning the 40 remaining hostages were being made. The plan was to put them on one flight to perhaps Kennedy International Airport in New York, then connect them to their desired destinations. The main consensus among the hostages was get home as soon as possible.

Then I received a phone call from the White House. "How are you getting these people back home?" my inquisitor asked.

"Will TWA bring them all back into Andrews Air Force Base so that the President (Reagan) can welcome them home?" He asked. I answered that I would look into it, as we would have to get an aircraft to Germany from the U.S. as all trans-Atlantic capable aircraft were in scheduled service.

But the next question surprised me. My caller said the President was concerned that the returning hostages would perhaps not feel up to the worldwide attention of being welcomed home by the President for whatever reason, be it survivor's remorse, or just wanting to get home or not wanting to be perceived as being used for positive publicity. The president did not want to this so publicly if the returning hostages didn't want it to happen.

We decided to take the direct route and ask each of the hostages if it was all right with them if we flew them into Andrews Air Force base where their families would also be flown, and the President would welcome them back to American soil. They would then be bussed to a commercial airport in Washington and flown home. I told my White House contact that I would get back after we had asked the released hostages. That was accomplished through the medical officers that were in direct contact, and 30 of the 40 chose to return as group. By then, 17 days of captivity had served to form a bond among them.

I was very impressed by the fact that the President was so concerned about the preferences of the returning hostages. He was fully prepared not to do a public greeting if it was something they did not want. A question came up as to whose aircraft would fly the hostages back to America. Was it their desire to provide military transport? No, the expectation was for TWA to fly them back on a dedicated aircraft.

Obtaining the plane that would fly them back into Washington wasn't an easy task. And I already had a mark against me regarding access to an aircraft. Previously, the Delta Force had asked for access for the same type of aircraft as the hijacked plane so they could prepare for possible rescue operation. I found an aircraft that had a five-hour layover. The Delta Force did their "walk through" and managed to damage the aircraft so badly that it had to be taken out of service and I believe the flight cancelled or at least delayed so another aircraft could be flown in.

We finally managed to obtain a widebody aircraft, but not until my boss went to the president of TWA, Ed Meyer, and asked that he make it happen, since it meant adjusting schedules significantly. It got done.

And when the plane arrived at Andrews, I continued to be impressed by President Reagan's great consideration when, according to a *New York Times* account that day:

The plane landed, relatives boarded first, then the President. "This isn't time for speeches. This is a time for reunions and families coming together. There's only one thing to say and I say I from the bottom of my heart in the name of all the people of our country, WELCOME HOME."

*It was the President's desire not to intrude on their personal lives any more than he had to and it was his sole intention is to make absolutely certain that they know that the nation welcomes them home and rejoice in their being there according to his spokesman.***

This attitude and concern was unexpected, and a poignant memory to a tragic and violent situation.

* I had an added connection with Navy Seabee SW2 Robert Stethem. I was in the Navy Reserve. Just prior to the hijacking, I had done a tour of duty at the Pentagon on the Navy Desk at the Office of the Secretary of Defense and as a Navy Public Affairs Officer, so I knew who to connect to at the Pentagon, knew not identify Navy personnel on board the flight or even acknowledge that they were there until cleared by the Pentagon.

** New York Times, July 2, 1985

LTJG Kyle Wagner, U.S. Navy, Public Affairs Officer, USS Stethem
Named after the murdered sailor, the USS Stethem (DDG 63), an Arleigh-Burke class guided missile destroyer is seen during a port visit.

OPINION: Lessons from the Hijacking of Flight 847

By David C. Venz

When my telephone rang at 2:30 on the morning of June 14 this year, I just had a feeling that it was not going to be a good day. That call signaled the beginning of a very close and constant relationship between TWA and the worldwide news media, one that would continue for every moment of a succession of seventeen 24-hour days. The news that call brought me was this: TWA flight 847, a Boeing 727 carrying 145 passengers, four flight attendants and three cockpit crew members, had departed Athens, Greece, for Rome and had been hijacked by two armed fanatics brandishing hand grenades, whose pulled pins they were holding clenched in their teeth. The hijackers said they wanted to go to Algiers. When the captain told them that there was not enough fuel on board for such a long flight, they opted for Beirut instead.

In addition to generally terrorizing the passengers and crew while they awaited fuel at Beirut, they trussed up a young Navy man -- Robert Dean Stethem --- beat him with the arm of a chair, kicked him and jumped on him with the full weight of their bodies. I have been asked not to be overly sensational in these remarks, but those are the regrettably violent facts of what took place aboard the plane. As the result of a lot of sensitive, courageous persuasion on the part of Captain John Testrake and Purser Uli Derickson, 17 women and two children were released before the plane took off again for Algiers. In Algiers, another U.S. serviceman was bound, beaten and left unconscious on the floor of the airplane. Once again, the crew persuaded the hijackers to release more passengers. This time 20 women were allowed to go. Four hours after landing, its fuel tanks full again, the plane returned to the air. Three and a half hours later, once more approaching Beirut, the crew had to threaten to make a crash landing if obstacles were not removed from the runway. When the plane landed, the terrorists stood Mr. Stethem in the open doorway of the 727, shot him in the head and let his body drop to the tarmac.

At sun-up, its tanks filled again, flight 847 once again headed for Algiers. On arrival there, the hijackers released the remaining women and all male passengers except the Americans and one Greek citizen. The next morning, the hijackers told Captain Testrake that they wanted to go to Aden. When the Captain convinced them that that would be hopelessly beyond the plane's range, they demanded to return to Beirut. As it developed, this was to be the last flight in this strange odyssey of terror.

During the time the plane was shuttling back and forth across the Mediterranean, we slowly put together a mass of confusing bits and pieces of the story. For example, it appeared the hijackers were Shi'ite Moslems, but at this point not one of us yet knew exactly what they wanted. We learned that a group of men with "Jewish-sounding" names had been taken from the plane during its second visit to Beirut and separated from the rest of the hostages -- but for what reason was not clear. We were told also that the original hijackers had been replaced by a substantial group of terrorists. Along with the rest of the world, we tried to puzzle out the meaning of these disjointed facts.

About 1:30 in the morning local time, the remaining passengers were removed from the plane, but the cockpit crew remained aboard. They would be the focus of world attention for long days to come, and we at TWA would play a difficult dual role. On one hand, we were looked to be the media as a source of news about ongoing events. At the same time, we often found ourselves dependent on the media for information about our own personnel and equipment involved.

We have been asked, on occasion, about our "communications strategy," and how it enabled TWA to emerge from what was potentially a very reputation-damaging situation smelling like a rose, or at least not "de-flowered" by the experience. In answer, I can only say that our strategy, if it merits such a description, was a simple determination to tell the truth and try not to hold anything back other than information that could prejudice the hostages' safety. Certainly, there is no way we can complain of the media's treatment of our company. Most reporters and their associates were very understanding and sympathetic to our predicament. More than once, I had to call upon their sensitivity to understand why I could not confirm or comment on a given piece of information -- and they reacted most responsibly. Nevertheless, there were some incidents during and shortly after the hijacking that many people feel are worth reviewing and evaluating. And the preponderance of such incidents -- perhaps inevitably -- grow out of the conduct of the television medium.

Not long ago, a senior executive at one of the networks suggested that it might encourage the production of more and higher quality documentary programs if they were somehow declared exempt from the ratings process. I would go further, I think, and suggest that such treatment might usefully be applied to all forms of news broadcasting. I speak as one who has seen first-hand the excesses this contest for ratings can produce in the coverage of an ongoing news event. I recall, for example one morning after the crisis had ended, when I escorted members of the TWA flight crew to an appearance on one of the network morning news and entertainment shows.

Perhaps that should that be run together, as one word: newsentertainment. We had finished the interview and were driving away, when a representative and crew from another newsentertainment show took off in hot pursuit of us. At our destination the young representative hopped from her car and cut me off, demanding that I immediately take the two pilots to her show for an interview. When I said that was not possible at the moment, she changed her tactics and pleaded, telling me that otherwise she would be fired. Then, seeing that that would not work, when I was some 30 feet away from her and well into the lobby of an office building, she yelled after me that her boss, Mr. Big, would have me fired. Lo and behold Mr. Big did call my superiors the next day, but I am happy to report that I still represented TWA.

While that young lady's misplaced zeal may have been less than professional, and momentarily embarrassing for me personally, there was another incident that was downright chilling. I received from a network radio reporter telling me that they were about to broadcast a report saying that the arms used by the terrorists had actually been placed aboard the plane by TWA employees in Athens. After a discussion of how he had come by that information, and whether he could be sure of its validity, I asked him to give me the names of the individuals suspected. He said that he would have to check with his boss. He called back a few moments later to say that under no circumstances was he prepared to betray his sources by revealing the names.

"Wait a minute," I said. "You've just made a serious accusation. If it's true, those same people next time might just as well put something even worse on the plane. And your telling me you won't identify them to me, or the authorities, because it would betray one of your news sources?"

"That's right," he said proudly.

But even more upsetting than this little personal unpleasantness was the scene that occurred at a press conference held at Kennedy Airport for Purser Uli Derickson, just minutes after her return to the United States. Not only was there an actual fistfight between two photographers scrambling for a vantage point, there was a far more serious and distressing event. I am sure everyone is familiar by now with the unfortunate flap concerning whether Mrs. Derickson did, or did not, single out for the benefit of the terrorists a group of passengers who had "Jewish-sounding names." The source of this preposterous accusation was the combination of a reporter's poorly phrased question and a physically exhausted and emotionally drained Mrs. Derickson, who desired to be properly responsive to the press. When a reporter asked her the double-barreled question, "How many passengers with Jewish-sounding names did you select for them?" she focused on the "how many" rather than defending herself against the

implied accusation that she herself had done the selecting. It is perhaps not surprising that many viewers got the totally false impression from that exchange that she was doing the hijackers bidding in a particularly ugly way, whereas in fact her strenuous effort was to persuade them that no such judgments could be made on the basis of name alone. A few moments later, one of the questioners did attempt to set the record straight about just who did the selecting, but that exchange went largely unnoticed and the harm was done.

It was only with some difficulty that we were able to put this unfounded and vicious rumor to rest, but not before there were actual bomb threats directed against Mrs. Derickson and her family from some home-grown terrorist extremists within her own society. Within a day or two of the first erroneous news reports of Mrs. Derickson's comments, a major Midwestern newspaper carried a lengthy editorial, castigating her. I guess that it is probably not surprising that they never called, prior to publication of the article, to ask if TWA or Mrs. Derickson cared to comment. But neither did I hear from the editor, even after he had received my letter of protest, buttressed with written support of Mrs. Derickson from the FBI and a number of major Jewish organizations. I wonder to this day if they ever got around to retracting their mean-spirited, totally false opinion piece.

Fortunately, along with these episodes of total exasperation, there were also welcome little moments of a kind of comic relief. About a week into the hostage taking, a man from Arizona wrote me, offering a 12-point program for resolving the situation. Part of the plan involved using a 400-kilowatt U.S. Air Force "duterium fluoride" laser to "cut and quadrant" the aircraft -- thereby exposing the terrorists so they could be dealt with further. Now, I have no idea whether or not there actually is such a thing as a "400-kilowatt Air Force duterium fluoride laser," but I can tell you this; If there is, I am pretty unhappy that this guy knew about it!

And it will be a long time before I forget the absolutely bizarre conversation I had early in the a.m. with one good old boy who said he and a colleague would be only too happy to go over there to "Bay Root" and spring the captives plus our plane. All we had to do was provide two Browning automatic rifles, 500 rounds of ammo and two first-class tickets. I told him I would get back to him.

I tell you these stories for a reason. More than one reporter asked me if I could provide any amusing anecdotes they could use. The anecdotes existed, and I think I have a sufficient sense of the absurd to appreciate them -- but they really had no place in a story like the one that was then unfolding.

Others in the forum are perhaps better equipped to discuss the media's function and impact from a political standpoint, but I would like to acknowledge believing there were positive results from journalism's presence in the action, and particularly television's. To begin with, there was the great comfort provided the loved ones of the hostages by their being able actually to see them, right there on their home TV screens, in good health and (under the circumstances) and apparent good spirits.

As for us at TWA, the television coverage of the ongoing events, and in particular the famous tarmac interview of our flight crew through the open window of the cockpit, was of great value in assessing the physical and mental condition of the pilots, not just for the human reassurance it provided us, but also for the very practical purpose of judging whether or not they were capable of continuing to operate the aircraft if called upon to do so.

Most important of all, though, was the fact that the unremitting bright spotlight of media attention on this event was undoubtedly a primary factor in preserving hostages lives. As many people pointed out, the fate of the group of American hostages still being held captive in Lebanon was far less certain than that of the group from flight 847, for the very reason that the TV camera is not a daily witness to their plight.

But this positive benefit of protective TV visibility for the hostages did not come entirely free. It was balanced by a negative consideration: The continued well being of the captives was important to the terrorists only because it allowed them to manipulate the media to champion their cause. The hostages' survival was the terrorists' admission ticket for ongoing access to the media and world opinion.

By and large, I would have to say that, with a few exceptions, such as the misunderstanding about Mrs. Derickson's actions, TWA came out very well in the media coverage. Also, our attitude of openness paid dividends in other ways than just getting "favorable press." It also helped us get a lot of timely and useful information from our friends in the media that we might not have obtained through any other channel, or at least not as fast. There was, of course no question of the immense public sympathy for and approval of the flight crew, Captain John Testrake, First Officer Phil Maresca and Flight Engineer Christian Zimmerman. To the best of my knowledge we as an airline didn't suffer any significant loss of respect as a result of the incident.

But there's also no denying that the cause of the Shi'ite Moslems got one of the greatest free rides on world television in communications history.

In pursuit of news pre-eminence, the networks rushed onto the air virtually anything transmitted from Beirut, including some highly politicized video conceived, orchestrated and produced by the very same bad guys who were holding several dozen of our fellow citizens at gun-point.

I'm happy to note that as a result of the considerable discussion of ethics and methods this situation has set off, signs emerged showing the networks have not only learned some things from the experience, but are actually prepared to put what they've learned into practice.

One company adopted a new set of guidelines for the handling of similar stories, and also for network conduct in connection with that coverage.

Those guidelines say that the network will no longer issue press releases or publicize competitive claims about ratings, scoops or special programs during major crises, and will also avoid airing unedited tape or interrupting scheduled programs when there's no major news development, just to be competitive.

I would just note that I think it's this very kind of enlightened self-governance that's called for, rather than some clumsy form of government regulation.

You all know how we in the airline business feel about government regulation.

David Venz delivered these remarks at The Center for Strategic and International Studies in Washington, D.C., on October 9, 1985. He first joined TWA in 1966 as a Public Relations Representative at JFK Airport. Follow a brief tenure in Chicago, Dave returned to New York to manage media relations. He left to work for two major New York public relations firms in 1973 and returned to TWA in 1979, as Director – International Public Relations. In 1985, he became Vice President – Corporate Communications North America for Airbus, and retired in 2005, settling in Athens, Ohio, with his wife, Lucy.

My Incomparable TWA Experiences

By C. Keith Riggs

Jon Proctor

Mount Rushmore, in the Black Hills of South Dakota, where the author grew up.

Growing up in the remote yet beautiful Black Hills of South Dakota, I always enjoyed traveling. I motorcycled through much of the United States as a young man and hitchhiked through Europe and Asia up to the Persian Gulf. In my senior year at Brown University, my counselor suggested given that passion for travel, I should look for a career that suited me and he suggested I seek employment at an international airline. I applied for work at Pan Am and TWA, and TWA offered me an airport management-training job.

I was asked if, given a choice, would I prefer being based at London, Paris, Frankfurt or Rome. Because I already spoke English - albeit with a South Dakota accent - and my wife was Italian and I had German as my foreign language in college, I said that I would prefer Paris -- what a menu selection!

It worked out, and I became an airport management trainee in September 1967. Later, following a TWA reorganization, I received training in sales and reservations and accounting. Such began a life full of adventures that few can match while many can only live in their dreams. Join me for some of those exciting journeys.

France

In May 1968, there was a large strike and violent student movement that shut down Paris and the airport. At first I was assigned to accompany passengers on a bus to Brussels, but eventually we operated out of a small military airport southwest of Paris. I did all kinds of things thanks to my experience in all the departments. After about four or five days, the manager asked me to take care Ambassador Shriver, his wife Eunice, sister of the Kennedys, and her brother, Edward Kennedy, who were visiting the Shivers in Paris. It was at the time that Robert Kennedy was assassinated, and they were going back to the USA for services. I did what I could for them, serving them coffee and escorting them later to the airplane.

Libya

On Monday, September 1, 1969, driving to work a bit early, I noticed a few army vehicles, but as I approached the town center, there were more and yet fewer private cars. Closer to the port, I suddenly realized there were only military vehicles. Traffic was stopped, and a soldier came to my car with a rifle. He pointed it at me,

Paris Service Is Maintained

PARIS—TWA on May 25 temporarily transferred its Paris flight operations to Bretigny-sur-Orge, located less than 30 miles from the center of Paris, to relieve passenger inconvenience caused by the closing of Orly Airport on May 19 by a general strike throughout France.

Richard W. Wilson, vice president-sales and services for the International region, said that TWA had been granted temporary authority to serve the Bretigny airport, which is under French military control. With the positioning of ground support equipment, the first flight was dispatched to New York.

Mr. Wilson said TWA's operations at Bretigny-sur-Orge greatly eased the movement of Paris passengers who had been diverted to Brussels following the interruption of all air service at Orly. Previously during the shutdown of Orly TWA had rerouted its Paris flights to Brussels, providing charter bus service between the two capital cities. During a four-day period, more than 1,200 passengers were protected.

The bus trip took approximately six hours, including a lunch or dinner stop, and each bus was accompanied by a ground hostess or customer service agent. In contrast, ground time between Paris and Bretigny-sur-Orge is less than an hour. A fully-staffed TWA check-in facility, established at the Paris Hilton at the start of the Brussels service, continued to process departing and arriving Bretigny passengers in an efficient and orderly manner.

TWA Skyliner

shouting something (I didn't understand Arabic); then kicked my door (denting it) and motioned for me to get out, which I did, of course, walking to the edge of the road.

Then I saw a young officer sitting on the front of a kind of tank with wheels, with his legs over the front edge. He called the soldier over, spoke with him, and the soldier came back, motioned for me to get back in the VW and to drive off the road, which I did. I drove back toward our house, but I stopped at a bar and used the pay phone to call my boss, who had a home phone. I told him what happened, and suggested that it might be a military coup. He told me to go home while he called the US Embassy, and would get back to me. An hour later he confirmed that it apparently was a coup, and that we should not leave home.

There were shots all over the place, even down our street if the soldiers saw someone moving. I think they shot over people rather than trying to kill them. Unfortunately our running water was out at the house. I talked with a neighbor across the street, and he said that if I could get a hose over, he would hook me up to his water. I managed to do that, and although soldiers fired a shot from time to time down our street, I don't think they could really see me when working with the hose. We finally had water and could shower on the lawn and give our baby a bath.

It was still quite warm, and being just a block or two from the sea, we figured out a way to go down to the beach without being seen. It was like a mini-vacation. Luckily there was enough food to get by for the five or six days until the coup ended. I later saw photographs of Gaddafi, and am convinced that he was the officer on the tank behind me. He was born in June 1942 so we were about the same age. I was a sales rep, and he was ruler of a country.

London

Upon arriving at work on June 18, 1985, I found the office it in turmoil. TWA 847 had been hijacked shortly after takeoff from Athens, en route to Rome. Later in the morning my boss Peter McHugh and another director took off on a private plane to Algeria, where the aircraft had landed. Leaving the office in a rush, Pete asked me to stay on the open telephone conference line to organize and respond to the events from his office. It was an intense and long day and night, not just for me but for so many people involved. TWA's president and others were often on the line, giving information and asking questions. In the afternoon the next day, someone in New York asked me how long I had been on line. I told him that it had been since the morning before, or about

32 hours. He told me to find a replacement and to go home for some rest, so I asked another director to take my place, went home, had a whiskey, and got some sleep.

Back at work the next day, I flew on another private plane to Algiers, to help with some of the released passengers. I helped other TWAers, who were extremely fatigued. We eventually flew to Athens to meet with others, including the pilot's wife. When it was finally over, we returned to London.

Later I was sent to Libya in sales, and remained there until our office closed, then was assigned to New York headquarters in product and security. Returning to Paris, I held a position in the budgets and controls department, then went to London when TWA's headquarters were relocated there. I was eventually sent to Greece as general manager and returned to Paris in the same position, and finally came back to the United States at TWA's headquarters until the end of our proud airline.

I returned to Europe and now live in northern France, cherishing my recollections of life on the road with TWA.

C. Keith Riggs

Aviate, Navigate, Communicate

By Captain Jerry Lawler

Jon Proctor

TWA's extended-range 767-231.

The axiom "Aviate, Navigate, Communicate" is a reminder of the pilot-in-command priorities during emergency situations.

Aviate-Maintain control of the aircraft.
Navigate-Know where you are and where you intend to go.

Communicate-Let someone know your plans and needs.

TWA Trans-Atlantic Service

TWA assisted the United States in World War II by providing airplanes and flight crews flying missions over the Atlantic Ocean. This gave our company invaluable experience in oceanic operations. TWA began trans-Atlantic service in 1946 using DC-4s and the elegant new Lockheed Constellation. In 1969 TWA opened a trans-Pacific link to complete its round the world network that lasted until 1975. These flights were flown with 4-engine aircraft including the 707 and the 747.

We began flying the twin-engine Boeing 767 in late 1982. It was the first Boeing widebody to be designed with a two-pilot crew, digital glass cockpit. New automated electronics replaced the flight engineer role by enabling the pilot and co-pilot to monitor aircraft systems directly. In the mid-1980s, TWA spearheaded the growth of twinjet flights across the northern Atlantic under extended-range twin-engine operational performance standards (ETOPS) regulations. ETOPS tests include shutting down an engine and flying on the remaining engine to a diversion airport, in order to demonstrate that, during the diversion flight, the flight crew is not unduly burdened by extra workload due to the lost engine and that the probability of the remaining engine failing is extremely remote.

767 Pilot Training

Boeing's philosophy maintained that the autopilot flies more efficiently than the pilots. We were expected to use it as much as possible. This troubled me. Why? Every six months, captains are required to take a proficiency check in the simulator or airplane. Maneuvers such as stall recovery, steep turns, emergency descents, visual approaches, non-precision approaches, missed approaches and crosswind landings are all flown manually and are required on the check.

One of the most challenging training maneuvers was flying the 767 with one of its two engines shut down. All the engine thrust is either on the left wing or the right wing. The wing with the power wants to turn toward the wing with no power. This requires the pilot to control the rudder with one leg and foot to keep the plane going straight ahead. An engine failure requires a strong muscular leg effort on the side of the operating engine to keep the rudder in balance. Fortunately the pilot can relieve the pressure on his leg by applying rudder trim to balance the airplane.

Having already been qualified on the Convair 880, L-1011, 707, 727 and 747, I was disappointed to find out that the engine-out procedure on the 767 was markedly different. With all the other aircraft, the pilot was allowed and expected to use rudder trim during an engine out approach. The rudder trim would be removed as the throttle power was reduced for landing and the airplane would stay aligned with the runway. But it was not the case on the 767. TWA's procedure at the time was to fly around on one engine with rudder trim until arrival at the final approach fix, which was generally 5 miles from the runway and about 1,500 feet above the ground.

Approaching the final approach fix, pilots were required to remove the rudder trim and use leg muscles to keep the airplane aligned with the runway using the high engine power required during the approach. Remember, one engine on one side is now doing the work of two engines. When power is reduced on the operating engine to land, some fancy footwork moving the rudder is required to keep the airplane aligned. I was told the reason for this procedure was that the nose wheel steering was tied to the rudder. That is fine except we touch down on the main landing gear before the nose wheel.

Twin-engine Atlantic Service

The FAA and ICAO concluded that a properly designed twin-engine airliner could make intercontinental transoceanic flights. TWA was awarded an extended ETOPS rating in May 1985, for Boeing 767 service between St. Louis and Frankfurt, Germany, allowing us to fly up to 90 minutes away from the nearest alternate airport.

On June 6, 1985, a beautiful summer day in Germany, I was excited to command TWA Flight 745 from Frankfurt to St. Louis. The flying time was scheduled for 9 hours, 27 minutes. Flights over 8 hours required a relief pilot and he was sitting in the cockpit jump seat. There was a full load of passengers and fuel.

Our route took us northwest over the Netherlands and the United Kingdom towards Iceland, where a suitable alternate airport was located. Several hours into the flight, everything was operating smoothly. In the cockpit, the relief pilot was standing between the pilot seats discussing our international operations. We were

Author

Posing with members of the famed first Marine Division, returning from Saudi Arabia on a military charter flight.

about an hour southeast of Iceland over the North Atlantic when a red emergency light illuminated, indicating the left engine oil pressure was low; the left engine oil quantity gauge indicated zero.

Shutting down an engine while cruising at 39,000 feet in the middle of the ocean was not on my wish list. The Emergency 767 Checklist procedure for an engine failure contained 10 steps to be followed. The engine was secured according to standard operating procedures. Although the airplane is able to safely fly on one engine, it cannot maintain level flight at higher altitudes and must descend. In order to do so we had to divert off course so as not to interfere with aircraft that may be below us. Our procedure at the time called for a turn in the direction of the nearest suitable airport.

Once again, it was time to Aviate, Navigate, and Communicate. I disconnected the autopilot and trimmed the rudder for flight on one engine. We descended and headed for Iceland. The non-flying pilot communicated with Oceanic control that we were declaring an emergency, descending and diverting to Keflavik.

We also had to communicate with TWA dispatch to advise them of the emergency. The passengers and flight attendants could tell something was amiss and I advised them of our plans.

Murphy's Law states "Anything that can go wrong, will go wrong." With an engine shut down, I wanted the entire crew to mentally prepare for the possibility of an ocean ditching in case the other engine failed.

TWA's training included an engine inoperative Instrument Landing System (ILS) approach procedure. Having demonstrated proficiency in this maneuver only months ago, I was confident of flying a successful single engine ILS approach. However, Murphy's

Law was lurking. We were informed that the ILS at Keflavik was shut down for maintenance. We would have to do a non-precision Visual Omni Range (VOR) approach to an altitude well below the prescribed safe landing minimums. A non-precision approach is a misnomer in that it requires more precision flying due to lack of vertical guidance the ILS glidepath provides.

In the 1980s, a non-precision VOR approach was flown as a series of step-down fixes. After reaching one fix, pull the power off and descent to a set altitude and then level off by adding engine thrust until reaching the next fix. At the Final Approach Fix start descent to a Minimum Descent Altitude (MDA) altitude and level off until you see the runway or execute a missed approach. Descent requires reducing power and level off requires adding power and maintaining that power for some distance.

Managing the rudder trim on a multiple step down approach can be very challenging. TWA had a published procedure for an engine inoperative landing in good weather. There was also a published engine inoperative procedure for an ILS approach in bad weather, but there was no procedure for an engine in operative VOR, non-precision approach in bad weather. I discussed my plan with the flight deck crew and informed them of my intention to manually hand fly the entire approach with the required rudder trim; I would not remove the rudder trim prior to the final approach fix. This was an emergency and I intended to Aviate. I briefed the relief pilot in the jumpseat how and when to remove the rudder trim on my command as we landed.

This would be far different from a normal approach. The 767-200 was designed without a fuel dumping system, used to reduce the landing weight. An overweight landing with a higher landing speed was our only choice. Also, the approach has to be flown at 20 knots faster than normal. Full landing flaps create too much drag, severely limit the aircraft's ability to climb if necessary, so only partial flap settings are used. This approach speed would be close to 200 miles

per hour. A missed approach was not an alternative since there was nowhere else to go. So we had to get it right the first time.

TWA Flight 745 was cleared for the VOR, Runway 20 approach. We crossed the Final Approach Fix at 2,300 feet, reduced power to descend to published minimums, 440 feet above the ground, and leveled off. Level flight required more engine power and more rudder trim. This was an emergency and using captain's authority I was ignoring the prescribed procedure of removing all rudder trim. At 440 feet, we were still in the clouds and could not see the ground. We descended to 300 feet and started to see some of the ground.

The control tower was watching us on radar. We were below the inoperative ILS glide slope and the tower, thinking we were too low, advised us to go around. We were right on course and I told the non-flying pilot to report that we had the field in sight. We did not see the runway but at 250 feet the runway approach lights came into view. We started down and crossed the end of the runway. As I reduced the power for landing, the relief pilot removed the rudder trim and we made a normal landing using a time-tested technique.

We touched down very fast and I decided to use moderate braking to prevent overheating the brakes and possibly having a tire blowout. We turned off at the end of the runway and began a long taxi back to the airline ramp.

This adventure led to some procedure changes. TWA pilots were advised to hand fly at least one approach on every flight to maintain manual flying proficiency. Also, the requirement to remove all rudder trim prior to the final approach fix was removed. One more change since the Iceland adventure 30 years ago; the newer Boeing 777s and 787s have automatic rudder compensation during engine out operations. Called thrust asymmetry compensation, it greatly reduces the pilot workload and most importantly, keeps the aircraft in proper trim.

Thirty years after this diversion, there are still many cases of veteran pilots losing control of the aircraft when hand flying. For example, an Asiana

Author

Airlines 777 crashed during a manually flown visual approach in good weather at San Francisco and an Air France Airbus A-330 went down in the South Atlantic when the relief pilot hand flew the airplane into an aerodynamic stall. Once again, Aviate, Navigate, Communicate.

About seven weeks after the Iceland incident, I received a report detailing the cause of the oil leak. A metal bolt, not part of the 767, was found in the oil system drain pan. The bolt had torn a rubber seal that allowed the oil to leak from the engine. How it got there is a mystery. Could it have been "Murphy's Law?"

Jerry Lawler was hired by TWA in 1964 and promoted to captain four years later. He served in various positions within the Air Line Pilots Association (ALPA), and was a volunteer 747 pilot flying troops to and from Saudi Arabia in the first gulf war. Jerry retired in 1998, at age 60. Captain Lawler and his wife, Sue, are pictured on the flight deck during his retirement trip.

TWA Flight 885 TLV – ~~JFK~~ – TLV
By Captain Jim Breslin

T. L. Brown

A TWA 747 receives service at Tel Aviv.

As I round the Clubhouse turn at age 79 and start down the home stretch, I sometimes steal a few quiet moments to bask in the sunshine of my life and to reflect upon those events that still remain vivid in my memory.

One such event happened on November 23, 1986, some 24 years ago.

We had just taken off from Tel Aviv's Ben Gurion Airport and were loaded to the gunnels with fuel for the 11-hour journey to New York. Climbing through 5,000 feet there was a catastrophic explosion out on the wing that rocked the whole airplane as the No. 1 engine came apart in a hail of shrapnel and fire.

What must have seemed like an eternity to those in the cabin as they waited for word from the cockpit, but it took time to run our check lists and consult with Air Traffic Control for an area where we could jettison some 55 tons of fuel, or 14,000 gallons, depending on which unit of measure you might choose to use to describe a whole lot of it, in order to lower our weight for a more acceptable overweight landing. I got on the public address system just as soon as I could to assure everyone that the engine had now been secured, the event was over and would be followed next by routine cleanup procedures to prepare the plane for a landing back at Ben Gurion Airport. I went on to explain the fuel jettison procedure and what they could expect to see out on the ends of both wings as the fuel was being sent overboard.

Once on the ground I filled out a "Flight Debrief Report" and a "Pilot's Use of Emergency Authority" report to explain our overweight landing, then went back to the hotel, not thinking very much more about it.

I don't remember how it came into my possession but I have an oversized postcard with a cartoon on the face of it depicting a herd of passengers all jamming the aisles as they scramble to retrieve their belongings from the overhead bins, while the caption reads "Fasten your seat belts!" for landing in Israel.

While on the reverse side are the following inscriptions: "Thanks for the best landing in this situation. (signed) Martie." "They say stress is the spice of life, but some is more enjoyable than others. Thanx for a great job! Benji." "Thank you! Pleasurable trip with a captain as yourself (not to mention the feeling of safety). Janette Eldredge (flt 884 survivor)" "If I have to be in an emergency you are the one I want for my captain. You're great." Linda Cuppy Flt. 884." "Great simulator drill. International Reserve Officer Ray Carlucci" "Some people will do anything for a living. First Officer Blaire Thompson" "Thanx for a good landing & a good memory of Israel. Simone Schmidt" "Thanks for a good landing. You are the greatest!" "Thanx so much for being the wonderful Captain that you are. It definitely was a good experience in my new career. A great memory in Israel and thank you once again. I had a feeling of total safety. Thanks again. D. Sulison ." "I feel so lucky you were there. Mary." "Okay, Jim. Thanks for those extra ray hairs today. You truly did a great job. Craig Stevens." "Good show. Barney Rawlins." "Words just can never express how I feel Barney Rawlins" "Words just can never express how I feel." "You are truly a wonderful captain and a wonderful gentle man! Linda Britton."

I was so humbled by these generous comments that I had to remind them all that this was not a one-man show by a long stretch of the imagination. Rather, it was supported by a superb team of professionals, both in the cockpit and cabin. I don't recall the exact number of passengers on board that day but do know that there were very few empty seats when we took off from Tel Aviv for New York.

And I was acutely aware that when you get nearly 400 people restricted to a confined space, and in a stressful situation for what must have seemed like an eternity, the lid could come off at any time. But that didn't happen because of those who took charge of the cabin without knowing themselves what the outcome might be, and made sure that the element of panic was defused and taken out of the equation.

Oh, there was one person who took us to court because of her emotional stress and I was called to testify in that instance but never heard the outcome.

A depiction of the incident by Captain Russ Day, whose drawings were well-know among TWAers.

I wanted to give each of my crewmembers some lighthearted memento of the event that we had all shared in together that day and called upon Captain Russ Day to create an animated caricature of the event that I could present to each one of them, and he did an outstanding job for me as well.

In the foreground is a bloated rendition of a 747 casting a mother's scornful eye back towards a naughty No. 1 engine pulling a tantrum beneath the wing and flinging nuts and bolts into the air like a Fourth of July show, while over the engine in large bold letters is the caption "Ker-Pow!" And in the distant background the skyline of Tel Aviv can be seen from afar.

Thanks again to Russ for a magnificent memento. I have the caricature and the postcard both framed and hanging on the wall in my office.

Captain Jim Breslin

David Letterman's Fourth Anniversary Show Aboard a TWA 747

By Charlie Musco

Photos: TWA Skyliner

David Letterman goes "on the air" in the air aboard a TWA 747 transformed into a television studio.

Even as a child airplanes fascinated me. Once old enough to fly, I wanted to see the world and began traveling in earnest following my junior year in college, traveling to London, England to visit my sister and her husband. They were living there while he was doing research for his doctoral thesis in English history. That was in 1968. I continued to travel as much as time and money would allow.

Flying began to interest me again in 1984, this time, as a career as a flight attendant. I was getting stressed out in my business as an equestrian professional, which included training horses and riders, managing my own boarding stable and officiating at riding competitions throughout the United States. Everything began to overwhelm me and I decided that I wanted to make a career change. The only career that really appealed to me was the airline business. I thought that becoming a flight attendant was the way to go, even though I knew it was highly competitive.

So, after attending classes in travel at a local community college in Winston-Salem, North Carolina, I applied with several airlines that were interviewing for the position of flight attendant. After several rejections, I was accepted by TWA in 1985. I think my final interview before being hired was the clincher that got me in. My interviewer loved horses and we talked a lot about that. I graduated from flight attendant training on June 17, 1985 after six weeks of rigorous training and testing at TWA's Kansas City, Missouri training center.

I was assigned to the New York base and began my career flying out of New York's La Guardia

Captains Wally Moran (left) and Clark Billie with Letterman.

Flight attendants for the special flight were (from left) Barbara Murphy, Suzanne Yanusz, Jean Shoemaker, Flight Service Manager Susan Lebert, the author (partially hidden), Neal Salth and Wendy Zweiback.

and JFK airports, as well as Newark, New Jersey. I thoroughly enjoyed traveling to different cities in the United States, meeting many other TWA flight attendants, and learning the many skills required to be an excellent representative of my employer. I was thrilled to be on the crew for an international trip to Rome, Italy even though I had just started my career. Along with Pan American and Eastern, TWA was certainly one of the most respected airlines in the world and, being one of their flight attendants, was an honor.

As 1986 began I was completely surprised to be chosen as one of 10 flight attendants from the New York base to be part of the crew that would fly on David Letterman's fourth anniversary flight from New York to Miami, Florida. The entertainer rented a TWA 747, which he used to film his anniversary television special. Needless to say, this was a big thrill for me as I had just started working the previous summer.

We had a wonderful time on that trip to. I gave my safety demo to David Letterman himself, who told me that he was actually not fond of flying. I have an autograph from him, thanking me for my service and was given a copy of the script from that show. It was a trip that I will never forget. I am still able to relive that moment on the Internet. The entire show is available for viewing on YouTube under David Letterman's Fourth Anniversary Special Parts 1-10.

One of my other shining moments with TWA occurred after the hijacking of TWA Flight 847 in 1985. The movie Delta Force, which came out in 1986 was based on this occurrence. I was honored to have Flight 847's captain, John Testrake, on one of my trips and, acknowledging and thanking him over the public address system, so that all the passengers knew of his heroism. He did pull me aside later and said jokingly that he would "get me" for that announcement because he didn't want the attention.

My career with TWA was short-lived when the flight attendants went on strike in 1986 and this ended my career. By the time of my recall, I was back in the horse business.

I still do a great deal of traveling in the United States and around the world. As I watch flight attendants going about their duties, I compare them to myself and my TWA colleagues. Occasionally I mention that I used to work for TWA and the usual reaction is to tell me what a great airline it was.

Being a flight attendant nowadays perhaps is a little bit of a different job. Planes are usually full and customers are more stressed and demanding. But for me, the ideal still exists; a poised, well-groomed, personable man or woman who does the best job possible to represent their airline.

I will always have these memories of being part of one of the world's great airlines, TWA.

Charlie Musco is now an official and announcer at equestrian competitions throughout the United States.

OPINION: Icahn the Terrible

By Barbara Peterson

Adapted from *Rapid Descent: Deregulation and the Shakeout in the Airlines*, by Barbara Sturken Peterson and James Glab, (1994, Simon & Schuster)

In the years since Rapid Descent *came out in 1994, I have often heard from members of the extended TWA community about the strange reign of Carl Icahn, who served as the airline's Chairman from 1985 until 1992. Icahn was perhaps the most unlikely airline chief that the industry has ever seen. He arrived in the executive suite with a long track record as a corporate raider; it is widely assumed that he was a model for Gordon Gekko, the quintessential 1980s villain in Oliver Stone's movie,* Wall Street. *Yet he had zero experience running a large company, and, it seems, even less interest in learning the minutiae of a complex airline operation.*

In Rapid Descent, *co-author James Glab and I set out to chronicle the aftermath of airline deregulation through the stories of how this landmark legislation affected the original "Big Four:" American, Eastern, TWA and United, as well as the most fabled of these legacy lines, Pan Am. Icahn makes his first appearance midway through this chronicle, in a chapter titled* Icahn the Terrible, *when he first homes in on TWA as a potential takeover target:*

The airline business in the mid-1980s was adjusting to the new reality of deregulation: companies like TWA, Pan Am and Eastern struggled to compete against lower cost upstart airlines while dealing with higher costs, and their stock prices slid accordingly. That drew the attention of financial buccaneers who smelled an opportunity for a fast profit. Among them was New York financier Carl Icahn, who'd made a fortune as a greenmailer: he'd identify a company whose stock was undervalued, quietly buy shares, threaten to take it over, and then back off with a substantial payment from management or from a "white knight" recruited to fend off the interloper. Icahn's first raids were on manufacturing companies, but in 1984 he'd turned his attention to the airlines, and TWA in particular, because their assets, planes and routes, could be easily spun off piecemeal. He'd already performed that trick at ACF Industries, a Midwestern maker of rail cars, selling off divisions for a handsome profit and leaving the core rail business as a leaner company and ultimately money-making company.

But the airline business had little in common with manufacturing, as Icahn would soon discover. A raid on a prestigious international airline with more than 30,000 workers, whose planes touched down daily in such places as Paris, Tel Aviv, and Bombay, would be another matter. Icahn also had virtually no management experience. The airline takeover, however, would display Icahn's predatory instincts at their sharpest, temporarily masking his unsuitability for the job of actually managing his prey.

Icahn's designs on TWA became public in the spring of 1985 when he was forced to disclose he had accumulated more than 5% of the company's common shares. When Icahn finally sat down with top TWA executives, he boldly pitched his plan to acquire the company and sell off the assets piecemeal to bolster the overall value, arguing this would allow him to acquire the airline without having to liquidate the *entire* company afterward. TWA's managers were shocked. Here was this coarse outsider who talked about an airline as if it were a collection of spare parts. After the session, the feeling of TWA was that it would be impossible to talk business with Icahn. (President Ed) Meyer described him as "the greediest man on earth." Icahn, on the other hand, portrayed himself as a champion of shareholders trying to oust incompetent management. He always claimed a genuine interest in acquiring TWA and operating it more efficiently. But since he had usually avoided ending up in the executive suite, his railing at bad managers seemed a thinly veiled rationalization for his plunder.

Meanwhile, Meyer and his allies on the board declared war on Icahn. They took out full-page newspaper ads to tell the world what they thought of him: his greenmail; his intention to dismantle a venerable company. They hired high-priced lobbying talent to take their case to Congress. It was a strategy based on the belief that their case, much like a political campaign, could be won on character. But TWA managers had failed to sense the great sea change in Washington and New York. Airlines were now just companies, no longer an extension of the U.S. government. Their book value was more important than any lingering value as a national symbol. Again the airline's leaders had failed to adapt to a new environment.

With their options running out, TWA's management came up with a last-ditch plan to rebuff the unwanted suitor, a white knight in the form of Continental Airlines chief Frank Lorenzo. That was a risky strategy, as Lorenzo's strategy of breaking the unions by declaring bankruptcy was widely reviled among airline employees. To management, Lorenzo was the lesser of two evils, compared with Icahn. "At least he's an airline man," said one executive. "But to labor, he was evil incarnate... The unions would have embraced the devil rather than work with Frank Lorenzo." That proved to be the case: Icahn finally gained control of TWA after high-stakes negotiations that culminated in the pilots' decision to throw their lot in with Icahn. In exchange, Icahn promised not to break up the company and to preserve core assets.

By early 1986, the unions may have already been regretting their eagerness to join forces with Icahn, who was firmly ensconced at TWA (he ultimately moved its headquarters from Manhattan to Mt. Kisco, NY near his Westchester County estate.) Word began to circulate around headquarters that he was getting the airline in shape in order to shed it. It was a rumor that some of his new employees, however, were already eager to believe. For while Icahn had rescued them from Lorenzo, the idea of this novice running a huge international airline was disconcerting. "We were trying to teach Icahn about the airlines," said one long-time executive "But he seemed to have a short attention span. He would go from one thing to another; it was really chaotic." Experienced managers tried to convince him he needed a marketing plan, but, as one of them recalled, Icahn resisted the idea, protesting that "it'll make people think I'm hanging on to the airline." Icahn was obsessed with keeping people guessing, as if managing an airline were a poker game.

Shortly after he'd won his airline, in fact, he set in motion two plans right out of his playbook: selling part of it, and acquiring another one. He'd already identified TWA's profitable PARS computer reservations system as a choice asset: it wasn't like international routes or other airline pieces whose sale would upset his accord with the pilots. While orchestrating this spinoff, he was then literally handed a merger with Ozark Airlines, whose management had been talking with TWA before Icahn came on the scene. The deal gave TWA a monopoly at its St. Louis hub, and it quickly won the blessing of a friendly Washington regime (which rubber stamped virtually every airline merger put before it in the 1980s).

Dealmaking aside, Icahn's limitations as a manager of people were on full view when the flight attendants' contract came up for renewal. His tendency to go for an opponent's weakness, honed by years of financial gambling, would have unforeseen consequences. First, he demanded that the mostly female flight attendants take bigger pay cuts than the mostly male pilots or machinists. "He told us that we were secondary incomes, that we were not the main wage-earners in our families," reported union leader Vickie Frankovitch. Icahn denied that claim, but wouldn't back down and the union went out on strike March 7. Icahn hired replacements, who were hustled onto planes after only superficial training, without any concern for the quality of inflight service. Striking attendants started picketing in front of Icahn's mansion, and sometimes the boss would stroll down the long driveway and give the assembled troops his now-familiar "If I hadn't come along, this airline would have gone under" diatribe. A few months later, the attendants ended their strike but Icahn refused to hire most of them back; as positions opened up, some were allowed to return but only

at reduced pay levels they'd rejected months before. Icahn viewed it as a total victory; the pay cuts saved TWA around $320 million a year. But the strikers who'd been left out in the cold did not let him forget it, continuing their picketing and denunciations of Icahn at every opportunity. When, a year later, news came out that Pope John Paul II had joined TWA's frequent flier program, still-unemployed workers protested loudly on the grounds that TWA's labor practices went against the social teachings of the church.

By the late 1980s, Icahn's obsession with saving money had impaired his ability to make the major spending decisions that running an airline required. He refused to buy the next generation of fuel-efficient jets that American and other rivals were flying and TWA's maintenance and operating costs were soaring. Icahn instead got distracted by other deals, pursuing unsuccessful attempts to buy USAir and Eastern, and he took the airline private, recouping his initial investment. By late 1989, TWA's losses were mounting, and Icahn got the deal he wanted: he began selling off TWA's crown jewel, its prized London routes, to American. This sent TWA's union into a frenzy, for it meant Icahn was finally planning to dismantle the airline, something they had warned about since he took control four years earlier.

None of this stemmed the red ink flow; TWA ultimately declared bankruptcy and Icahn finally bowed out of the airline business in January 1993, nine months before his troubled airline finally emerged from Chapter 11 under new ownership of its employees and creditors. It seemed unlikely that the crafty financier would ever venture back into the business. Icahn called TWA "the worst investment I ever made," and *The Wall Street Journal* estimated he lost more than $100 million on the airline.

Barbara Peterson is a writer specializing in aviation, travel and consumer issues and is author of two books on the airline industry, Blue Streak: Inside JetBlue (2004) *and* Rapid Descent (1994.) *Her articles have appeared in* Condé Nast Traveler, The New York Times, Daily Beast, The Wall Street Journal *and* The Guardian. *She is the winner of the Lowell Thomas Award for Investigative Reporting and the Gene DuBois Award for Excellence in Travel and Aviation Reporting.*

Operation Desert Shield

By Jon Proctor

Operation Desert Shield involved the buildup of troops and defense of Saudi Arabia in preparation for the Persian Gulf War; also known as Operation Desert Storm the majority of troops were transported to Saudi Arabia for deployment to Iraq in conjunction with the Civil Reserve Air Fleet (CRAF) program. TWA operated two 747s for this purpose, painted all white. Crews were scheduled on a voluntary basis, although plenty of cockpit and cabin crewmembers stepped up to the task.

T. L. Brown

Two 747-200s were stripped of TWA colors for the CRAF flights operating to Saudi Arabia.

On January 1, 1991, as a Flight Service Manager, I departed from JFK with a full load of military personnel and minimum cabin crew, operating nonstop to Rome.

It struck me at how young our passengers were, many of them barely 20 years old and all military

volunteers; none had been drafted since Vietnam days. Weapons were brought aboard and stowed in the overhead racks, without ammunition.

Although only nine cabin crewmembers were on board, the service was easy. In fact, I had to make an announcement to the effect that we appreciated everyone bringing their meal trays back to the

Author's photos except as noted

*En route to the Kingdom, I posed with Flight Attendants
Megan Chase (left) and Margo McConnell.*

hurry to minimize exposure to hostilities that might come our way.

The big 747 was empty on the way back to Rome, with only the cabin and cockpit crews. I put on another movie but most of us stretched out instead, contemplating the day we had witnessed. Five and one-half hours later CRAF Flight 9770 touched down at Rome. We had been scheduled to ferry the airplane all the way back to New York 24 hours later, but plans changed and the cabin crew instead deadheaded on Flight 841.

galleys but it was causing traffic jam. Two movies were shown, and the flight attendants engaged soldiers in conversation. We placed sandwiches and other snack food on galley work surfaces so the troops could serve themselves throughout the night; all of it was consumed by daybreak, yet continental breakfasts were eaten as well.

Following a 1-night layover, we operated another 747 on to Dhahran in eastern Saudi Arabia. The 6-hour segment left Rome early in the morning with an augmented cockpit crew to permit a quick turnaround and return to Italy. It was a much more somber atmosphere aboard as the reality of impending war set in.

We landed at King Fahd Airport late in the day. Taxiing to our assigned parking spot, I saw endless rows of military vehicles and aircraft lined up as far as the eye could see. It was quite evident we were going to war, to be fought in part by the brave men and women on board this 747. I wished them well on the public address system and added that we were also anxious to bring them home.

Minimum time was spent on the ground. The aircraft bellies had been boarded on freight pallets and were quickly unloaded by the first soldiers to disembark. We took on some fuel and left in a

Our participation in CRAF operations intensified when Operation Desert Storm began in mid-January. Still on the volunteer list, I received another trip assignment, departing February 14, this time on a daylight trans-Atlantic crossing to Frankfurt. The flight somewhat mirrored my earlier experience, again with minimum cabin crew and a full passenger load.

We disembarked on the military side of the field at Frankfurt and then retired to a hotel in Darmstadt just as snow began falling. By morning the town had taken on a storybook appearance with a white coat blanketing the countryside. At breakfast someone from the front desk brought me a note with instructions to call TWA's airport operations. Instead of proceeding to Dhahran, six of us were to deadhead later in the day to Rome and await further disposition, while the others were told to stay in Germany. No explanation was given for the change of plans.

An Alitalia MD-80 brought us to Rome on the short segment, less than two hours. We were served a cold lunch of very high quality, with wine and yes, everyone was out of uniform. I thought the meal was a bit of overkill on such a short flight until referring to my ticket: $700 one-way.

A Rome operations agent met us on arrival with a roster sheet for a downtown hotel and put us in a limousine. Instead of Saudi Arabia, we were, 36 hours later, going to operate an L-1011 charter to Sharm el-Sheikh, Egypt, carrying United Nations peacekeeping troops, relieving a contingent there and bringing back those soldiers.

A few of us went out on our day off but the weather was cold and damp, not conducive for sightseeing. Plus, our onward flight was scheduled to depart at 3 a.m. the following day, after arriving from Griffiss Air Force Base in New York State. As with my earlier trip we were scheduled to turn around and come back to Rome later the same day. This would not have been possible except for suspension of all work rules during a time of war.

The crew call came about the time most of us had barely fallen asleep and six weary souls rode in silence to the airport; the pilots had stayed at an airport hotel. Just as we were about to depart, it was discovered that return food provisioning had not been thought of, and I delayed the flight about 30 minutes while our operations people scared up enough meals. We only had 88 troops on the way down and a like number returning.

As our flight approached Sharm el-Sheikh around daybreak, there was no answer from the airport control tower. It turned out the field was not scheduled to open until 7 a.m. While the L-1011 was put into a circling pattern, TWA's Cairo operations people attempted to get our destination airport opened up earlier, but it was all for naught and an extra hour was spent burning jet fuel.

On the ground things were not nearly as organized as Dhahran and it took nearly two hours to get in and out of there. As a result Flight 9777 touched down at Rome in the late afternoon. We had been on duty for nearly 14 hours and looked forward to the hotel, a

A spliced-together picture shows the desolation of the Sharm el-Sheikh Airport. The U.N. peacekeeping troops we were to pick up wait on the ramp.

light supper and to bed before deadheading home to New York the next day.

Instead, JFK inflight supervisor Mark Mosciki, doing temporary duty at Rome, came aboard to tell us there was a problem. Although our flight was to fly back to Griffiss posthaste the crew that we relieved the night before needed three more hours of hotel rest before returning to duty. Fine, I said, take the troops inside; give them something to eat and a place to wait. But no, Rome officials said they were armed and therefore could not leave the plane, even if they left their weapons aboard. In turn, the cabin crew would have to remain on board for the duration.

With plenty of unoccupied seats on the airplane, I assigned half the flight attendants to a period of rest and let them nap for an hour, then reversed the process. It wasn't exactly like sleeping in a hotel, but we made do. To his credit, Mark stayed with us the entire time to offer moral support and help keep the troops occupied.

Finally, the onward crew arrived and received a hearty welcome. One flight attendant looked at us and, realizing we had been up since they left the airplane 27 hours earlier, exclaimed, "Oh my GOD!" Indeed, it was a long night and day.

That crew brought the flight back, technically,

During a lighter moment, I tried on a gas mask, issued to all of us while on the ground at Dhahran.

from Rome (Italy) to Rome (New York), where the military base is located. For my fellow crewmembers and me it was nonstop to bed for about 18 hours. In fact, one flight attendant slept right through the wake-up call the next morning.

TWA's European schedules had been drastically reduced because of the hostilities. Instead of returning nonstop to JFK on a 747, we rode a packed 767 home via Milan. It was my last CRAF trip and TWA Atlantic crossing. I took early retirement two months later, but will long remember my CRAF adventures.

Inflight Supervisor Mark Mosciki chats with soldiers during our extended duty day on the ground at Rome.

Opinion: The Sale of TWA's Routes to American Airlines

By Jamie Baldwin, J.D.

On July 1, 1991, Trans World Airlines Boeing 747 Flight 701 pushed back from its gate at Terminal 3 of London's Heathrow Airport and began its taxi to runway 27-Right, passing through an arch of water sprayed by the airport's fire brigade. After takeoff, the pilot executed a fly-by, over the length of the runway as airline workers waved and cheered. As the aircraft banked away from Heathrow for the last time, air traffic control transmitted to the pilot, "Cheerio 701, it's been nice knowing you."

The departure of flight 701 that day for New York marked the end of TWA's more than 40 years of service at London's Heathrow Airport, service that began in 1950.

The following day, July 2, American Airlines took over TWA's operations at Heathrow, following United Airlines, which had earlier that year taken over the Heathrow routes of Pan American World Airways. Just like that, two iconic airlines, airlines that pioneered overseas travel, ceased to exist on the most important international route in the world.

How did that happen?

In the early 1980s, TWA was facing the pressures of deregulation and as a result consolidated its route system around a hub at St. Louis and an international gateway at New York Kennedy airport. In 1985, Carl Icahn bought the airline operations from the TWA's holding company, Trans World Corporation, and appointed himself as chairman of the newly independent airline.

During that time, TWA had a large European operation with temporary pilot bases in several cities. These bases provided crews for Boeing 727s, which TWA operated across its European route network, serving cities such Athens, Rome, London, Paris, Geneva, Frankfurt, Hamburg, Stuttgart, Zurich, Amsterdam, Lisbon, Barcelona, Madrid, Oslo, Vienna Cairo and Istanbul.

In 1988 TWA carried more than 50 perecent of all trans-Atlantic passengers with daily Boeing 747, Lockheed L-1011 and Boeing 767 departures to more than 30 cities in Europe, fed by a small but effective domestic operation. A similar intra-

European operation fed passengers to TWA's European gateways for travel to the United States.

On the corporate side, TWA was recapitalized in 1988 when Icahn took the company private, withdrawing in cash all of his own investment and leaving the company so highly leveraged that it fell into a perilous financial condition.

In 1989, TWA's managers decided to replace its overseas Boeing 727 aircraft with more economical DC-9s. Preparing for the transition, the airline positioned several million dollars worth of spare parts in Germany as required by the German government. They also sent senior DC-9 pilots to observe operations in preparation for the changeover of crews that was to follow. Shortly before the DC-9s were to arrive in Germany, however, the entire plan was canceled because the aircraft lease contracts specifically forbade any operations outside the United States.

This exacerbated TWA's already perilous financial condition and, coupled with some serious operating losses, the company agreed in December to sell its Chicago–London route authority to American Airlines for about $110 million. The two airlines filed an application with the Department of Transportation (DOT) for approval of the transfer.

Going into 1990, TWA continued to suffer losses and for the first nine months of the year lost 54.3 million dollars on revenues of $3.58 billion. The Iraqi invasion of Kuwait in August that resulted in an increase in fuel prices and a serious drop in trans-Atlantic traffic further increased the company's losses and it was becoming a real possibility that the airline would be forced into bankruptcy. Therefore, in December, while the Chicago transfer application was still pending, TWA agreed to sell its three other London routes, Boston, Los Angeles and New York to American for about $500 million.

TWA's foreign business had been the core of its operations and the London routes were actually profitable. In fact, for the year ended August 31, 1990, the profit was about $130 million. These London routes were essentially the only moneymaking assets TWA had.

On January 30, 1991 the DOT approved the Chicago route transfer, effective January 31. And on April 24, the DOT granted the Boston, Los Angeles and New York routes, effective July 1. In approving Chicago route transfer, the DOT said that the public would be better served by American because the airline had the strength to adequately compete with the British carriers in the Heathrow market. In other words, the transfer was consistent with the public interest.

TWA did not tell what it proposed to do with about half a billion dollars in the cash to be paid by American, nor did the DOT inquire. The airline's management did say it needed funding to enhance its competitive position and that the money was more important to it than the routes.

One speculation was that TWA (specifically Icahn) wanted to buy Pan American with the proceeds. Earlier, while Pan American was in the process of selling its London routes to United Airlines, Icahn approached the airline and made an offer that the Pan American board virtually ignored. He later renewed the offer, suggesting that by combining the two airlines cash could be raised by selling overlapping routes.

Icahn's bid for Pan Am was $1.50 a share, with $1 in notes. The notes would trade at a large discount from their face value. Some suggested that a merger between the two airlines would make sense, resulting in making a "stronger 'one' out of a weaker two," but it never happened.

In the end, TWA was one of the weakest airlines in the country, deeply in debt estimated at $2 billion, with a fleet of aging airplanes. It had defaulted on some notes. Operating losses were in the tens of millions and it was becoming quite clear the company would have to file for protection under Chapter 11 of the Bankruptcy Code. Basically TWA needed to reduce its debt, and the only way to substantially do so was to use the proceeds from the sale of its London routes.

Thus, on May 16, 1991, from the proceeds of the sales, TWA offered to purchase for cash five classes of its debt securities: equipment trust certificates, to be bought for 73 cents on the dollar;

15 perecent senior secured notes, to be bought for 65 cents on the dollar; 16 perecent senior notes due in 1992 and 17 1/4 perecent senior notes due 1993, for 35 cents on the dollar; and 12 perecent junior subordinated debentures for 17.5 cents on the dollar. This represented retirement of $1.37 billion of current debt at an estimated cost of $482 million. However, even then, TWA's financial picture was still hardly bright. However, the picture probably would have been much darker if TWA did not have the cash to make that offer.

An ancillary issue related to TWA's sale of its Heathrow routes, along with the Pan American sale, was the potential impact on the then bilateral Air Services Agreement between the United States and the United Kingdom, known as "Bermuda II".

Before the route transfers were approved by the DOT, talks were being conducted between the United States and the United Kingdom over landing rights at London's Heathrow Airport. The U.S. was intent on increased authority at Heathrow. Under Bermuda II, each party was limited to two designated carriers, then Pan American and TWA on the U.S. side. However, with the sale of the routes pending, speculation arose as to whether the British government would scrutinize the impact of the change of ownership on those routes. And if the British government denied United and American permission to take over Pan American's and TWA's rights at Heathrow, they would have been restricted to operating from London's Gatwick airport and both deals could have died.

Another issue on the agenda for these talks was foreign ownership. The British were seeking permission for foreign airlines to own a greater share of U.S. carriers above the then limit of 25 perecent. Should that limit be raised, it was speculated that Icahn, when he renewed his bid for Pan American, might have been trying to forge a TWA that would be an attractive investment for a British airline or other foreign carrier.

However, none of this happened. Both deals went through and American and United became the two U.S.-designated carriers. Pan American and TWA would be relegated to London's Gatwick

Airport, with TWA operating a daily 747 rotation from St. Louis.

At first blush, one would consider the timing of the sale of the Heathrow routes by Pan American and TWA to be a strange coincidence. Maybe it was, however, would Carl Icahn had sold those routes had not Pan American? He certainly was aware of what was going on and, but for Pan American's sale, he might have lost it all.

The 1988 recapitalization triggered the start of a downward trend that ultimately led to the sale. Being heavily leveraged, the company walked a tightrope to survive. The perilous financial state of the TWA was further exacerbated by the ill-advised plan to switch from the Boeing 727 to the DC-9 in Europe. What added insult to injury was apparently no one was aware the leases on the DC-9s limited operations to the United States. As the company was closely held, it is likely only Icahn and his closest advisers were privy to the terms and conditions of those leases. This begs the question, how could management of a sophisticated international air carrier overlook such an obvious restriction?

It would appear, going into 1990, Icahn was desperate. But redemption came in the form of Pan American's sale of its profitable Heathrow routes. However, during the previous two years, profits on these routes were deteriorating and, with new competition from United, the earnings would almost certainly continue to erode. It became quite obvious. TWA's debt had to be dealt with, or certain bankruptcy would ensue. Sale of this asset would solve the problem.

While the sale was pending before DOT, speculation arose regarding what TWA was going to do with the money. What is hard to understand is how Icahn could have seriously thought he could buy Pan American, knowing full well the amount of debt that burdened his company. However, it played well with the media and little was said about the extremely serious nature of the debt.

At the end of the day, the $1.37 billion of secured debt was retired at a cost of about $482 million, the approximate amount of the proceeds

TWA received from American for the London Heathrow routes.

Carl Icahn did his best to paint a rosier picture of the sale than what it really was.

Jamie Baldwin is an author, speaker and consultant in the airline industry. With more than 30-years experience in commercial aviation, he lectures on aviation matters as a Visiting Lecturer at the University of Westminster (London) and teaches Business Law at the University of Maryland University College (UMUC). He formerly was an Adjunct Professor at Embry-Riddle Aeronautical University where he taught Airline Management and Business Law. His areas of expertise include aviation regulation, aircraft leasing and financing, contracts and commercial issues.

Mr. Baldwin is the author of Pan American World Airways - Images of a Great Airline *and the blog "The Pan Am Series". He also co-edited* Pan American World Airways - Aviation History through the Words of its People *with Jeff Kriendler. He is currently working on a new book,* Aviation Regulation - History and Practice, *to be published in 2016.*

Jon Proctor

TWA 747s served London-Heathrow daily for 20 years.

TWA - A Collegial Innovator

By Craig Jenks

Jon Proctor

The Boeing 767 opened additional route opportunities for TWA.

The challenge for TWA was... how to deal with tough guys! It competed with much stronger airlines both domestically and internationally. TWA employees and managers also had to cope with difficult owners: the legendary and tyrannical Howard Hughes, and later, investor Carl Icahn. TWA people had to somehow navigate these external and internal tough guys, and in doing so they developed a corporate culture that was above-average collegial, collaborative and conducive to bold innovation.

This was TWA's reputation when I started as a consultant in New York the late 1980s. I observed it, and experienced it directly in my own work.

Truly innovative was the TWA launch of ETOPS: extended twin, over-water operations. I recall being interrogated by an incredulous head planner at a European airline. Could TWA be really serious about twin-engine transatlantic services? Indeed they were: TWA was about to pioneer ETOPS flights to Europe with its Boeing 767-200s, up to then deployed by U.S. carriers only domestically. This was the first time any airline operated regularly scheduled twin-engine overwater, now normal globally. At that time, nothing smaller than three-engine, DC-10 or L-1011 equipment could be operated on trans-Atlantic routes. ETOPS substantially expanded the options route planners could realistically evaluate.

A TWA 767-200 would have been part of an imaginative trans-Atlantic project I chanced to be directly involved in. TWA almost entered the JFK-Turin, Italy market in the summer of 1994. The city and airport of Turin lobbied TWA to launch this service, not allowed for in the restrictive US-Italy bilateral. My job was to assist in persuading TWA,

and making the case for a bilateral exemption to the governments.

Turin is a large city and the capital of Italian manufacturing, but it lacked lobbying clout against Alitalia and its focus on. The client and I used every argument we could think of. TWA's then Vice Chairman, Robin Wilson, was open to new ideas and bright TWA youngsters Mike G. Whitaker, Assistant General Counsel, and Nikos Kardassis, then TWA head for Italy, were dispatched to check realities on location. We convinced them, and in March 1994 TWA filed for a four weekly 767-200 JFK-Turin-Vienna schedule. The US Department of Transportation (DOT) gave the okay but the Italian government stalled until it was too late for TWA to start summer service. Kardassis later became CEO of Jet Airways in India. Mike Whitaker held senior positions at United and another Indian carrier, Indigo and is now the FAA's Deputy Administrator.

My one other project with TWA started in a surprising way. Mr. Kazuhisa Shin, the then new

Jon Proctor

A morning TWA departure from La Guardia Airport was timed to connect
at Washington-Dulles with the All Nippon Airways nonstop to Tokyo.

Resurrecting the old-fashioned interchange service, a TWA/Gulf Air partnership provided the TWA late-day Heathrow departure to New York.

All Nippon Airways (ANA) New York offline head, was unusually ambitious and resourceful. The first-ever incumbent of this position, he wanted to boost ANA's penetration in New York City by upgrading from off-line to on-line ASAP. The fact that ANA had rights only for Tokyo-Washington Dulles (IAD) and not New York did not faze him at all. My instructions were clear: "Jenks, ANA needs La Guardia to Washington Dulles feeder service".

Shin's idea was that the negative of one-stop New York–Tokyo against nonstop competitors would be countered by the convenience of La Guardia (LGA) versus JFK. Of course there was no provision for such a service under the bilateral, or even for a code-share on an existing service. The only solution would be to commercially incentive some US carrier to schedule LGA-IAD-LGA at times connecting with the five weekly ANA Dulles-Tokyo and then buy seats from them. Another hurdle: the flight would have to leave La Guardia at about 8 AM, diverting a scarce airport peak morning slot from some other profitable use.

This was the post-deregulation heyday of turboprop regional carriers. The CEO/owner of one such carrier, Kingsley Morse at Command Airways, was willing to countenance our unusual not to say outrageous request. This was also when Japan's economy was at its strongest: money was no object for growing Japanese companies. The deal was done, and ATR-42s diverted to IAD on ANA's five days. An ANA Japanese media ad showed the miniscule Command Airways ATR-42 connecting with the giant ANA 747.

Unfortunately, a few months later Command founder Kingsley Morse sold out to American Airlines. The new owners took one look at our rogue LGA-IAD flight, exclaimed "what's this" and cancelled it. My (by then) friend Kazuhiza Shin came back to me with new instructions: "Jenks, we need LGA to IAD jet feeder service." Another reason for upgrading to a jet: Japanese passengers were apparently uncomfortable with the turboprop. But this was prior to the regional jet era and I had to reply to Mr. Shin that jet feeder would be horrifically costly. Yet again, cost was no object and my consultancy, Airline/Aircraft Projects Inc., was given its marching orders.

We approached TWA. They proved to be the ideal partner: Carl Icahn had taken over and was focused on near-term profitability, while rank-and-file TWA managers (led for this deal by Larry Thierman) were collegial and resourceful as usual. This time, the chosen instrument was a Boeing 727-200, no less. Lawyers and operations staff from both airlines completed the deal. The service started December 15, 1988. Dedicated LGA check-in desks had Japanese language signage. Timetables for 1989 show an 8 a.m. TWA LGA-IAD flight daily except Tuesday and Friday, to coincide with ANA's IAD-Tokyo operating days. The deal lasted more a year. Soon after, ANA obtained JFK nonstop rights.

A precedent for this ANA deal was the aircraft interchange with Gulf Air in 1987. TWA needed a 6 p.m. London Heathrow-JFK departure, to compete with Pan Am and British Airways late flights, attractive to business passengers. But TWA's U.S. flights all arrived at LHR in the morning, rendering prohibitively inefficient a 6 p.m. departure. However it happened at about this time that Gulf Air wanted to start U.S. flights. So an interchange flight was established, with TWA sub-leasing a Gulf Air L-1011 arriving at Heathrow mid-afternoon from the Middle East and deploying it onwards to JFK, then returning to LHR the following morning. Gulf Air was thereby able to market virtual U.S. one-stop service, and TWA got its evening LHR-JFK service.

One of TWA's earliest collaborations was as launch co-investor and then for 30 years primary adviser to Ethiopian Airlines. TWA helped it to become the leading airline of Africa, a position it retains to this day, with its Addis Ababa hub the crossroads of the continent.

A problem TWA never resolved, and arguably contributing to its undoing, was the tremendous, multi-tiered peaking of the JFK hub operation. Multiple levels of peaking were at play. The excellent Saarinen Building and an armada of Boeing 747s were certainly quite full:
- at the early evening hub peak times
- in summer
- on weekends
- in years that the notoriously cyclical trans-Atlantic routes were doing well.

Pan Am faced the same issue, but had some JFK long-haul routes with different time-of-day and seasonal peaks, and less leisure-oriented flights to southern Europe. This was a summer-intensive TWA niche, with JFK nonstop flights to/from Lisbon, Madrid, Milan, Rome, Athens and Tel Aviv, based largely on legacy route rights going back to the negotiating prowess of Howard Hughes.

TWA's JFK-Europe, mostly 747 network had very high load factors, when these peaks all converged. But this was the exception not the rule. TWA did not have a sufficiently diversified network to offset transatlantic peaking.

Craig Jenks Ph.D. is founding President of the Airline/Aircraft Projects, Inc. consulting firm, based in New York City. Its website is: http://www.aap.aero

Wings of Pride: A TWA Plane Nearly Forgotten

By J. L. Johnson – The Airliner Reporter

James Ferris

On August 7, 2015, I had the honor of welcoming an iconic piece of aviation history back home to Kansas City, MO. I watched the event unfold while standing on the roof of what was once an early Trans World Airlines (TWA) stronghold.

Looking into the sky, I could see a tiny red speck on the horizon that slowly grew into a beautiful red/white DC-9-83, N948TW. It was something unique, and certainly not common at the Charles B. Wheeler downtown airport (MKC).

Soon one of the most familiar, albeit nearly forgotten, planes to grace the TWA fleet landed and taxied to within a few yards of the airline's first Kansas City. The TWA Wings of Pride, after 27 years of service had finally reclaimed its greatest livery and arrived back to the home of its former airline, courtesy of TriStar History and Preservation, Inc. (doing business as TriStar Experience) and their patrons.

The Plane

This DC-9-82, manufacturer's serial number 49575, 1,414th off the assembly line, belonging to an Irish leasing company, got its start in 1987 with Spantax, a Spanish carrier. Months later, it went to another short-lived Spanish airline, LAC. After less than a full year with the Spaniards the plane migrated BWIA West Indies Airways, where it operated until 1994. The plane came to TWA as gift from its employees, who raised the monthly $233,000 lease payments and painted it in a unique reverse of the normal double-red-stripe livery, sending a message that the airline was reinventing itself "from the inside out."

After TWA's final color scheme appeared in 1995, it was applied to Wings of Pride, along with a special red banner above the window line. Finally, when American Airlines purchased major assets of the airline, the scheme disappeared altogether, but not before it fittingly operated the ceremonial last TWA flight, on December 1, 2001.

But Wings of Pride's story doesn't end there.

In 2014, the plane was saved from salvage in a deal between American Airlines, TriStar Experience and a number of sponsors. Wings of Pride returned to the former TWA overhaul base at Kansas City International Airport (MCI). For nearly a year, it sat on the ramp as funds were raised to remove the American Airlines livery and apply the reverse color design.

Wings of Pride will now remain at the downtown airport with the TWA museum as a reminder to Kansas City citizens of their rich aviation history. It will be kept in flying condition and pending various FAA approvals may be used to provide flights to patrons who supported the acquisition and repaint and for educational purposes. Additionally, TriStar History expects to provide some support to honor flights, shuttling military veterans to Washington, DC to visit their memorials.

TWA's Link to Kansas City

TWA was headquartered in Kansas City for much of its existence. Its headquarters building at 1735 Baltimore, in the historic Crossroads District, opened in 1956. Even after the executive offices moved to New York City in 1964, TWA maintained a presence at the building for a number of years. It was added to the National Register of Historic Places in 2002. On the roof of the southwest corner of the building sits a 20-foot tall replica (of a replica) of the TWA Moonliner from Disney's Tomorrowland exhibit. The original replica is on display at the National Airline History Museum (NAHM), which also houses a Lockheed Constellation, Douglas DC-3 and Martin 404, all three in basic TWA livery, plus an L-1011.

Kansas City is also home to the TWA Museum. It occupies a portion of 10 Richard Roads at the

Jon Proctor

downtown airport, the same building that served as TWA's original Kansas City headquarters and now owned by Signature Aviation. As the name suggests, it is dedicated solely to preserving the history of TWA and is believed to host the most comprehensive collection of TWA artifacts anywhere. Its crown jewel is a Lockheed Electra Junior 12A, the world's oldest former TWA airplane still flying.

TriStar Experience

One of the newest organizations to enter Kansas City's aviation-related, non-profit markets is TriStar History. As its name implies, the organization's people have a special place in their hearts for the L-1011 TriStar. In fact, they own one, which is being made ready for a ferry flight to MCI from Tucson, Arizona. Also in the inventory is a rare BAC One-Eleven twinjet.

Rather than operate a museum, TriStar is taking a unique and much more active approach in looking to cultivate the next generation of science, technology, engineering and math (STEM)

workers. The organization's mission is "inspiring greater achievement through higher altitude." TriStar aims to use flyable aircraft (and simulators) in educational and experiential programs to inspire youthful students to pursue STEM careers by offering rides on historical airplanes. As a lover of aviation history I could not be more excited about the future of this organization.

Visit the TriStar Experience website at: *www. tristarhistory.org.*

This story is reprinted from August 7, 2015 edition of the on-line aviation newsletter Airline Reporter.com, with permission of the author.

J. L. Johnson holds the title of Senior Correspondent, Airline Reporter (www. airlinereporter.com), based in Kansas City, Missouri. A resident of nearby Lee's Summit, he is a twenty-something Senior Business Analyst, semi-frequent traveler and lover of all things aviation. He attributes his love of aviation to his grandfather, a U. S. Air Force Colonel. J. L. can be reached at jl@airlinereporter.com or at @User47/ AviationGeek.net/YouTube/Flickr/Instagram.

Jon Proctor

Blessed Charter

By Bradley Sunshine

Photos: Courtesy of George Alexander

TWA First Officer George Alexander peered down from the Boeing 767-300ER's cockpit and marveled at the surrounding ground equipment. A train of baggage carts whisked by, their fresh red-and-white paint gleaming in the sun. The tug below was also spotless, free of the exhaust stains and grime that inevitably plaster such vehicles. Its massive black tires shined with thick coats of Armor All.

"Wow, they really covered every detail." Alexander said to his captain and friend Willard (Van) Van Wormer.

After entering the takeoff speeds into the flight management computer, Van Wormer looked out of his side window. The mobile staircase against the forward left door was immaculate, but his eyes focused beyond the polished silver railings. Thousands of people had come to see his flight depart from the cargo area of Newark International Airport for a short flight to Baltimore/Washington International Airport. "Agreed," he replied. "I've never seen such a shiny tug, or so many people for that matter."

Both men were experienced and in the upper echelons of TWA's seniority list on that 8th day of October 1995. Van Wormer was hired 30 years earlier, at the age of 20, as a first officer on the Lockheed Constellation. He eventually became a Douglas DC-9 captain and flew nearly all of TWA's aircraft types. Early in the '90s he became triple-qualified as a DC-9, L-1011 and 767 check airman. By 1995, he was the standards manager of the airline's 767 fleet.

Alexander was initially hired at Ozark Air Lines in 1974 following stints with commuter carriers and two corporate flight departments.

First Officer George Alexander (left) and Captain Willard "Van" Van Wormer.

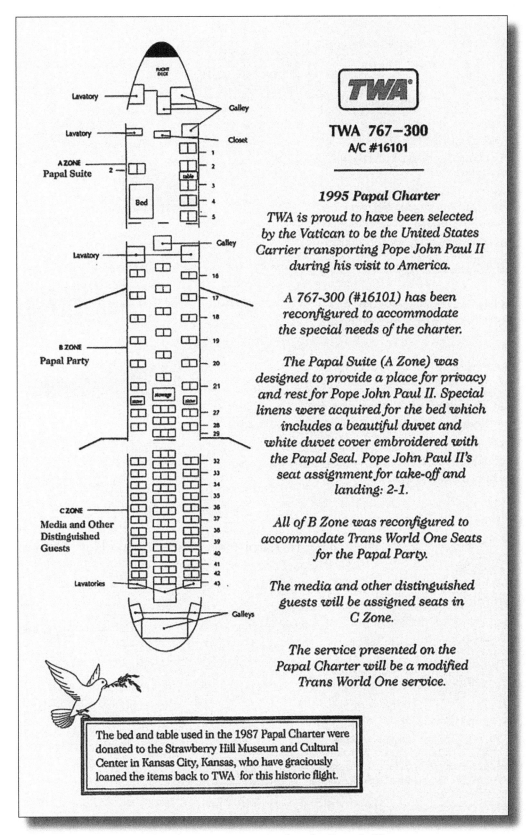

Special cabin arrangement for the Papal Charter.

After the airline merged with TWA in 1986, he became a check airman/designated examiner on the DC-9, McDonnell Douglas DC-9-80 series and L-1011 before transitioning to the 767. Van Wormer conducted Alexander's 767 initial operating experience in 1993, and the two became friends.

Each airman accrued thousands of hours over their careers, including many flying 767s on long international pairings. Yet through all the years and trips, the most momentous flight was arguably the 35-minute hop from Newark to Baltimore that sunny morning.

Some pilots can claim they once flew noteworthy figures such as movie stars, politicians, or athletes. But Van Wormer and Alexander had the honor and privilege of flying an individual blissfully removed from the paparazzi and petty endorsement deals. Their VIP passenger was a man known throughout humanity as an ambassador of peace, virtue, and faith. He was Pope John Paul II (born Karol Józef Wojtyla) the Holy Father and head of the Roman Catholic Church. As Alexander later summed it up, "the highlight of my career was being selected to fly the papal charter in 1995. Hands down, no contest; it was just a wonderful experience all the way around."

Pope John Paul II was in the midst of a five-day visit to the US East Coast. Arriving in Newark aboard an Alitalia flight on October 4, the following days entailed addressing the United Nations General Assembly, celebrating Mass and delivering homily at Giants Stadium and in Central Park. He met with regional bishops and Jewish leaders at the Cardinal's residence. The Baltimore portion of the journey (the Archdiocese of Baltimore is the oldest in the United States) included mass at Camden Yards and a parade through the city.

TWA was selected by the Vatican to transport the Pope from Newark to Baltimore and then on to Rome's Ciampino Airport. The charter was welcome news for employees as the airline had just exited bankruptcy for the second time within a 3-year period, and was in the midst of

promoting the "We're Up to Something Good" advertising campaign.

This was actually the fourth papal charter in TWA's history. The airline flew Pope Paul VI from New York to Rome (Fiumicino) in 1965 aboard a Boeing 707. In 1979, a TWA Boeing 727 took Pope John Paul II on a 6-day domestic tour, and then a 747 flew him from Andrews AFB, Virginia, to Rome. John Paul II again travelled by TWA in 1987, aboard a 727 that undertook an 11-city, 12-day tour starting in Miami; he returned to Rome from Detroit on a TWA 747.

By the time Van Wormer and Alexander were selected to operate the first leg of the 1995 charter, the airline managers were able to plan and execute these flights with impressive detail and coordination. Hundreds of flight crewmembers volunteered for the assignment, but only those recommended by TWA management were ultimately selected. In addition to Van Wormer and Alexander, the Newark-Baltimore segment was crewed by 10 flight attendants with a wealth of cultural experience. Led by Flight Service Manager Gil Bernal and flight attendants that spoke 11 languages between them, including Italian, Polish, Spanish, Japanese, Lithuanian, and Greek.

The Baltimore–Rome flight was crewed by Captain Fernando Arenas, Captain Doug Craighead, and First Officer Gregory Dohrn. Virginia Kelly was the FSM. The nine flight attendants supporting her represented the airline's St Louis and JFK crew domiciles, and mirrored the cultural diversity of the Newark–Baltimore team.

In the days before departure, both crews attended several meetings that covered every operational detail. Van Wormer and Alexander were briefed on parking locations at Newark and Baltimore, schedule, route of flight, planned altitude, and their additional passengers consisting of papal party members, foreign press, and other distinguished guests. Acceleration during takeoff was also discussed. Because the 767 would carry a light fuel load, there was concern that a brisk takeoff roll could damage the papal china if it was not properly secured. "From top to bottom, everything you could think of was covered," Alexander remembers.

The 767-300ER, fleet number 16101 named *Shepherd 1* for the charter was integral to these preparations. Pre-flight modifications were conducted at TWA's JFK maintenance base before the airplane was ferried to Newark. The cabin had an elegant "Papal Suite," with brand-new galley equipment, carpeting, and overhead bins. "The aircraft looked incredible," Alexander recalls. "Every inch of that airplane was waxed and detailed by hand; even the forward lavatory was repainted in papal colors."

A few days before the big event, Van Wormer decided that Alexander would fly the Newark to Baltimore leg. It was an acknowledgment of their friendship and the significance of the event to Alexander's family. Alexander's wife, Mary Jane, prepared several loaves of paska, a type of religiously symbolic bread traditionally eaten during Easter in eastern European countries, including the Pope's native Poland. The Holy Father not only ate the delicacy, but the Vatican later mailed an official thank-you note and blessing the Alexander residence in Missouri.

As the 767 taxied to Runway 29 at Newark using the *Shepherd One* call-sign, Van Wormer and Alexander witnessed a sight neither has seen since: One of the world's busiest airports at a standstill. As this was a "head of state" flight, all traffic except for *Shepherd One* was stopped on Newark's crowded taxiways until the Boeing was airborne.

Alexander rotated about halfway along the runway in front of the grandstands, and climbed to a cruising altitude of 16,000ft. Airspeed was maintained at 250 knots to minimize cabin noise and potential turbulence. Shortly after level-off, the New York Center controller promptly cleared *Shepherd One* direct to Baltimore. Van Wormer made light of the unusual clearance in such busy airspace. "You know, I'm flying the same route next week, " he good-naturedly transmitted. "No chance," the controller immediately replied. It was clear this shortcut was a one-time occurrence.

Before handing *Shepherd One* off to the next control sector, though, the controller asked what runway at Baltimore they planned to use considering the northwesterly surface winds and security precautions. Van Wormer and Alexander decided Runway 28 was preferable to 33L. The latter piece of pavement was (and still is) known to be a challenging landing surface because of its upward slope and crown.

Alexander remembers making the greatest landing of his career as he rolled the 767 onto Runway 28. Years later, he jokes about the smooth outcome: "If I would have known that the landing was going to be on TV and on the big screen (at Oriole Park at Camden Yards,) I probably would have been sweating bullets."

Van Wormer taxied the 767 to BWI's cargo area. Approaching the parking spot where the governor of Maryland and mayor of Baltimore were among a large awaiting crowd. He slid open a cockpit side window, allowing the maintenance supervisor riding in one of the jumpseats to hold out the papal flag in the autumn breeze.

"Hold onto it," Van Wormer cautioned. "If that falls, you know where it's going to go." (He didn't have to explain that he meant the number one engine.)

After the Boeing was safely parked, Pope John Paul II would not deplane until he talked with the crewmembers. He spent several minutes with each individual, the subject matter of each conversation personal and unique. It was a moment Van Wormer and Alexander would never forget. "You can hardly find the words for it," Alexander explains, "It was such a fantastic one-time experience."

Their portion of the papal charter successfully completed, both men continued their careers. After joining American Airlines, their gold epaulets were exchanged for silver ones. Van Wormer retired in 2004; Alexander's three years later

For Van Van Wormer and George Alexander, flying the 1995 papal charter was one of great pride. Their 35-minute flight was a flash amidst decades, but the experience remains vibrant and all encompassing. Flying and meeting Pope John Paul II was a once-in-a-lifetime occurrence.

Van Wormer and Alexander view the fight as a testament to their friendship and a reminder of TWA as one of the world's original and most distinguished global airlines. They certainly experienced the carrier's tumult and uncertainty during their long tenures, but they also witnessed its grandeur and achievements. The papal charter represented the finest of TWA: numerous individuals across the airline working together to facilitate a successful travel experience for one of the world's most pre-eminent religious leaders.

This achievement will inevitably persist in the hearts and memories of Van Wormer, Alexander, and every other crew member of *Shepherd 1*. TWA's red-and-white markings are gone, but the airline's finest qualities will forever be part of the papal colors and history - the enduring legacy of a very special and memorable charter.

This story originally appeared in the September 2013 issue of Airways Magazine *and is republished with permission.*

Left from top: Captain Van Wormer, James Daly, Don Albert, Mary Lynch, Barbara Chevigny, Flight Service Manager Gil Bernal

Right from top: First Officer George Alexander, Barbara Pollem, Donna Heron, BJ Jawn Collins, Kelly Bender, Stan Teramoto

TWA Career Memories

By Milo Raub

My love for aviation began 70 years ago. As a wide-eyed, eight-year old boy, I was led out to an Allegheny Airlines DC-3 for the first leg of an unaccompanied flight from Erie, Pennsylvania to Oakland, California. I could not have imagined that this trip was the beginning of a relationship with aviation that would span a lifetime.

By the early 1960s, I had completed my bachelor's degree in aeronautical engineering at Tri-State University in Angola, Indiana. My mentor was Dr. Quentin Hawthorne, who not only headed the aero department, but was also an industry consultant. The consulting aspect was intriguing to me. He hired a few willing students to make drawings of parts for a Volpar tricycle conversion modification for the venerable Beechcraft Model 18. I never realized how these circumstances might come together to shape my life in aviation. During the summer break of my senior year in college, I met Edie, the love of my life, and married her the following year.

After working a few years at Ryan Aeronautical Company in San Diego, I accepted an offer in 1969, for an engineering position at TWA at the Kansas City Overhaul Base, beginning a 31-year career. Warren Jones, Manager of Interiors Engineering hired me. Our Director, John Roche, was one of TWA's first engineers.

My group supervisor was Gene Allen, who was also an FAA designated engineer (DER). Being part of the engineering department interiors group presented me with extensive opportunities for creative design and technical development. It was an incredible experience visiting Norm Parmet's technical development offices on the third floor of the overhaul base. New airplanes were being delivered regularly, and this department was in charge of their specifications and acceptance. Bud Spannuth, Gene Palmer, Mike Walker and other wrote the specifications and approved the first production at the Boeing, Lockheed and Convair factories.

I spent countless hours on the drawing board with my drafting equipment, a slide rule and drafting pencil. Combining my art ability and engineering skills, I produced endless drawings for cabin furnishings and interior modifications. My college courses lacked training on consultation with flight attendants and pilots on design details. Nor did they prepare me for negotiating with experienced mechanics that had to actually build my creations.

Whenever I had a field assignment at one of the major bases, the regional director became my boss for the time, people like J. P. Cooper at MKC, Roy Davis at Chicago. Bill Keller at Los Angeles once picked me up at the gate and we headed for a damaged 707. Herman Jaffe at Tel Aviv always met me at the airplane and accompanied me through Customs. Much of my time during the 1970s was devoted to designing and installing coach lounges in 707s and 727-200s. I had an early assignment on a new 707-331BAH that had been fitted at Boeing with doors in the old-style hat racks. I had to modify the doors for our standard movie equipment and other stowed items. It was my first time aboard a brand-new plane from the Boeing factory in Seattle. That project evolved into an on-going assignment for development and installation of overhead stowage bins on 727s, DC-9s, and 747s.

I took particular pleasure in engineering TWA's fleet paint schemes. Gil Prince was the engineer responsible for many years. When he retired, I eagerly volunteered to take over the responsibility. Soon after corporate managers decided to replace the iconic "double globe" and rocket stripe livery with a new one designed, by Jules Rondepierre in New York. I was provided with 1/100-scale models and renderings of the new red and white double stripe markings to be used in creating engineering drawings and full-size patterns for each airplane. This led to many hours working with Ray Davis and the painters at MCI. Each first application had to meet with Jules' and corporate management approval. Of course the unveiling of a new livery was a huge media event. I would get to repeat the experience in 1995, when New York consultants designed what became the final TWA livery. I am still very pleased that the final scheme was both tasteful and classic.

My lifelong passion for commercial aviation history found fruition when I read in the *TWA Skyliner* about a project to restore a former TWA Northrop ALPHA 4A. NC-11Y had been discovered in a barn on a Wisconsin farm, and an effort was underway to restore it for the new National Air and Space Museum in Washington, D. C. I made a beeline for Jerry Cosley's office to get the details. By chance, a rather large smiling Irishman from Flight Safety Training confronted me, and introduced himself as Dan McGrogan. I soon discovered he was heading up the effort. It only took brief conversation to discover we were both interested in aviation history. The two of us became good friends for many years, and I became an "Alpha Volunteer", and their only engineer. The airplane restoration was completed and trucked to Washington in time for the museum opening on July 4, 1976, Dan and I along with other volunteers, went on to restore other TWA airplanes including *Star of Switzerland*, an 049 Constellation at Tucson, and the Douglas DC-2

Jeff Burch/Proctor Collection

The first TWA airplane to wear the then-new twin-stripe livery, seen at Chicago-O'Hare.

now owned by the Museum of Flight in Seattle. Dan made a lasting impression on my life as an engineer.

Much of the time I found myself in various desert storage yards evaluating used airplanes. Typically we had a team of engineers, pilots, maintenance foremen and flight attendant supervisors to do the survey. In 1982, the FAA delegated me as a TWA Designated Engineering Representative (DER). I later received a parallel appointment as a Consultant DER, allowing me to approve non-TWA modifications. The latter delegation was useful in the sale and modification of two 747SPs to American for its newly awarded Dallas–Tokyo route. That project took me to Hong Kong for three months. Tower Air and Hawaiian also contracted with TWA for maintenance and modifications. These projects took me on assignment to Tel Aviv and Honolulu. When TWA acquired a 747-200 from Athens-based Olympic Airlines, I was teamed with Bill Keller,

Jon Proctor

One of two TWA 747SPs sold to American Airlines, see at Marana, Arizona.

Jerry Maag

Now on display at the National Air & Space Museum in Washington, D.C., an immaculately restored Northrop Alpha.

Arnold Spinelli, Frank Miller and others to work with the Olympic mechanics and engineers who standardized the airplane prior to delivery. The assignment took us nearly three months before the airplane was ferried to Kansas City.

On June 14, 1985, TWA Flight 847, a 727-231, operating intra-Europe flights at the time, was hijacked by Palestinians and flown to Beirut, Lebanon. Our brave captain, John Testrake, maintained composure as spokesman through the ordeal. After long days of negotiations, the hostages were released and it was expected that the terrorists would destroy Ship 4339. Instead it was back in our hands, thanks to a daring TWA crew, with cooperation from Lebanon's Trans Mediterranean Airlines. When the airplane was finally returned to Kansas City, Bob Holmes and I were the first engineers aboard following its security release, to survey the cabin damage. The terrorists, without knowledge of vital airplane systems, had done only superficial damage in an effort to deface the interior. They slashed seats, scribbled Arabic on window shades and overhead bins, and ripped up carpeting; all were all replaceable items. I was honored to meet Captain Testrake at St. Louis as we waited for a flight back to Kansas City, and able to express my appreciation of his bravery and Christian testimony throughout the struggle.

I returned to Athens just a few years later when another intra-European 727-231A, Ship 4340, was able to return to Athens after a passenger placed a briefcase containing an explosive device under Seat 10F. The explosion blew a 6-foot hole in the side of the fuselage, below the window line and above the floor. Had the explosion occurred just inches further inboard or outboard, the plane would have likely been lost. Once again our TWA team received excellent work and cooperation from the Greek technicians at Olympic Airways as the plane was prepared for the ferry flight back to the United States. Final repairs were the completed at Kansas City.

I particularly admired Robin H. H. Wilson when he ran the overhaul base. Later when he became vice chairman and executive operations officer, he

TWA Skyliner
*Captain John Testrake sits
in the hijacked airliner after
its return to Kansas City.*

visited the base often. On one such visit with CEO Ed Meyer, they inspected a newly overhauled and reconfigured 747. I was asked to give them the tour.

Later, as manager of the interiors group, the challenge became one of continuing my design and development work, but now by remote control. Fortunately, I hired some excellent new engineers who became protégée material.

I was able to continue to survey potential acquisition airplanes with a management team. The most significant survey trip took us to Germany to review Condor Boeing 767-300s. TWA needed the type for resumption of Polar, Los Angeles–Paris service. As Manager, I was responsible for the engineering work changes and experienced a new sense of pride when Ship 16101 departed Los Angeles enroute to Paris.

The used airplane acquisition projects gave me the opportunity to pursue my career goal of new airplane development. In the mid 1990s TWA's Board of Directors authorized a fleet renewal acquisition program, introducing the Boeing 757-231 and adding more McDonnell-

Douglas DC-9-83s. As Manager, I participated in cabin and equipment selection and design, making numerous trips to Boeing and equipment vendors. After delivery of the first few airplanes, the position of director of technical development became available and I was selected. The following four years included regular trips to Seattle and Long Beach for acceptance and delivery flights of the 757s and DC-9-83s. In the midst of this activity TWA contracted with McDonnell-Douglas to acquire 25 MD-95s. As Boeing completed its takeover of the McDonnell Douglas, the airplanes were renamed Boeing 717s in the FAA type certification process. TWA also added three new airplanes, and one used, to the 767-300 fleet.

I carry with me the memory of projects and people I worked with. The feeling of family at TWA, and sense of aviation community, is something that will be cherished for a lifetime. There is an unexplainable bond whenever I meet alumni TWAers, especially those I've known and worked with. There is a dedication that does not fade with time. It was one of the world's great airlines made up of great people and historic aircraft.

Jon Proctor

One of the 757s accepted by the author is seen at Boeing Field, Seattle.

Checking conference table for Shepherd I are (from left) Glenn Eaton, manager-aircraft maintenance; tech services coordinator Art Boucher and project engineer Milo Raub.

TWA Skyliner

Following his retirement in 2000, Milo Raub formed his own engineering firm, described at www. raubaero. com, and is now an aviation industry consultant.

Proctor Collection

The restored Star of Switzerland *is a featured attraction at the Pima Air Museum in Arizona. Fleet number 517 accumulated more than 37,000 flying hours before being sold in 1961. It was turned over to the museum and placed on permanent display, following renovation by volunteer TWA employees who gave more than 7,000 hours of their time to complete the project.*

The Grandeur of TWA's Flight Center to Live On

By Jeff Kriendler

The Flight Center as it will look with the two hotel towers in the background.

After languishing since 2001, TWA's beloved Flight Center at John F. Kennedy International Airport in New York will re-open in 2018 as a multi-use, world-class hotel, rekindling fond memories of the stunning futuristic JFK landmark and symbol of the Jet Age.

The project calls for a 75-year lease agreement with Flight Center Hotel LLC, a partnership of MCR Development and JetBlue Airways Corporation, to remake the TWA Flight Center and its nearly six-acre site into JFK's only on-airport hotel. MCR Development will maintain 95

Douglas Corrigan

This December 2011 photo shows how the Flight Center has been surrounded by the JetBlue terminal and adjacent construction.

MCR Development CEO Tyler Morse said, "We are proud to help advance Governor Cuomo's plan to modernize our region's aviation infrastructure by bringing the TWA Flight Center, the most storied symbol of the Jet Age, back to life. Accessible to the general public as well as all airlines from all terminals, the 505-room hotel at the rehabilitated TWA Flight Center will be a tremendous amenity for the entire JFK International Airport. It will be an opportunity to celebrate and preserve Eero Saarinen's historic masterpiece while also creating 3,700 construction and permanent jobs and 40,000 square feet of desperately-needed onsite meeting space."

The TWA Flight Center opened to critical architectural acclaim in 1962, a year after Saarinen's death, and served as TWA's terminal at JFK until 2001. Since its completion the terminal evolved as an icon of both modern air travel and design. Its daring gull-winged construction, reinforced concrete sculpture tested the limits of its material was also the source of its distinction and downfall. The building's stand-alone, sinewy form made it difficult to adapt to the constantly modernizing airline industry. When the building was deemed obsolete as a terminal because it could no longer accommodate today's passenger volumes or modern aircraft, the Port Authority undertook an intricate renovation to preserve a part of aviation history.

In 1994, the city of New York designated the terminal a historic landmark and in 2005 the National Park Service listed the TWA Flight Center on the National Register of Historic

percent ownership of the hotel and JetBlue will have 5 percent.

Flight Center Hotel LLC will invest approximately $265 million to continue renovations of the historical TWA Flight Center, while developing 505 hotel rooms, 40,000 square feet of meeting space, restaurants, a spa and a 10,000-square-foot observation deck. The complex will feature two six-story hotel towers and a micro-grid energy management system, allowing the building to generate its own power.

Additionally, preservationists will see the curving 1960s-era stark white concourse with plush-red lounge area, designed by legendary architect Eero Saarinen, remain as it first looked a half-century ago following a $20 million renovation by the Port Authority to comply with the building's historic designation.

Port Authority Executive Director Pat Foye said, "The Port Authority is proud to ensure the TWA Flight Center plays a critical role in JFK Airport's future, while acknowledging its importance in aviation history. The new hotel will serve the growing needs of our passengers throughout the 21st century, with a touch of the bygone era of glamorous mid-20th Century Jet Age travel."

Places. The soaring white landmark building is adjacent to Terminal 5 and is part of JetBlue Airways' JFK operations.

Over the past decade, the building has had a limited role for special events, such as Open House New York public openings, and the 50th anniversary celebration of the Beatles 1964 arrival at JFK for the rock band's first visit to the United States that kicked off Beatlemania and the British Invasion.

Saarinen's original design featured a prominent wing-shaped, thin shell roof; unusual tube-shaped departure and arrival corridors wrapped in red carpet; and tall windows enabling expansive views of the ramp activity. The design straddled futurism, Googie and Fantastic architecture. It was among the early terminals with enclosed passenger Jetways.

The plan, which was unanimously approved by the Port Authority Board of Commissioners in September 2015, will rehabilitate the landmark to its 1962 glory through a privately funded investment. The New York City Planning Commission plan has certified the hotel conversion plan for public review through the Uniform Land Use Review Procedure (ULURP).

"The rich history of TWA and its employees is a beloved piece of our heritage and one that all 100,000 American Airlines employees are very proud of," said Mike Minerva, Vice President-Government and Airport Affairs for American Airlines. "We are honored to be playing such a critical role in the development and planning for the TWA Flight Center Hotel and are thrilled that the proud name of TWA will continue to live on in such an iconic way for generations to come."

"Since its debut more than five decades ago, the TWA Flight Center at JFK has been among the most admired buildings in modern architecture and a symbol of the golden age of travel. The redevelopment efforts will maintain the structure's heritage while enriching the passenger experience, enhancing the airport's infrastructure and adding to the ongoing development of one of the world's busiest gateways, something Lufthansa as a managing partner of JFK's Terminal One can only welcome," said Juergen Siebenrock, Lufthansa German Airlines Vice President – The Americas.

MCR Development is the seventh-largest hotel owner-operator in the United States, with a $2.0 billion portfolio of 88 premium-branded hotels featuring more than 10,000 rooms spread across 23 states in 62 cities. MCR developed the High Line Hotel in Manhattan. Its JFK hotel plan includes the creation of an innovative museum focusing on New York as the birthplace of the Jet Age, with the storied history of TWA, and the Midcentury Modern design movement.

Courtesy of MCR Development

The interior as it will look, with a portion of the hotel service counter to the right.

Looking Back – Forty Years Out on the Line
By Daniel F. McIntyre

I have collected TWA memorabilia since 1953, and conversations with visitors to my display room help keep my memories fresh. Here are random thoughts from the viewpoint of 40 years out on the line.

I began my career in 1952 loading galleys and passenger service supplies at Chicago Midway Airport. After loading, it was customary to show the hostess where everything was stored. This often became a social event where conversation and coffee were sometimes shared. Casual friendships grew out of these brief but frequent contacts.

I remember when our address was 10 Richards Road, Kansas City, Missouri, and the bottom line of every manual page stated that, "Nothing in this manual replaces the exercise of good judgment on the firing line."

Back then you did not board a terminating flight until Fleet Service put a rug runner on the floor to protect the carpet. We changed all the headrest covers and pillowcases during a "Triple A" cleaning of the plane's interior and provisioned fresh lavatory cloth hand towels. Fleet servicemen

carried toilet cans down the stairs. We helped agents push the passenger loading steps up to the aircraft and provided umbrellas for passengers when it rained.

Red carpets and chrome stanchions were in place for our then-new 1049G "Super G" Constellations. Hat-adorned hostesses were handed a toy broom and dustpan to tidy up the cabin during station stops.

Two-gallon beverage jugs are seen in a Connie galley.

*The LAX ticket counter in the old
Avion Drive terminal building.*

I remember when, on a certain date each year, TWA ferried airplanes out of California to avoid tax liabilities, and when we operated a crew bus 24 hours a day, between the hangar and terminal at Midway. I recall one night when employees from various departments gathered to applaud a captain as he deplaned, having set a new speed record between cities. I also remember one morning when a vintage, World-War II B-25 bomber, painted in TWA red and white, taxied into the west bay of the hangar. This would have been a major No-No, but it was there to pick up someone named Hughes.

I recall those wonderful little sandwiches, one half ham and Durkee dressing and the other half sweet brown bread with cream cheese. Two of the best Royal Ambassador items were Beef with Oyster Sauce and Iron Skillet Chicken. Ah, those days of ice cream sundaes with coffee and cognac on a high-flying 707.

I remember when beverages were loaded in two-gallon jugs; entrees were boarded in warming carriers, and I made up berths for the crews on the 749A international flights as well as for domestic passengers on Super and Super G Connie flights. Hostesses placed pillows on passengers' laps to support the meal tray and cardboard airsickness "burp cups" were stowed under seats.

The cockpit door was left open in-flight and passengers were encouraged to come forward.

I remember when liquor was boarded only in fifths. Then miniature "shooters" arrived. During the daily inventory we spent hours trying to find a shortage of just one or two bottles, then kept a stash of overages that were not on the previous inventories, and whenever a new one occurred we dipped into the overage box.

The passenger service kit (PSK) contained Dramamine, aspirin, baby food, diapers and pins, along with baby certificates, coat/parcel tags and green Class 44 equipment "out of service" tags. I remember the card playing board with the elastic band to hold the cards in place. We boarded an ice

Howard Hughes' private B-25 complete with window blinds.

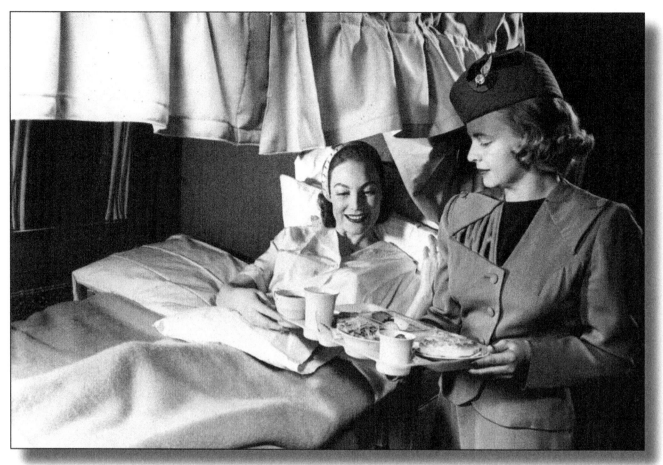

A sleeper Connie with berths made up.

pick and small silver ice tongs. Overhead racks were used just for pillows, blankets, coats and hats. Railroad-format timetables showed only one class of service. Snacks were packed in white paper boxes and hostesses passed out "Wrigley Chiclets" chewing gum. Electric hot cups warmed baby bottles and poached eggs. We occasionally boarded a Bon-Voyage cake or bottle of champagne. Little tent cards on meal trays advised Catholic passengers of special dispensation from the Holy See that allowed them to eat meat when flying TWA on Fridays.

I recall the staccato rhythms of Teletype machines blending with sounds from the hand-cranked adding machines in Operations, and interesting conversations on the Private Line Fone - PLF; all calls started with the same question: "Line clear?" The first St. Louis Ambassador lounge was a bottle club and each member had to

bring and store his or her own booze. Nearly all of our planes had names. My personal favorite was *Star of Paris,* assigned to 049 Connie #555.

The last thing boarded on a departing flight was that "greenie" weight slip. Then the transportation agent crisply saluted the captain at departure time. Our uniform shirts got little black oil spots from Connies pulling out the gate.

Before Xerox machines, there were rolls of carbon paper behind the original, that teletype operators used to make copies of the messages we called "long lines." The door marked "ARINC Radio" (Aeronautical Radio Incorporated) was always closed, hiding operators who never seemed to leavet he room.

I remember June 30, 1956, when we lost Flight 2 in the Grand Canyon, and the night a cargo Connie went in just south east of Midway Airport.

The author has put together a "TWA Museum" in his home basement in Granite City, Illinois. He welcomes visitors. Contact Dan at: dmcintyre52@aol.com

In 1960, the O'Hare terminal had but four TWA gates and an Ambassador Club, small but nice. At MDW in 1952 the contractor was not finished with our two-bay hangar. I recall the night they tried to park a 707 in the smaller St Louis hangar. Everyone was watching the wing tips when the tail struck a ceiling-mounted heater vent.

In the flight kitchen, a "Tele-autograph" machine sat on the flight kitchen supervisor's desk, receiving messages from other departments. The text was always difficult to read.

Non-revving was an adventure on our piston fleet, but the flights were longer and there was more interplay between the passengers. I recall one Super Connie flight from Chicago to Phoenix when, after lunch, the hostess set up a poker game in the forward cabin. Passengers played for matchsticks and she even wore a green visor.

For 10 years starting in 1964, I was a weekly commuter between St Louis and Los Angeles. Another employee gave me a rule to fly by: Never ever leave the gate room or get too comfortable in your seat on board until the aircraft is off the ground; sage advice. More than once I was told to wait at the airplane doorway, with engines running, while the agent and hostess took another head count, searching for an open seat.

Traveling during seasonal peaks and holidays was risky, often creating the dreaded announcement: "Would the following passengers please collect their personal belongings and proceed to the gate area." Or worse yet, after deplaning: "Flight 72 is full. Our next flight to St Louis leaves in six hours."

Back in the day there was a pack of Philip Morris cigarettes on each meal tray. It seemed to me that the smoke was thickest on flights to Las Vegas. I remember once, standing in the aft galley holding a cigarette for the hostess, who would steal a drag when she could.

TWA carried many celebrities back then. In the late 1950s my wife Diane and I were flying to Los Angeles on a 707, along with our infant son. Actor William Bendix asked if he and his wife could hold the baby while we ate. After dinner, he said, "I don't suppose you would let us keep him!" I was once Walt Disney's seat companion; he was a friendly man.

I tried to give Col. John Glenn a free upgrade not long after his first flight in space. He refused the offer but shook my hand.

I recall descending for landing at Los Angeles around Christmastime in the 1950s. It was a crystal-clear night and the crew turned down the lights. There must have been billons of festive lights visible out the window. These memories you don't forget.

I have so many TWA memories and much to be thankful for. Even now I continue wearing my TWA 40-year service pin with pride

Epilogue

I was fortunate to ride TWA's ceremonial last flight, on December 1, 2001, from Kansas City to St Louis. Flight 220 operated with DC-9-83 N948TW, christened Wings of Pride several years earlier, commanded by TWA President and CEO Bill Compton.

Following a brief ceremony, we departed from Gate 34, receiving a water cannon salute from the Kansas City fire department. Turning onto the

Courtesy of John Mays – TWA Museum at 10 Richards Road
TWA employees posed for this picture upon arrival of Flight 220 at St. Louis.

active runway, I noticed the distinct outline of the TWA Overhaul Base across the field. So many memories in that building.

On-board television crews filled the aisle as flight attendants passed out box snacks containing a bottle of wine and a TWA glass, fruit, cheese and crackers. It reminded me of boxed meals I had boarded on Connies so many years ago. Other mementos included a commemorative last-flight route map and certificate, plus a small toy 747.

An incredibly smooth landing followed a fly-by at Lambert Field. TWA personnel were lined up at the arrival gate to meet us. One last water canon salute showered the airplane.

Refreshments were served in the gate area and many took pictures. There were red eyes and tears, hugs and good-byes to our alma mater. All too soon the terminal grew quiet as people dispersed. It was over; Trans World Airlines had "flown west," into history.

Dan McIntyre began with TWA in 1952 and held a variety of positions in Station Operations at Chicago-Midway, O'Hare and St. Louis. He retired in 1992.

A Career of Challenges and Rewards

By Don Fleming

During my teens, I visited Philadelphia International Airport and saw a Lockheed Super-G Constellation for the first time. Her incredible curves, big jugs and beautiful tail, made quite an impression on me as a teenager. It was Connie that seduced me to TWA.

I had been an aircraft mechanic when I was discharged from the Navy in 1965 and intended to become FAA certified to do the same at TWA. But President Johnson passed the GI Bill for veterans of the Cold War, so I decided to go to college instead.

I was wearing the white coveralls with TWA logo, ready to clean airplanes on the graveyard shift at Los Angeles International Airport (LAX) on

September 16, 1965. I polished the exteriors of the planes for the six months that I spent in Fleet Service. One night, a shift foreman named Johnny Green, took me up on a scaffold to give me a bird's eye view of a 727 wing that I had been polishing

Jon Proctor

Polishing Boeing 727 wings began a long TWA career.

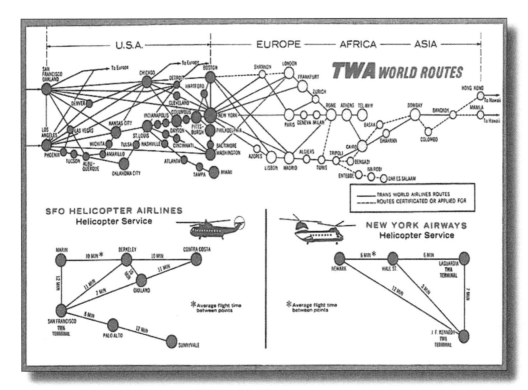

TWA's 1966 route map.

and said, "The right wing looks clean, but the wing that you have been working on shines. I wanted to bring you up here so that you could see what the good job looks like." His example demonstrated to me how powerful it could be to help others see "what the good job looks like."

I became an agent in the Los Angeles Reservations Office in early 1966. It was a great place to learn about TWA, its routes, the service product and its competition. Just after joining "Res," American, United and TWA introduced excursion fares and for many months the low prices had the phones ringing off the hook and non-stop coast to coast flights filling up.

TWA's marketing staff in New York wanted us to use branding terms like "Starstream Jet" "Royal Ambassador First Class" and "Golden Banner Coach." And in 1967 they added that "TWA, the all-jet Airline" should be the greeting when answering the phone. But it took time to use and explain the obscure terms to customers and worked against our ability to reel in business already on the hook, so when calls were holding I stopped using the buzz words.

My supervisor was administering a reprimand and had written a letter of warning to place in my file. But he couldn't ignore the fact that I was in the top 10% of the office for the volume of calls that I handled and number of reservations booked. He said that my numbers were so good that he would nominate me for the quarterly Award of Excellence had it not been for the letter being placed in my file.

Obviously we had a difference of opinion in "what the good job looked like" here. Normally, when you have a difference in philosophy with your boss, it is the boss who has the philosophy and you have the difference, unless an agreement on your position is reached.

Explaining my position, I asked that my own letter be attached and that a copy be sent to the district sales manager. In it, I pointed out that explaining that buzzwords were increasing the time it took to handle calls for customers who already wanted to book. Those who got put on hold could call American or United and some probably did. The reprimand letter disappeared; I was nominated and won the Award of Excellence for the third quarter of 1967.

At about 6:30 p.m. on November 20, 1967, I was about to leave the office for school when the callboard totally lit up. An operator ran out of the Teletype room with tears streaming down her cheeks. She held a short message in her hand confirming TWA Flight 128 that departed LAX earlier in the afternoon had crashed short of Cincinnati Airport.

I was assigned to lead the disaster control desk with five other agents. Calls from anyone related to or who knew passengers on board or who might have information, were transferred to us for four days following the crash. This experience seeing this wonderful industry filled with fun and adventure could suddenly turn deadly and traumatic shaped my approach to operational accidents and incidents forever.

In 1968 I became a TWA sales representative for the Los Angeles Wilshire District. Two years later, I became manager of convention sales for Southern California and Nevada while attending California State University at Los Angeles.

The year after taking delivery of our first 747, TWA put a management person on board as a cabin crew supervisor with focus on customer relations. One of the objectives was that the Director of Customer Service (DCS) would later take a position of increased importance where the perspective gained while flying would be valuable. The outcome was a job that most young people would have designed for themselves. While the Director of Customer Service (DCS) had a multitude of managerial responsibilities, the work schedule was much like that of a cabin or pilot crew member flying to exotic overseas destinations with liberal time off between trips.

After earning my Bachelor's degree in Business Administration in 1971, I applied for the DCS position for the third time, and was accepted. My class consisted of five furloughed pilots, three pursers, two flight attendants, a ticket agent from JFK and me as the only one who was already in TWA management. Upon completion of training, we all reported to the JFK domicile.

Cause Sought In CVG Crash

CINCINNATI — Investigation is underway by TWA and the National Air Transportation Safety Board in the crash of Flight 128 at Cincinnati on November 20. The recovered flight and voice recorders are being studied to help determine probable cause.

There were 13 survivors—including hostesses Sheila O'Brien and Eleanor Kurtock—among 75 passengers and seven crew members. The two hostesses suffered serious injury but were reported in satisfactory condition.

Others in the crew, all Kansas City-based, were Captain Charles Cochran, first officer Robert P. Moyers, flight engineer Jerry Lee Roades and hostesses Barbara Jean Posthumus and Marilee Kivett. No other employees were on board.

Expressing deep personal sympathy for families of victims and concern for the injured, Mr. Tillinghast joined investigators at the scene. He then visited Miss O'Brien and Miss Kurtock at St. Elizabeth Hospital in Cincinnati.

The two hostesses were cited for their heroism, in spite of their own injuries, in helping to rescue a five-year-old boy. All three were assisted by an unidentified passenger to a nearby farmhouse to await help.

TWA Skyliner

I became identified with Madrid when I started importing Spanish classical guitars. My 20-year-old guitar teacher and I became my partners in the guitar business. I took him to Spain and he stayed at the layover hotel for a few weeks to set up business contacts. During that time he walked in the footprints of Hemingway to the bullfights, had dinner at Casa Botin and enjoyed nightcaps called "flaming crocodiles" with the TWA crews at a bar behind the Plaza Hotel. The guitar business

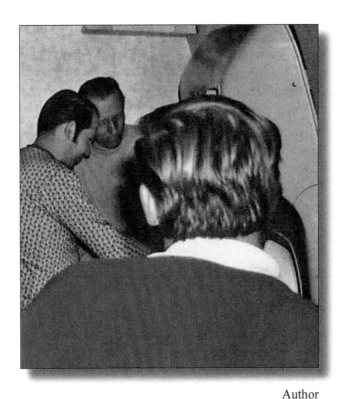

Author

*Don Fleming (left) receives instruction
in the 747 cabin trainer.*

was good but I had to phase it out when I was promoted and stopped flying. Last I heard my business partner was still selling guitars out of a shop near Swarthmore College.

The families of about a dozen JFK-based DCSs settled in the Danbury area of Western Connecticut. None of us had family close by so the DCS types, their wives and kids bonded quickly and watched out for each other. We spent holidays together and twice a year got gathered for picnics at Macedonia Brook State Park in Kent, Connecticut. This unique enclave became known as the Danbury Commuting Society (DCS).

Egos were large among the pilots and it wasn't unusual for the DCS to get a little pushback from those who resented "management suits" being in charge of anything on their airplane. There was occasional friction from the union-represented pursers and flight service managers who viewed the DCS as redundant and a challenge to their

leadership role. Diplomacy at all levels was not a virtue but a necessity to get by in this DCS adventure. The best way to deal with those trying to mark their territory was to hold your ground and try not to get wet if they peed in the corners.

The DCS program came to an end in 1976 and the three years that I spent as a DCS working alongside the brightest and the best having sharing the excitement, fun and camaraderie of their unique flying world was an honor and a privilege for me. It gave me the insight to fully comprehend what "the good job looked like" from the TWA flight attendant's perspective. That understanding helped me continue a rewarding relationship with them as a domicile manager at JFK and LaGuardia airports from 1976 through1980.

The loss of the DCS from domestic L-1011 flights left a void that was filled by creating a flight service manager position for those flights. But the selection process would only require that they had the interest and seniority to get the bid for this new, premium-pay job. A specially formulated leadership course was the core component of training because skills required to be a good leader are not exactly the same as those required to be a good flight attendant.

Going to graduation ceremonies for new flight service managers became a priority for me. It was important to reinforce that, as new leaders, they had a "license to make mistakes." Unless someone got hurt, a mistake was just a learning experience. They should not punish themselves and rest assured that their supervisors, who were specially selected to support them, would not punish them either, unless they did the same thing over and over again. We worked closely with them so that everyone had the same understanding of "what the good job looked like."

I felt satisfaction when flight service managers occasionally showed up on my doorstep and announced "I had a learning experience today," in effect putting themselves on report. That demonstrated that trust and mutual respect prevailed over frustration and fear. I think the implementation of the expanded flight service manager program and watching fledgling leaders develop to be great was one of the best things I was involved with at TWA.

I spent few years at the corporate headquarters in Manhattan as Director In-flight Services operations and returned to JFK to serve as General Manager In-flight Services from 1984 until 1991.

My career at TWA ended in August 1998. It was a good one and I would not have had the opportunity to do many of the things that made it a wonderful 33 years had the airline not experienced such significant challenges. To all of TWA's former employees and specifically the TWA flight attendants …thank you for making it a great ride!

From his position as general manager of the JFK domicile, Don Fleming became TWA's director of public relations in 1991 and then staff vice president of corporate communications in 1994. As head of "P.R." Don served five TWA CEOs, starting with its controversial chairman, Carl C. Icahn, through the airlines most tumultuous years. He assumed responsibility for the company's corporate re-engineering program in 1996 through 1998. When asked to comment on his unique TWA experiences, Don replied, "It certainly was an education that you can't get in school." Now retired except for occasional real estate ventures, he lives with Linda, his wife of 52 years, in New Milford, Connecticut. Their son, Tim is an autistic adult who lives and works close-by. Their daughter, Rebecca, is a Seattle-based pilot for Alaska Airlines.

Author

Proud father and daughter, Rebecca, in the cockpit of an Alaska Airlines 737.

Thoughts on Two Memorable Decades with TWA

By Robin H. H. Wilson

My good fortune was to be hired by TWA in 1964, arriving at its then new headquarters at 605 Third Avenue as an Analyst in the new Route Structure Research Department. Our task was to find potential opportunities to strengthen the route system in the then stiff regulatory environment of the Civil Aeronautics Board (CAB). For me this was a dream job, offering exciting opportunities to learn the key drivers of the airline business at a desk beside two great tutors, Mike Philburn and Julius Maldutis, later Dr. Julius of Salomon Brothers, the premier Wall Street airline analyst of his era.

During that period TWA expanded its routes to East Africa and Hong Kong. At the same time, retirement of the last of the Connies made it the first all-jet US airline. Happily, another venture failed, the setting up of Kingdom of Libya Airlines, thereby avoiding any unpleasant future dealing with Colonel Qaddafi.

Subsequent years were not as frantic, but nevertheless interesting and often amusing. During a stint in Pricing, Julius enabled us to show the CAB how its statistical formula that claimed to prove that airlines could profit from huge growth by reducing their fares, would also prove that the death rate would increase similarly if funeral parlors reduced their charges. A damaging fare cut was thus avoided.

Later, in Marketing Services, Dieter Buehler, in charge of Food Service, persuaded me to avoid a budget overrun by replacing expensive Salisbury steak in coach with lasagna and cannelloni, a first in the industry. Passenger complaints immediately followed; however, those came from first class passengers wanting those choices. I saved my job, and Dieter was honored later with the Gold Plate award from his professional organization.

In that department, we were also able to develop the broader capabilities of the then new IBM PARS reservation system, the handiwork of Bob Crandall, then IT VP, to create the industry's first computer-generated tickets and boarding passes. By coincidence, I was at the spear-end of the smooth introduction of that system at San Franicsco, where I was then City VP, smoothness greatly helped by Art Hurst, one of my former colleagues in Marketing giving up weekend time to train our agents. American, (pre Bob Crandall's arrival there) had to call in police at Los Angeles to calm angry passengers when AMR's catch-up system was introduced six months later.

Transfer to Technical Services in Kansas City brought me to the heart of the airline and immediate challenges from aircraft ground (AOG) without serviceable engines, amid unhappy mechanics understandably upset by seemingly endless contract negotiations. With respect to the AOGs, one name stands out for me, Joe Nemecek, who pointed to a fundamental flaw in our engine overhaul policy. Its rectification effectively eliminated the problem, reduced the need for spare engine purchases and cut down on overtime during the summer while permitting a much more popular summer vacation schedule for mechanics. On the second issue, Jerry Cosley took a step out of his PR role to introduce me to a small group consisting both of management and IAM employees that became of a Northrop Alpha airplane flown by TWA in the early 1930s, found in a Wisconsin barn. Would we be interested in restoring it? The group was volunteering their labor, if the company would purchase the material, permit the use of tooling and provide the space. It became an opportunity for management and shop floor to work together was much too good to be missed. Now that TWA Alpha hangs proudly in the Air & Space Museum in Washington, D.C., blessed on its way by Jack Northrop himself at its roll-out at the base in 1976.

As I left TWA in April 1981, I can offer little comment on the period 1981 to 1992, largely the Icahn era, which left TWA much weaker at its end than its start. The sale of the London routes was the deepest cut, but the sale of Boeing 767s that had been ordered on my watch was galling, knowing that we had bought them on very attractive terms and that they would serve TWA's route system well. The Flight Attendant strike caused major damage and left a horrible aftermath that lasted longer than Icahn. The Ozark merger, sad for its employees, did breathe some oxygen into TWA and St. Louis,

but the Atlanta hub effort was a travesty in spite of the best efforts of management and employees.

The Bankruptcy in 1992 left Icahn still controlling the Board, but he had agreed to a new three-person management committee running the airline, one each appointed by Icahn, the creditors and unions for the employees. The creditors made a wise choice in selecting the then-current CFO, Glenn Zander; I was very gratified to be asked to be the employees' representative; Carl chose not to designate anyone.

With the company running on fumes, its market reputation in tatters, its fleet ancient and its employees in shock, although still hopeful for miracles, survival was far from certain. Glenn and I divided our day-to-day responsibilities, largely on the basis of our backgrounds with Glenn managing the Finance and Administrative elements and I, the operating side. We each had offices in Mount Kisco, New York and in Kansas City, Glenn at KCAC and I at the maintenance base, reoccupying the office that I had had in the 1970s as Vice President - Technical Services.

I was actually grateful to the head of the IAM local at MCI who, when asked about my return by a reporter from the Kansas City Star, commented that he did not know me well but remembered I had an interest in toilets – hardly sounding flattering, but true and a useful reminder. So I made it a point in my new role, as I had in the past, to visit the area where lavs, galleys, seats and other cabin items were refurbished during an overhaul. It's not a big status item to tell family and friends what a good job you have done fixing toilets, so it's important to tell those who do that essential work that it is appreciated.

My first such visit subsequently had remarkable results, stimulated by a mechanic whose name I deeply regret not recalling, to whom I and every TWA employee as well as multiple thousands of passengers have reason to be grateful. Specifically, he told me that TWA needed to comply within the next three months with an FAA order that seat spacing around exit rows be expanded, a requirement that every airline other than TWA had already met. As, practically, this meant moving all the seats as well as overhead lighting and air vents, he added astutely that now would be a good time if Marketing wanted to make any changes in seating arrangements.

At that point, TWA's reputation for service was poor; old airplanes and cutbacks in on board and ground services made for unhappy passengers, reflected on flight attendants still feeling the understandable morale impact of the earlier strike. Icahn's response to attract passengers was to offer frequent fare sales. A pattern of repeated sales, however, is predictable and easily matched by competitors and therefore self-defeating. As a result, TWA had both low average fares and low load factors, creating wretched revenue per available seat mile.

What my mechanic colleague's comment suggested was that if TWA adjusted its seat spacing to create a provable and attractive advantage over competitors, we would not need to cut fares. And although its seat capacity per flight would diminish, little revenue would be lost since load factors were already low. Furthermore, since competitors had already suffered the cost of moving seats to meet the FAA order, they would be reluctant to spend again to compete with TWA.

Zander and I had previously orchestrated changes of both the Marketing head and the company's advertising agency. Both new parties were looking for, and very open to, ideas to create favorable differentiation for TWA in the marketplace. Legroom then, as now, was a highly marketable attribute, particularly if it was demonstrable and unmatched. The result was "Comfort Class," a program that opened up the coach seating in every aircraft to exceed competitive legroom. In one year, this took TWA from being way off the charts to winning the J D Power award for customer satisfaction. Importantly, it restored pride in TWA employees and established long lacking confidence in its management, all thanks to an astute mechanic!

While restoring the operating health of the airline was essential, there were other hurdles to

overcome. The most immediate was obtaining an agreement with the Federal Pension Benefit Guarantee Corporation (PBGC) that was critical to Icahn resigning as Chairman. Multiple meetings took place, one memorably at PBGC's office in Washington, D.C., where as a backdrop to our seats were motivational photos of former Eastern and Pan Am airplanes.

Eventually, a tentative agreement was reached in a meeting in Manhattan that started at 9 a.m. and continued to 4 a.m., leaving just enough time to shower, change clothes and catch a train to Delaware for a hearing before the Bankruptcy Judge, who approved the deal, as did the PBGC Board subsequently. This led to a meeting in the office of the creditors' law firm in Chicago, where the fax machine printed out Icahn's resignation from all TWA Board and Officer positions.

While this removed a substantial blockage to emergence from bankruptcy, it did little to move that process forward. That would require a credible business plan, blessed by creditors and backed by funding for which there were few if any conventional financial sources. The State of Missouri, however, was a possible source with TWA's major domestic hub in St. Louis along with its maintenance facility and administrative offices in Kansas City. Both the then Governor, Mel Carnahan, and the Majority Leader of the House, Dick Gephardt, whose Congressional District was adjacent to St. Louis, made serious attempts to help, but could not find Federal or State funds for the purpose.

Separately, fearing TWA's demise, Lambert Airport's management and its owner, the City of St. Louis, had sensibly begun discussions with USAir to potentially replace TWA's services at the airport in that event. However, they feared facing Kansas City's problem when it was unable to replace Eastern immediately as Eastern's creditors controlled its MCI Jetways & carousels. TWA's ownership of the same components at St. Louis thus enabled it to sell and lease back this critical operational equipment at attractive prices. With the kicker that we would move the corporate headquarters from the Icahn-owned facility it occupied in Mount Kisco, New York, we acquired funds sufficient to make the Business Plan work.

We could now file our application to emerge from bankruptcy and in November 1993, the Bankruptcy Judge called a Court hearing in Wilmington, Delaware to adjudicate it, a process that proved much more tense than anticipated. All the principal creditors were represented prepared to give their assent, with a single exception; the Port Authority of New York & New Jersey remained recalcitrant, largely over payment of JFK back rent. Only a court recess at the Creditor's request and granted by the judge, allowed a deal to be negotiated with the Port, after which the judge approved TWA's emergence from bankruptcy.

Some months earlier the creditors and unions agreed to designate a 12-person Board, with six named by creditors, four by unions and two by management. Bill Howard, former Chairman of Piedmont Airlines was designated Chairman and CEO, with Zander and me as Vice Chairmen. Howard's tenure was, however, extraordinarily short with his dismissal by the Board just two months later. Regrettably the Board chose not to replace him with Glenn Zander, who was well qualified for the job and under whom I would have been happy to serve. Zander resigned with a modest financial parachute and I departed some months later.

Following his departure from TWA in 1981, Robin Wilson served as President of the Long Island Railroad, Western Airlines and Burlington Express. Upon leaving the company again in 1994 he joined an aviation consultancy. Robin has an MA in Engineering from Cambridge, an MBA from Harvard and is a Fellow of the Royal Aeronautical Society.

The TWA Museum

By Jeff Kriendler

Photos: Jon Proctor except as noted.

In 1927 Charles Lindbergh first dedicated the airfield that would become known as the Kansas City Municipal Airport (MKC). Col. Lindbergh and Amelia Earhart subsequently consulted for Transcontinental Air Transport (TAT). On August 31, 1931, a ground breaking ceremony was well attended at the southeast corner of the airport to initiate the building of the first corporate headquarters for the newly merged airline named Transcontinental & Western Air (T&WA) at 10 Richards Road, which appropriately became home of the TWA Museum.

Through the years, 10 Richards Road saw many legends of commercial aviation walk its corridors - Charles Lindbergh, Amelia Earhart, Jack Frye, Paul Richter, Walt Hamilton, Tommy Tomlinson and later its legendary owner, Howard Hughes. For a period of time, The Lindbergh Line subtitles adorned company aircraft and advertising material. T&WA was later branded Trans World Airline. The "s" was added to "Airline" in May 1950 with an official corporate name change, making it Trans World Airlines.

Museum director Pam Blaschum says that the mission of the TWA Museum is to provide information to the public emphasizing the story, history and importance of the major role TWA played in pioneering commercial aviation. "The

Jon Proctor

The 10 Richards Road headquarters and hangar
appear in this vintage TWA advertisement.

Museum's vision is to assure permanent exhibits and showcase the growing collection of TWA artifacts which bring to light the strong partnership that has developed between TWA and Kansas City over many decades, culminating with the American Airlines purchase of TWA in 2001." She noted that the

Museum relates the important impact TWA had on local, national and global aviation. The Museum rents space from Signature on the building's first floor.

The first TWA Museum was established in 1985 with exhibition of items at the overhaul base. After four moves, it has come home to

roost in the original corporate headquarters of the iconic airline. The Museum is a 501(c)3 charitable foundation which was established in 2013. All of the staff at the Museum are volunteers, donating their time and passion for TWA. Many were never employed by the airline.

Blaschum noted that Charles Wheeler Airport (MKC) is also the home base for *Wings of Pride*, a McDonnell Douglas DC-9-83, operated by The TriStar Experience, conducting ground-based in-flight educational programs. The *Wings of Pride* lease payments were originally a gift from TWA employees to the airline they loved and wore a unique, one-of-a-kind livery. With the American Airlines acquisition of TWA in 2001

it was repainted and flown by AA. When TriStar acquired the aircraft in mid-2014 it returned the aircraft to original livery to continue flying and inspiring the next generation of aviation enthusiasts and professionals.

Wings of Pride will soon have a sister aircraft, a Lockheed L-1011 to be restored and painted in TWA colors. It will be based at Kansas City International Airport (MCI).

As to the Museum itself, it has captured the essence of TWA in several display cases, which relate to various aspects of the global airline, from flight attendant uniforms, to the rich history of Ozark Airlines, with a special case containing memorabilia from Pope John Paul II's first TWA charter trip to the United States in 1979. A room is dedicated to the three founders of TWA, featuring Jack Frye's original desk.

A special TWA Flight 800 employee memorial room provides a reflective opportunity honoring the memory of the TWA flight staff, employees and family members who perished on July 17, 1996 when Flight 800 bound for Paris exploded. The TWA Flight 800 International Memorial was dedicated on Long Island in a two-acre

(8,100 m2) parcel immediately adjoining the main pavilion at the park on July 14, 2004. The Families of TWA Flight 800 Association raised funds for the memorial.

The memorial includes landscaped grounds and flags from the 14 countries of the victims. The curved black granite memorial has names engraved on one side and on top an illustration on the other of a wave releasing 230 seagulls into the sky. In July 2006 the association added an abstract design of a 10-foot (3.0 m) high lighthouse in black granite designed by Harry Edward Seaman, who had lost a cousin in the crash. The lighthouse sits above a tomb holding many of the victims' personal belongings. The granite and crystal monument has since been moved to TWA Museum's memorial room after being housed for more than a decade in an ocean front park on Long Island.

The 4-foot high memorial found a permanent home in the Museum on July 15, 2012, when it was trucked 1,150 miles to Kansas City. In a fitting tribute the truck carrying the memorial was met in Liberty, Missouri by a 55-car escort motorcade made up of TWA employees, friends and family.

It was given a police escort from Liberty to the new hall of the Museum at 10 Richards Road.

Blachum pointed out that when it was announced that the old TWA hangar at Los Angeles would be razed, American Airlines was most generous in shipping salvageable memorabilia, saved by TWA volunteers from Los Angeles area, to the Richards Road facility.

The Museum staff welcomes volunteers to help at the facility, which is open Tuesday-Saturday from 10a.m. to 4 p.m. Funding for the facility is entirely generated by donations and modest paid entrance fees as well as rental revenue from special events held there. It is available for private events and makes a wonderful venue for a variety of aviation and personal milestones. Prospective business inquiries are invited to call 816-234-1011.

For Blaschum, the long hours are a "Labor of Love" for the airline that was a significant part of her life. Thanks to the efforts of Pam and her team of volunteers, the Museum is the glue that holds the large TWA Family together.

For more on the TWA Museum, go to: http://*www.twamuseumat10richardsroad.org/*

A Family Tragedy

By Jon Proctor

*A portion of the Flight 800 Memorial, located at
Smith Point County Park on Long Island.*

Perhaps more than other professions, airline employees have always felt a sense of "family" among their co-workers. Each carrier retains a camaraderie and closeness; in turn, the industry itself is a family. Although fiercely competitive, its individual members seem to understand each other, appreciating the unique lifestyles and challenges that exist in the business. Airlines often cooperate with each other more than it would appear to the traveling public. Maintenance personnel have, since early on, relied on their counterparts at other companies when in need of short-term loans of ground equipment, aircraft parts or physical assistance under unusual circumstances. One airline will rely on another to accommodate inconvenienced passengers, provide a spare gate or relay a message.

The July 17, 1996 loss of TWA Flight 800 was not just a horrible disaster widely covered by the media; it was a family tragedy, coming to an airline that had endured more than a decade of turmoil, dealing with its own family problems. Having experienced a divisive strike and corporate takeover, Trans World Airlines fought its way back to fiscal stability. The pioneer carrier, in the midst of celebrating a half-century of trans-Atlantic flying, suffered a tremendous personal loss on that summer evening. More than 50 employees and family members were aboard Flight 800.

While going through the nightmare of its first fatal crash since 1974, company employees still managed to maintain professionalism while privately grieving the loss of so many of their own. It is safe to say that nearly every TWAer knew someone on that airplane.

The airline community immediately embraced the airline, offering assistance of every kind. The company hangar lobby entrance at JFK, where flight crews, maintenance and administrative personal began their workdays, was flooded with floral arrangements and sympathy cards, all from other airline employees. When tragedy strikes, this industry always shows its true character.

We dedicate this book to all those who suffered with the loss of TWA Flight 800, but we should especially remember the people of Trans World Airlines, who endure a family tragedy even to this day.

Author

Acknowledgements: The Team

With so many of our readers and prospective book-buyers coming from the airline industry, you can appreciate that it takes a full complement of people to launch a flight from conception to completion. A large crew of engineers, crew schedulers, pilots, flight attendants, mechanics, sales personnel, catering teams and so many others ... the list could fill this page.

In putting together this book project, we also relied on an expert team of people to bring the book to fruition. Foremost, the editors would like to thank the writers who have provided their personal recollections of important events in the life of Trans World Airlines. These are stories from the heart, many stemming from those who dedicated their entire professional careers to TWA. We thank them for their time commitments to write the stories and most of all for their ongoing passion for an iconic airline.

We know that some might have submitted to this project but were unaware of it. In the end we could only accommodate a limited number of stories. For those left out, we apologize.

A few stories were selected from TARPA TOPICS, the official publication of the TWA Retired Pilots Association and are so noted in the book. We wish to thank Captain Dusty West, President of the Association, as well as the past President and TOPICS editor, Captain Bill Kirschner, Webmaster Bob Willcutts and acknowledge the cooperation from Cathy Gillespie, the magazine's designer.

We would also like to express gratitude to John Wegg, former Editor and Publisher of Airways magazine, who similarly granted approval for our reprinting of some excellent stories from Airways during his tenure there and Enrique Perrella, the magazine's Publisher and Editor-in-Chief. A word of thanks goes to Helen McLaughlin, author of Footsteps in the Sky of Island Press, who graciously gave re-print authorization for the story on Ida Staggers.

In addition, we would like to acknowledge the assistance provided by Pam Blaschum, Director of the TWA Museum at 10 Richards Road, in Kansas City as well as her most knowledgeable and efficient curator, John Mays and the museum's vice president, Karen Holden Young.

Many people provided assistance in recommending story subject matter and possible authors. We wish to express thanks to Captain Willard Van Wormer, Captain John Marshall, Captain Peter Sherwin and Marc Brécy, international dispatcher (Paris), Bob Woodling, Frank Lennon, Thomas Donahue, Gary Smedile, Douglas Corrigan, Thomas Livesey, Harry Sievers and Geoffrey Thomas. Finally, we wish to recognize the assistance of Harvey Bilt Photography, Bob Crandall, Michael Manning, Charlie Trippe, Steve Isenberg, Hector Adler, Carol Treutlein, Mark Schwab, Gerry Gitner, Jamie Baldwin, James Ferris and Curt Strand as well as Pat Rose, typist extraordinaire.

In closing we wish to acknowledge Ardis & Joe Clark, our Publishers at BluewaterPress LLC, whose patience, experience, talent and love of aviation are greatly valued by us both.

Jon Proctor   July 8, 2016   Jeff Kriendler

We hope you have enjoyed this account of
Trans World Airlines - A Book of Memories

For other interesting aviation books,
Please visit our website at
www.BluewaterPress.com